LEGO® STAR WARS™ IDEAS BOOK

LEGO STAR WARS™

IDEAS BOOK

WRITTEN BY
HANNAH DOLAN, ELIZABETH DOWSETT
AND **SIMON HUGO**

CONTENTS

Page 30

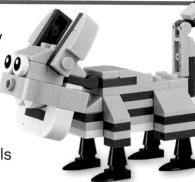

Page 37

Page 63

68 EXPAND

Enlarge the *Star Wars* galaxy!

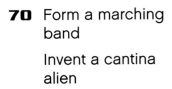

Page 70

Page 103

Page 85

5

Page 119

Page 151

Page 156

Page 176

Page 183

162 USE IT!

Build treasures to keep or gifts to give

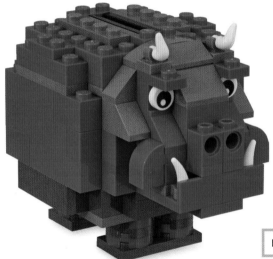

Page 164

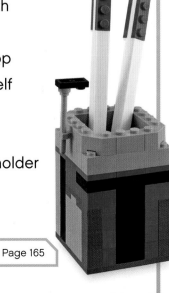

Page 165

We're gonna do this!

 EYE CAUTION
For models with shooting functions, do not aim the shooter at eyes.

Not sure what to build? Whether you've got five minutes or a whole day, a few bricks or a bucketful, answer these questions to find the ideal activity for you.

WHAT ARE YOU IN THE MOOD FOR?

BEING GENEROUS
Make someone's day with a fun buildable gift, such as one of these:

TAKING OFF
Try out some flight-based builds:

FEELING THE FORCE
Is the Force with you? Have a look at:

A CHALLENGE
Once the building is finished, it doesn't mean the fun is over! For builds that you can play with friends, turn to:

ARE YOU ON A SOLO MISSION?

YES
To build something for yourself, try one of these:

MIXING THINGS UP A LITTLE
Feel like making a build your own? Customize your own *Star Wars* themed builds with the following builds:

NO
Playing with friends? Take on one of these:

DO YOU WANT TO BE A ...

... WILDLIFE WATCHER?
Get to know the galaxy's many wonderful beasts with these builds:

HOW MUCH TIME DO YOU HAVE?

ALL THE TIME IN THE GALAXY!

If you are looking for a big challenge, try out one of these:

LESS THAN 15 MINUTES

Looking for a speedy build? Have a look at:

LESS THAN AN HOUR

If you have a little more time to work on a project, try taking on one of these:

HOW MANY BRICKS DO YOU HAVE?

JUST A FEW

Smaller builds can be found here:

LOTS OF THE SAME BRICK

For builds that use lots of similar pieces, take a look at:

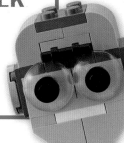

LOTS OF THE SAME COLOUR

Try out a build made up of almost all the same colour, such as these:

WHICH SIDE ARE YOU DRAWN TO?

I LIKE THE LIGHT

If you feel the pull of the light, turn to:

... SPACE EXPLORER?

For planet-based builds that are out of this world, take a look at:

I'VE TURNED TO THE DARK SIDE

Aligned yourself with the Empire? Take a look at:

MINI MAKES

There are so many ways to squeeze even more fun from your LEGO® *Star Wars*™ bricks. Make your own fleet of TIE fighters to add playability to a favourite set. Choose a model and see if you can build a version using different bricks. Make it in crazy colours and give it a whole new personality!

AT-DP (set 30274)

The stalking AT-DP looks menacing in black and grey

In colourful bricks, the AT-DP looks friendly rather than fierce

Page 113

RADICAL REBUILDS

So you've bought a LEGO *Star Wars* set and you've built a brick-perfect model. Well done! What's next? Break it down, let your imagination run wild, and rebuild the set into something completely different, that's what! Radical Rebuild pages will inspire you to use your LEGO *Star Wars* sets in new and exciting ways.

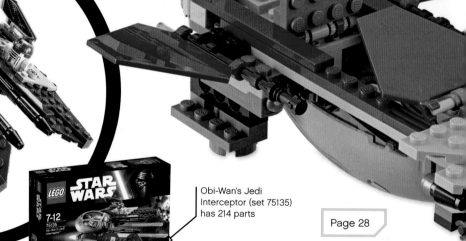

OBI-WAN'S JEDI INTERCEPTOR™

Most of the interceptor's parts have been used to build a sand-sailing barge

Obi-Wan's Jedi Interceptor (set 75135) has 214 parts

Page 28

When building *Star Wars* vehicles, droids and creatures, don't just stick to the obvious LEGO parts. Instead, try mixing and matching. You could turn a joystick into a droid's antenna, a piece of seaweed into a spiny creature's tail, or a pair of horns into speeder handlebars!

Spring-shooter missile

VEHICLE SPARE PARTS

Grille slope

Large angled flag

Printed 4x4 radar dish

DESIGN A DROID

Droid arm

Plate with a ring of bars

CREATURE FEATURES

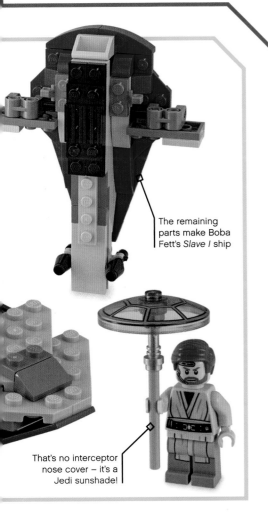

The remaining parts make Boba Fett's *Slave I* ship

That's no interceptor nose cover – it's a Jedi sunshade!

1x2 plate with ball and socket

The ingenious design of LEGO® bricks makes building easy – and full of endless possibilities. To get the most from your bricks, it is useful to know a few simple terms and to pick up some basic building tips from our experts!

These are your first steps...

LEARN THE LANGUAGE

Do you know your plates from your tiles? Learning the names of different pieces will be helpful when building with friends, or for identifying pieces when you are using this book.

BRICK

The most common LEGO pieces, bricks are the foundation of LEGO building. Bricks come in many shapes and sizes, but always have the classic LEGO studs on them.

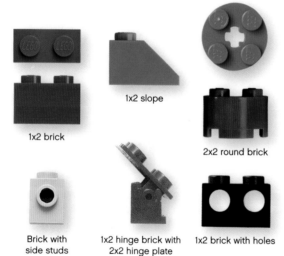

1x2 brick

1x2 slope

2x2 round brick

Brick with side studs

1x2 hinge brick with 2x2 hinge plate

1x2 brick with holes

PLATE

Plates are slim versions of bricks, and three plates stacked together are the same height as a brick. Plates also have LEGO studs on them, making them easy to build with. The jumper plate is super useful. It's a plate with a central stud, which "jumps" whatever you put on top of it over by half a stud.

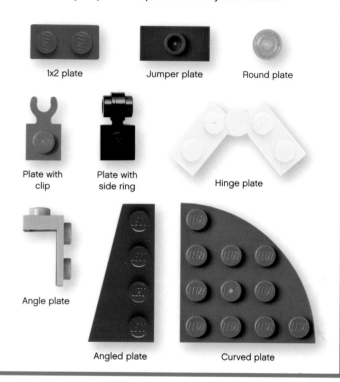

1x2 plate

Jumper plate

Round plate

Plate with clip

Plate with side ring

Hinge plate

Angle plate

Angled plate

Curved plate

TILE

A tile is similar to a plate, but without studs. Tiles are smooth and are great when you need a realistic effect, or for builds where elements have sliding functions. Printed tiles are available to give extra detail.

2x2 tile

Printed round tile

Tile with pin

1x6 tile

LET'S GET TECHNICAL

You don't have to be an expert engineer to build moving models! Thanks to LEGO® Technic elements, it is easier than ever to include working features in your builds. Combine gears and axles to bring your builds to life, or simply add them to your models to recreate the look of your favourite *Star Wars* movie set designs.

BUILD BASICS

Micro-scale builds make a few bricks go a long way

The *Star Wars* Universe is infinite, and so are the possibilities when you build with LEGO bricks! You can build to match the scale of your minifigures, or choose to go bigger or smaller. Why not create a mini Death Star that fits in the palm of your hand, or a mega-sized rathtar to frighten your friends!

Page 129

Building on a larger scale can make a big visual impact

Page 173

IT ALL ADDS UP

Often pieces are named based on how many studs they have on top. So a 2x4 brick is two studs across, and four studs long. Some bricks are higher than the standard brick height, so a third number is included, for example a 1x2x5 (one is the width, two is the length, five is the height).

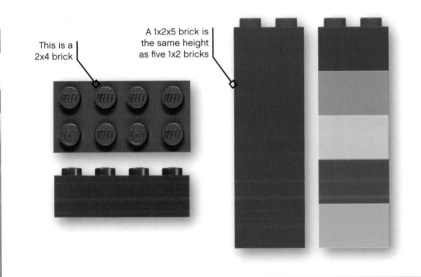

This is a 2x4 brick

A 1x2x5 brick is the same height as five 1x2 bricks

KEEP IT TOGETHER

The most amazing thing about LEGO elements is that they all fit together! Add strength and stability to your builds by overlapping different-sized pieces. When you use same-sized bricks, staggering them (making sure their sides don't line up) will lock the bricks together. After all, a shaky starfighter or a wobbly Wookiee are no good to anyone!

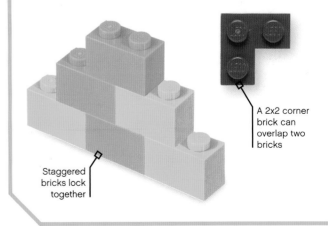

A 2x2 corner brick can overlap two bricks

Staggered bricks lock together

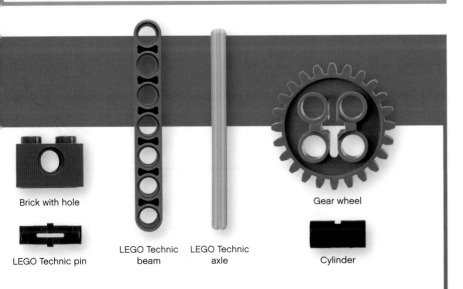

Brick with hole

LEGO Technic pin

LEGO Technic beam

LEGO Technic axle

Gear wheel

Cylinder

Anyone who loves LEGO® bricks and *Star Wars* is bound to have a great imagination. Let the ideas in this book spark yours – you'll soon be thinking up all kinds of exciting projects of your own. Remember, if you don't have the exact bricks shown, just use what you do have. It's all about being creative!

BE *STAR WARS* INSPIRED

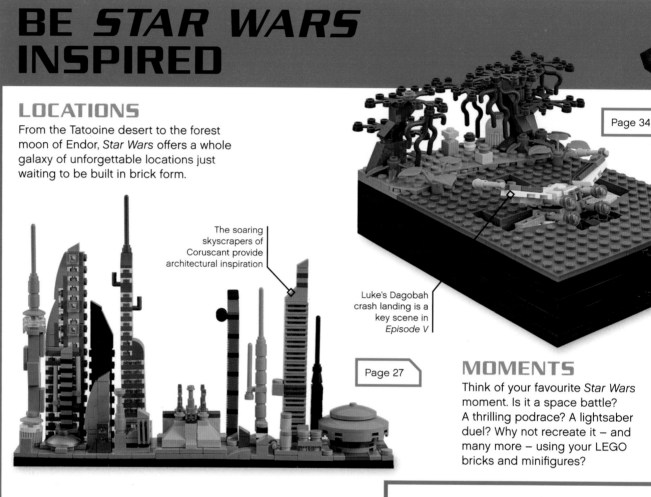

LOCATIONS

From the Tatooine desert to the forest moon of Endor, *Star Wars* offers a whole galaxy of unforgettable locations just waiting to be built in brick form.

The soaring skyscrapers of Coruscant provide architectural inspiration

Luke's Dagobah crash landing is a key scene in *Episode V*

Page 34

Page 27

MOMENTS

Think of your favourite *Star Wars* moment. Is it a space battle? A thrilling podrace? A lightsaber duel? Why not recreate it – and many more – using your LEGO bricks and minifigures?

CHARACTERS

The *Star Wars* series is full of unforgettable characters that will have you itching to recreate them in bricks. From a maxi-figure of Han Solo to a Yoda emoji, the possibilities are endless.

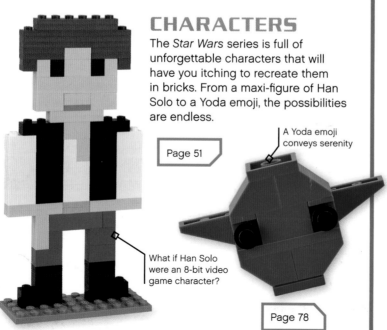

A Yoda emoji conveys serenity

Page 51

What if Han Solo were an 8-bit video game character?

Page 78

MOVE IT ALONG

Don't let the fun stop when you have finished your LEGO build. You could photograph it and start a picture diary of your best builds. If you are a budding director, why not write a *Star Wars* inspired movie script with your model as the star, then have a friend help you to film it?

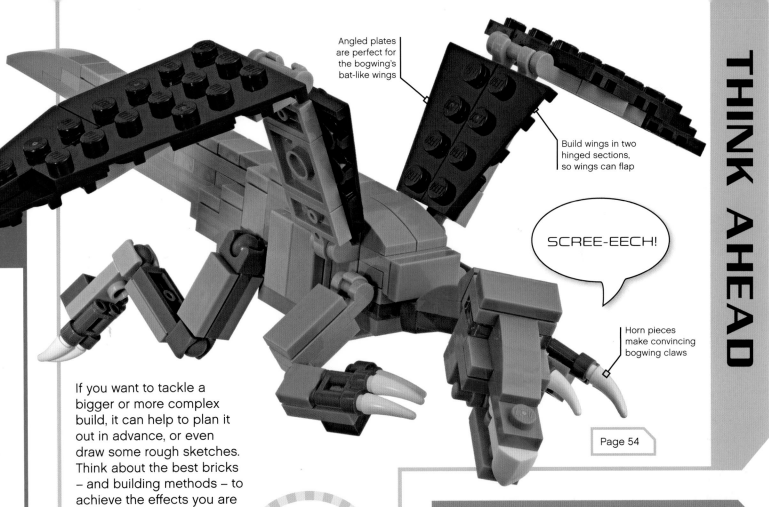

Angled plates are perfect for the bogwing's bat-like wings

Build wings in two hinged sections, so wings can flap

SCREE-EECH!

Horn pieces make convincing bogwing claws

Page 54

If you want to tackle a bigger or more complex build, it can help to plan it out in advance, or even draw some rough sketches. Think about the best bricks – and building methods – to achieve the effects you are looking for.

Discover more building tips throughout the book!

USE WHAT YOU HAVE

If you yearn to build Darth Vader's mask but you only have orange bricks, don't despair! Work with what you have and think creatively. The perfect solution might be staring you right in the face!

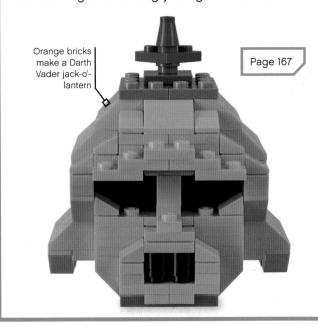

Orange bricks make a Darth Vader jack-o'-lantern

Page 167

Help me, Obi-Wan. You're my only hope...

Page 46

A smartphone flashlight adds a cool finishing touch to a model hologram

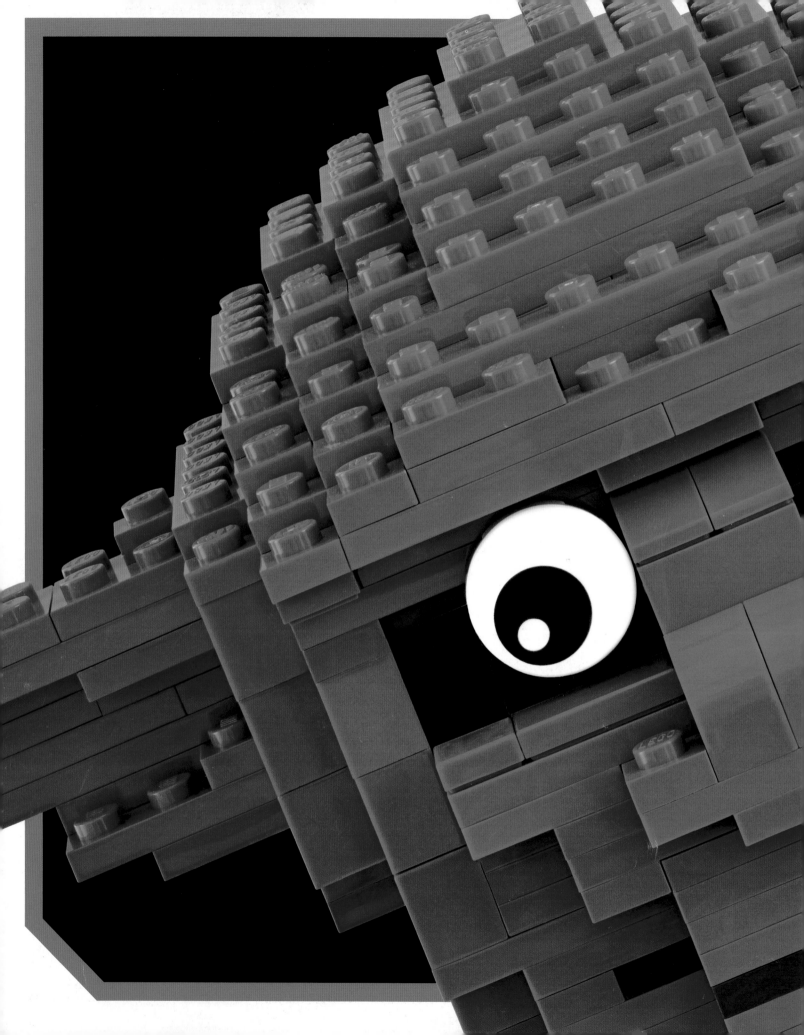

RECREATE

BUILD HAN'S ELECTROBINOCULARS

Build a pair of electrobinoculars just like the ones Han Solo uses on Hoth. Then create "far-away" scenery to survey! This pair is white to provide camouflage on snowy Hoth – you could build electrobinoculars for use on other *Star Wars* planets and their landscapes, too.

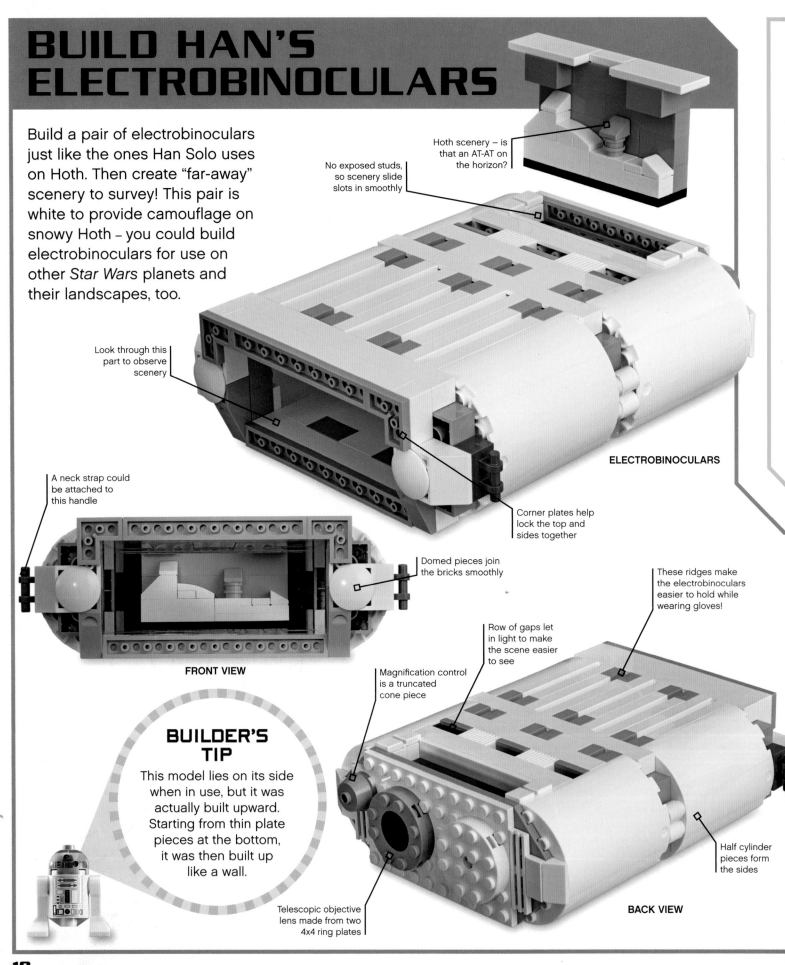

Hoth scenery – is that an AT-AT on the horizon?

No exposed studs, so scenery slide slots in smoothly

Look through this part to observe scenery

ELECTROBINOCULARS

Corner plates help lock the top and sides together

A neck strap could be attached to this handle

Domed pieces join the bricks smoothly

FRONT VIEW

These ridges make the electrobinoculars easier to hold while wearing gloves!

Row of gaps let in light to make the scene easier to see

Magnification control is a truncated cone piece

BUILDER'S TIP

This model lies on its side when in use, but it was actually built upward. Starting from thin plate pieces at the bottom, it was then built up like a wall.

Telescopic objective lens made from two 4x4 ring plates

Half cylinder pieces form the sides

BACK VIEW

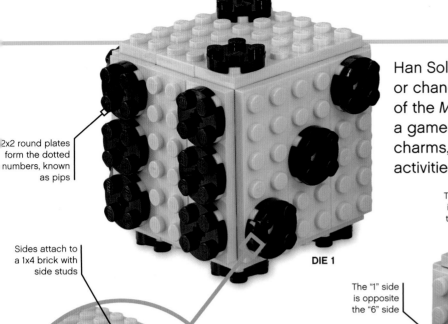

2x2 round plates form the dotted numbers, known as pips

Sides attach to a 1x4 brick with side studs

DIE 1

ROLL THE DICE

Han Solo has a pair of lucky golden dice – or chance cubes – hanging in the cockpit of the *Millennium Falcon*. They won him a game of sabacc! Build your own lucky charms, and use them to play some of the activities in this book.

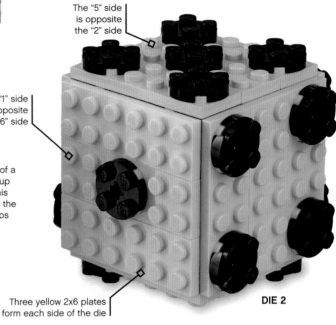

The "5" side is opposite the "2" side

The "1" side is opposite the "6" side

Opposite sides of a die always add up to seven – so this side is opposite the one with four pips

Three yellow 2x6 plates form each side of the die

DIE 2

CHANGE OF SCENERY

Are there other planets or people you'd like to keep an eye on? Create 2-D scenes from other lands to place inside your electrobinoculars.

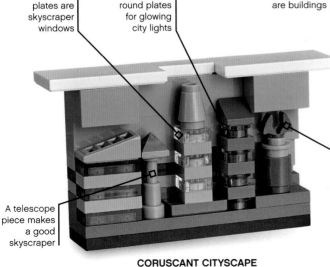

Transparent plates are skyscraper windows

Yellow 1x1 round plates for glowing city lights

Light grey tiles are buildings

Green slopes make grassy knolls

A telescope piece makes a good skyscraper

A spanner piece forms the striking shape of this Coruscant tower

CORUSCANT CITYSCAPE

NABOO VIEW

That's great building, kid!

STACK 'EM UP

Star Wars characters are so iconic, they are even recognizable in the form of small stacks of bricks. Two well-placed grey bricks become Chewie's bandolier, and 1x1 round plates attached sideways form Leia's hair buns!

LANDO CALRISSIAN

DARTH MAUL

AAYLA SECURA

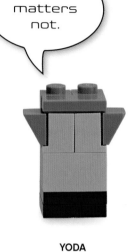

YODA

Size matters not.

BUILD A DROID

There are many kinds of droids, and all of them are assembled from multiple robotic parts. Build a droid workshop with a moving conveyor belt for droid parts and put your own LEGO® droids back together. Or, recreate a scene from *Attack of the Clones* where C-3PO gets mixed up before he gets fixed up!

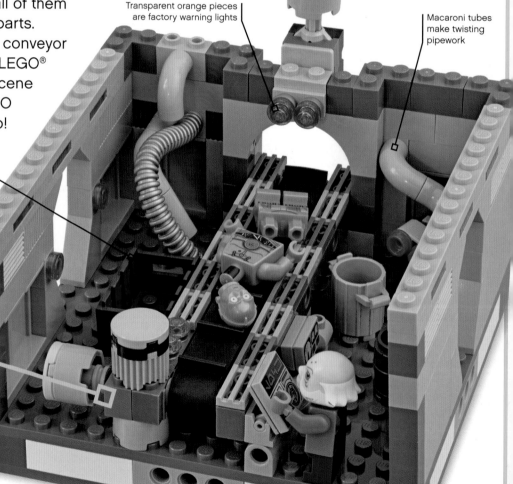

Transparent orange pieces are factory warning lights

Macaroni tubes make twisting pipework

Crate for faulty droid parts

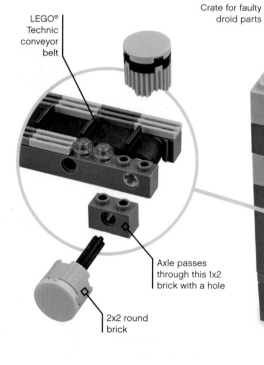

LEGO® Technic conveyor belt

Axle passes through this 1x2 brick with a hole

2x2 round brick

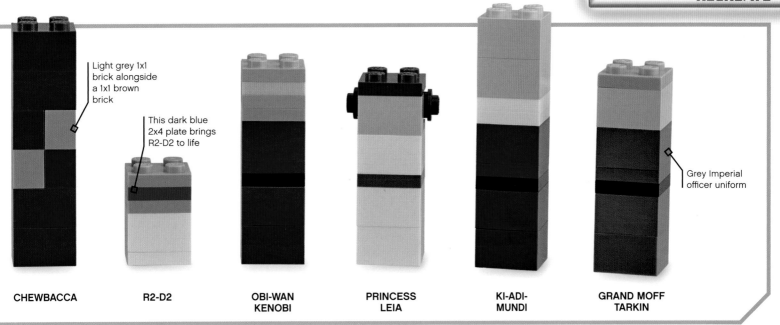

Light grey 1x1 brick alongside a 1x1 brown brick

This dark blue 2x4 plate brings R2-D2 to life

Grey Imperial officer uniform

CHEWBACCA **R2-D2** **OBI-WAN KENOBI** **PRINCESS LEIA** **KI-ADI-MUNDI** **GRAND MOFF TARKIN**

Put your stamp on the galaxy with postcard-style artworks. Explore ways of turning 3-D objects into flat images with LEGO plates and tiles. With so many exotic landscapes, iconic views and key moments, you'll be spoilt for choice. You could even make a gallery to display your pictures.

MAKE A SCENE

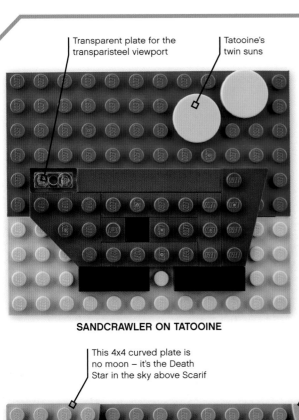

Transparent plate for the transparisteel viewport

Tatooine's twin suns

SANDCRAWLER ON TATOOINE

This 4x4 curved plate is no moon – it's the Death Star in the sky above Scarif

The dish on top of Citadel Tower in the Imperial security complex

SCARIF LANDSCAPE

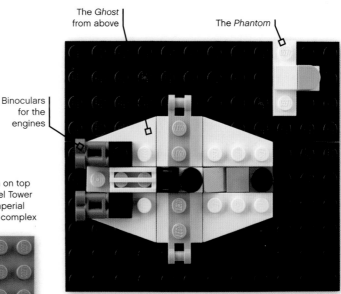

The *Ghost* from above

The *Phantom*

Binoculars for the engines

THE *GHOST* IN DEEP SPACE

KEEP IT SIMPLE

Choose objects with distinctive shapes, such as rebel ship the *Ghost*, that are easy to represent with flat bricks. Consider how to use colour, too – simple blue and tan pieces can become sea and land.

As a child, the future rebel hero Jyn Erso lived a simple life, playing happily with toys that were made for her by her loving parents. Here are a few favourites from her toy box that you can recreate with LEGO bricks.

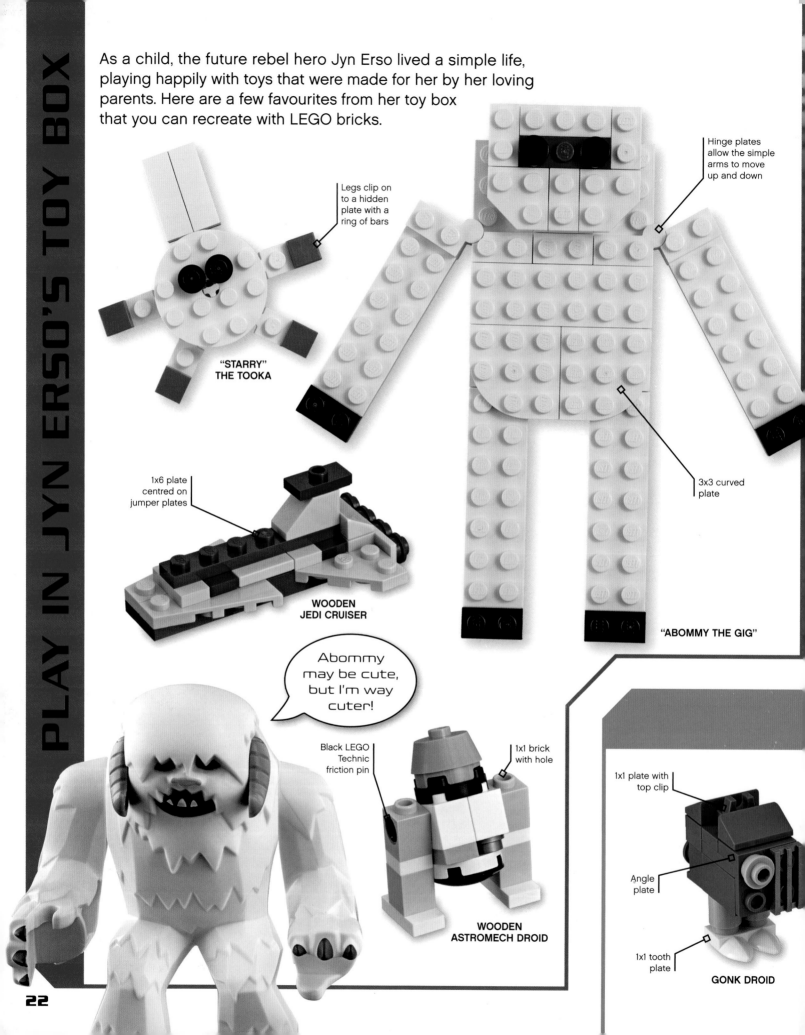

Legs clip on to a hidden plate with a ring of bars

"STARRY" THE TOOKA

1x6 plate centred on jumper plates

WOODEN JEDI CRUISER

Hinge plates allow the simple arms to move up and down

3x3 curved plate

"ABOMMY THE GIG"

Abommy may be cute, but I'm way cuter!

Black LEGO Technic friction pin

1x1 brick with hole

WOODEN ASTROMECH DROID

1x1 plate with top clip

Angle plate

1x1 tooth plate

GONK DROID

MAKE A CLASSIC SCENE MICRO

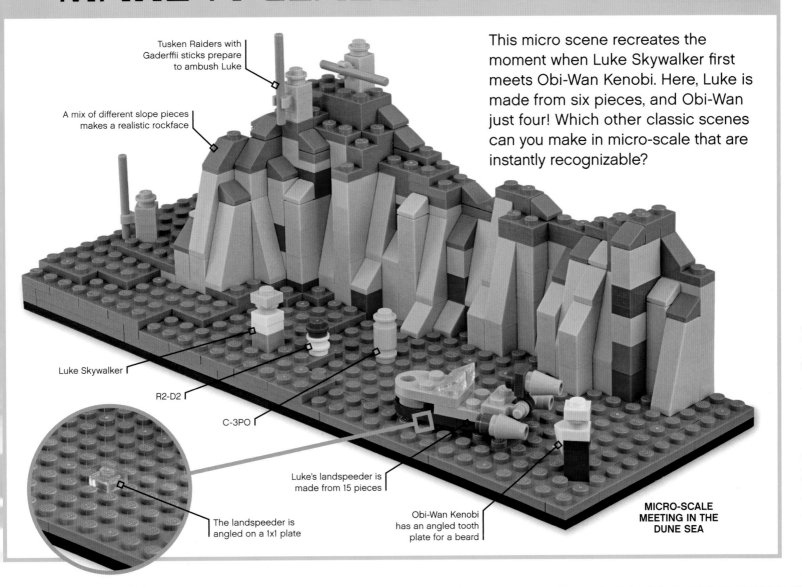

Tusken Raiders with Gaderffii sticks prepare to ambush Luke

A mix of different slope pieces makes a realistic rockface

This micro scene recreates the moment when Luke Skywalker first meets Obi-Wan Kenobi. Here, Luke is made from six pieces, and Obi-Wan just four! Which other classic scenes can you make in micro-scale that are instantly recognizable?

Luke Skywalker

R2-D2

C-3PO

The landspeeder is angled on a 1x1 plate

Luke's landspeeder is made from 15 pieces

Obi-Wan Kenobi has an angled tooth plate for a beard

MICRO-SCALE MEETING IN THE DUNE SEA

DEVELOP YOUR OWN DROIDS

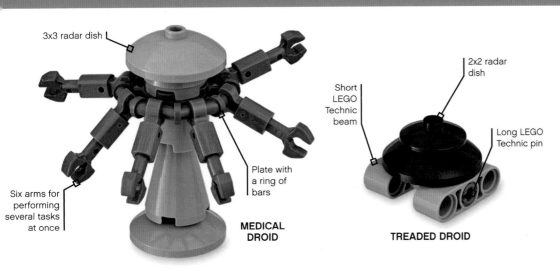

3x3 radar dish

Six arms for performing several tasks at once

Plate with a ring of bars

MEDICAL DROID

Short LEGO Technic beam

2x2 radar dish

Long LEGO Technic pin

TREADED DROID

Droids come in all shapes and sizes, and can be made with just a handful of LEGO pieces. Each of these droids has fewer than 20 parts and makes use of some unusual shapes for a one-of-a-kind look. Why not pick up 20 or so pieces at random and see what kind of droid you can make with them?

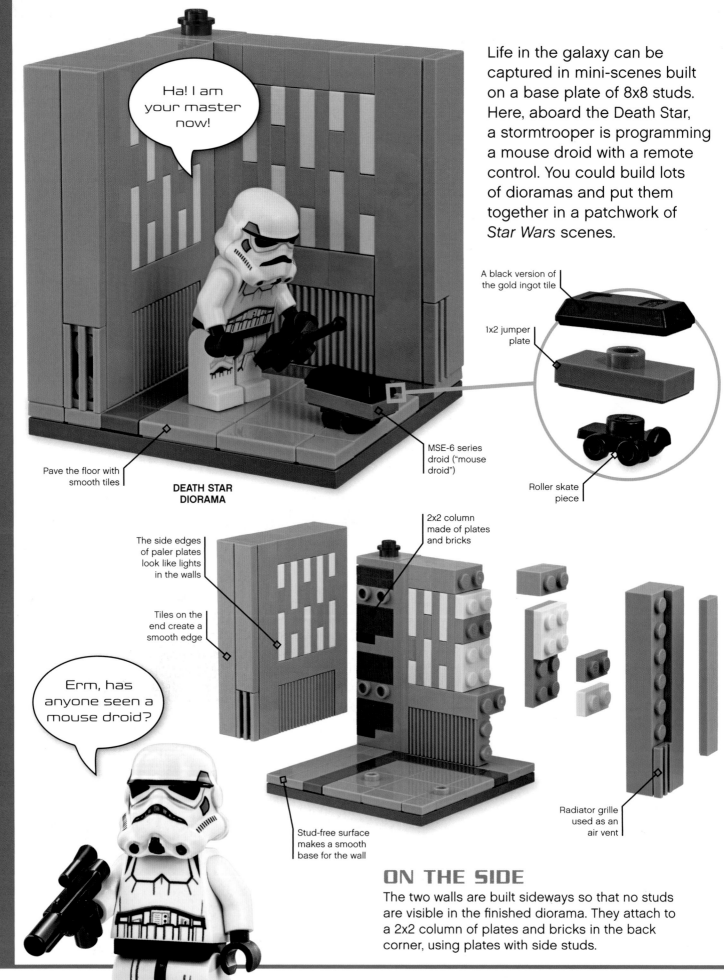

Ha! I am your master now!

Life in the galaxy can be captured in mini-scenes built on a base plate of 8x8 studs. Here, aboard the Death Star, a stormtrooper is programming a mouse droid with a remote control. You could build lots of dioramas and put them together in a patchwork of *Star Wars* scenes.

A black version of the gold ingot tile

1x2 jumper plate

Roller skate piece

Pave the floor with smooth tiles

DEATH STAR DIORAMA

MSE-6 series droid ("mouse droid")

The side edges of paler plates look like lights in the walls

Tiles on the end create a smooth edge

2x2 column made of plates and bricks

Erm, has anyone seen a mouse droid?

Stud-free surface makes a smooth base for the wall

Radiator grille used as an air vent

ON THE SIDE
The two walls are built sideways so that no studs are visible in the finished diorama. They attach to a 2x2 column of plates and bricks in the back corner, using plates with side studs.

PAINT A TATOOINE SUNSET IN BRICKS

Get your building down to a fine art. With this watercolour-paint effect, you can use bricks to capture landscape scenes from around the galaxy. Focus on the way colours blend together. Start with a 32x32 baseplate, use flat tiles for the background and add bricks, plates, and tiles on top for objects in the foreground.

SPECIAL BRICK
This 6x6 curved slope has just the right vibe for Tatooine: it was first made in this colour for Jabba's Palace in 2012.

Blend different shades of one colour together – like a colour wash in paint

The first of Tatooine's two suns is about to set

Tatooine-style domed architecture

Layers of sand built in different shades

Bricks in the foreground stand out from the 2-D background

TAKE A SEAT WITH THE JEDI COUNCIL

High in the Tranquility Spire of the Jedi Temple, 12 of the wisest and most distinguished Jedi Masters meet to rule over the Jedi Order. They sit in a circle, in 12 chairs of different sizes, shapes and designs. Build a seat for each of your Jedi Master minifigures.

Guys... was it something I said?

All chairs are grey with reddish-brown upholstery

Armrest juts out over a 1x1 slope brick

Each seat is a 2x2 plate so it fits a minifigure

YODA'S CHAIR

EETH KOTH'S CHAIR

MACE WINDU'S CHAIR

SCULPT BUSTS FOR THE JEDI ARCHIVES

Along the hallowed halls of the Jedi Archives are busts commemorating great Jedi. Why not sculpt them out of bricks rather than Bronzium? You can create your own designs of other characters or even people in your life. They're head and shoulders above other builds!

1x2 slope tops off tall Cerean head

Shoulders are an angled roof piece

Headlight brick

Bust raised off plinth with four 1x1 round plates

1x2 textured brick looks like Dooku's beard

A 1x1 plate and 1x1 slope make each of Yoda's ears

Head attaches to jumper plates

JEDI MASTER KI-ADI-MUNDI

LOST JEDI COUNT DOOKU

GRAND MASTER YODA

BE A STAR WARS ARCHITECT

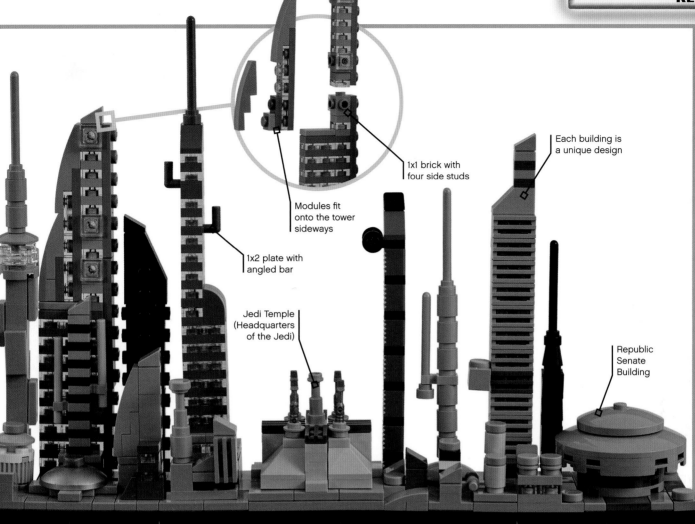

Modules fit onto the tower sideways

1x2 plate with angled bar

1x1 brick with four side studs

Each building is a unique design

Jedi Temple (Headquarters of the Jedi)

Republic Senate Building

In this build, the city-planet of Coruscant meets the LEGO® Architecture theme. LEGO Architecture sets are micro-scale versions of iconic buildings using mostly black, grey, tan and transparent bricks. They feature lots of sideways building, which gives a sleek, smooth look to builds.

Use antenna pieces to top off skyscrapers

Use transparent pieces for transparisteel windows

GALACTIC HUB

During the Republic era, Coruscant is a busy, thriving city. The sleek, high-rise buildings reflect its status as the galaxy's centre of politics, art, and culture. Pack your buildings together closely – Coruscant's surface is completely covered with skyscrapers. With a population of one trillion to house, the only way to build is up!

REAR VIEW

27

RADICAL REBUILD

Jedi Obi-Wan Kenobi goes on many rescue missions in his Jedi interceptor. In this radical rebuild, his ship can be reconstructed into new modes of transport: a sail barge and a mini version of a familiar-looking craft, plus a technician to keep all in working order. Don't forget to build in a space for Obi-Wan's astromech!

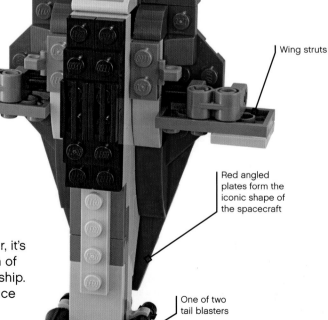

DATA FILE

SET NUMBER:
75135

LAUNCH DATE:
January 2016

PIECE COUNT:
215

BUILDER'S TIP

Why not set yourself an additional challenge to re-use every brick in the set? A combination of big and smaller builds makes for an interesting combination of models.

MINI *SLAVE I*

With clever use of the maroon pieces from the Jedi interceptor, it's possible to make a mini version of bounty hunter Jango Fett's starship. *Slave I* flies upright through space with a grey, hanging tail piece.

The two "wings" connect to LEGO Technic half pins

Wing struts

Red angled plates form the iconic shape of the spacecraft

One of two tail blasters

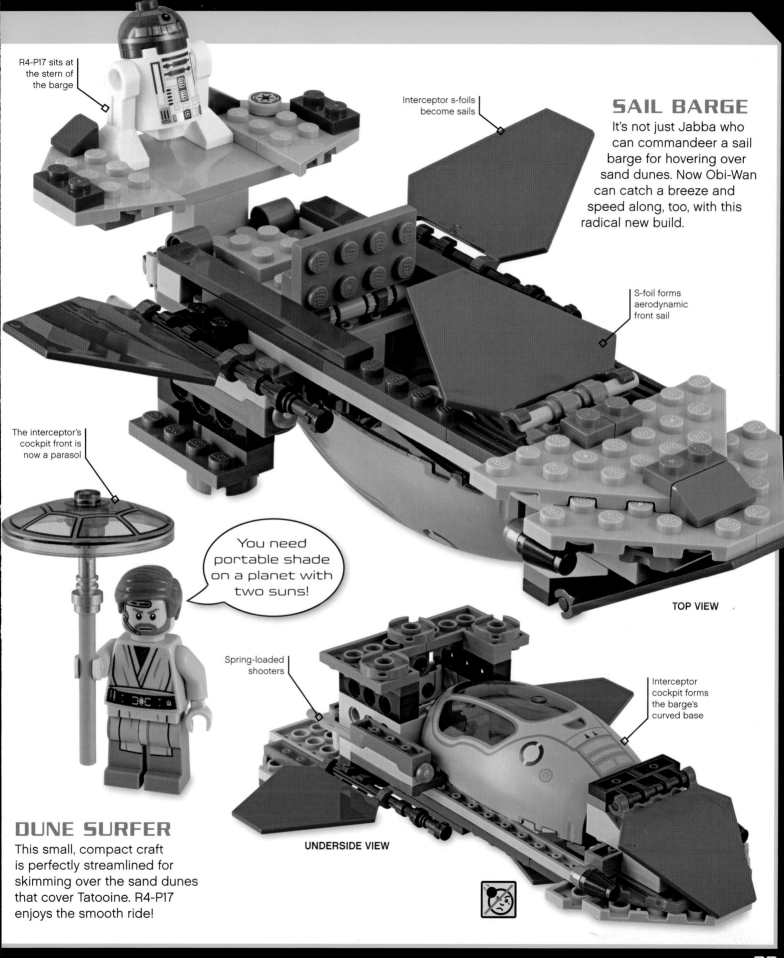

R4-P17 sits at the stern of the barge

Interceptor s-foils become sails

SAIL BARGE

It's not just Jabba who can commandeer a sail barge for hovering over sand dunes. Now Obi-Wan can catch a breeze and speed along, too, with this radical new build.

S-foil forms aerodynamic front sail

The interceptor's cockpit front is now a parasol

You need portable shade on a planet with two suns!

Spring-loaded shooters

Interceptor cockpit forms the barge's curved base

TOP VIEW

UNDERSIDE VIEW

DUNE SURFER

This small, compact craft is perfectly streamlined for skimming over the sand dunes that cover Tatooine. R4-P17 enjoys the smooth ride!

Step up the fun factor by recreating your favourite LEGO® *Star Wars*™ minifigures at a larger scale. These maxi-sized figures have posable parts for extra playability.

Cape attaches to a 1x4 brick with side studs

Breathing device is a 1x2 grille

BACK VIEW

Arm connects to a 1x2 plate with bar

An angle plate makes convincing eyes

2x2 round plates make Leia's trademark hair

DARTH VADER

YODA

PRINCESS LEIA

BUILDER'S TIP

When building at a bigger scale, you can add more detail. Look for pieces that provide a perfect finishing touch – such as 1x1 slopes for Yoda's elongated ears.

Stacked plates in R2's trademark colours

R2-D2

BUILD MINI MEAN MACHINES

These tiny craft are on a mission to defend the Galactic Empire – and if they can ruin a rebel's day in the process, that's even better!

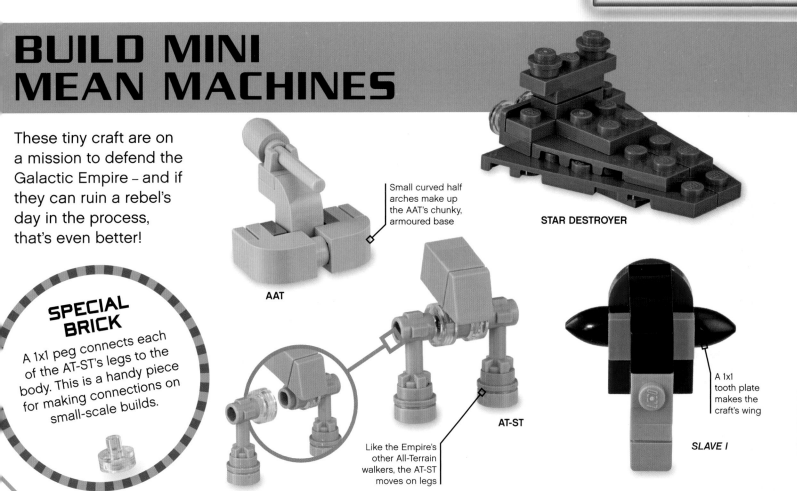

STAR DESTROYER

Small curved half arches make up the AAT's chunky, armoured base

AAT

SPECIAL BRICK

A 1x1 peg connects each of the AT-ST's legs to the body. This is a handy piece for making connections on small-scale builds.

Like the Empire's other All-Terrain walkers, the AT-ST moves on legs

AT-ST

A 1x1 tooth plate makes the craft's wing

SLAVE I

Bread is made of 3x3x2 quarter dome bricks

Once hydrated, polystarch turns into a loaf

Stacked bricks form the veg-meat slices

Round plates form the dehydrated polystarch

After a hard day's scavenging, Rey works up quite an appetite. Try building her a polystarch loaf and some green veg-meat for a bland but filling evening meal!

Um, a quarter-portion is OK, thanks!

SERVE UP REY'S RATIONS

Wouldn't it be nice to have a wise Jedi Master watching over you? With this build, you can slide Yoda's eyes left or right using LEGO Technic elements, so it looks like he can see you wherever you are in your room.

Build up a high-domed head

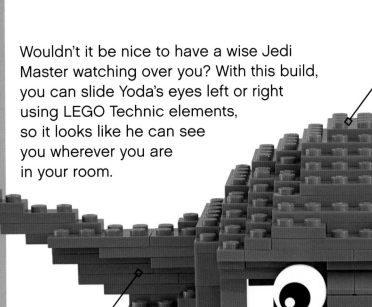

All-seeing eyes move sideways

Ears are built from stacked rectangular plates

BUILDER'S TIP

When you are building Yoda's face, take care to make the eye sockets one stud wider than the eyes. They need room to move from side to side.

EYES RIGHT... AND LEFT!

The key to the movement is a LEGO Technic gear rack built inside the head and attached to two eyes on the outside. A cog at the back of the build moves the rack – and the eyes – right or left.

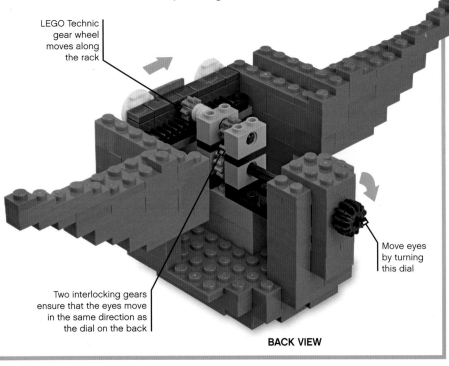

LEGO Technic gear wheel moves along the rack

Move eyes by turning this dial

Two interlocking gears ensure that the eyes move in the same direction as the dial on the back

BACK VIEW

Rey's Speeder (set 75099)

SET SCAVENGE

If you have Rey's Speeder set, you will find plenty of LEGO parts to reuse for this build. Get scavenging!

SIZE UP SEA BEASTS

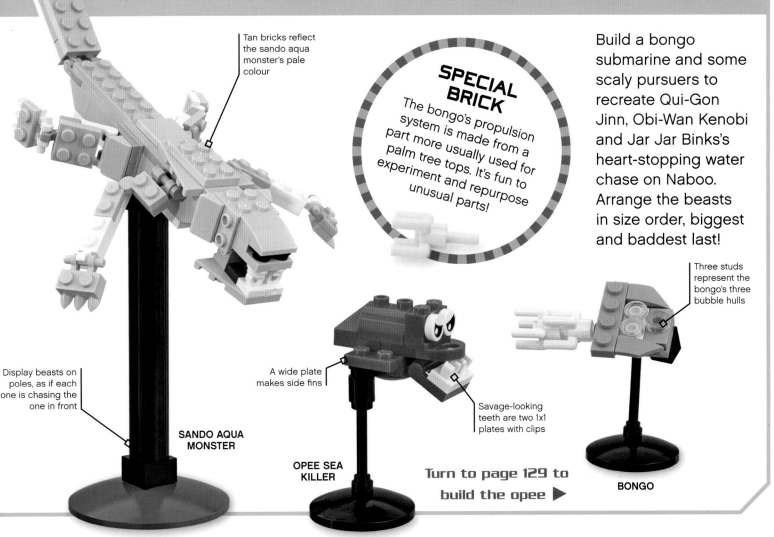

Tan bricks reflect the sando aqua monster's pale colour

SPECIAL BRICK
The bongo's propulsion system is made from a part more usually used for palm tree tops. It's fun to experiment and repurpose unusual parts!

Build a bongo submarine and some scaly pursuers to recreate Qui-Gon Jinn, Obi-Wan Kenobi and Jar Jar Binks's heart-stopping water chase on Naboo. Arrange the beasts in size order, biggest and baddest last!

Three studs represent the bongo's three bubble hulls

Display beasts on poles, as if each one is chasing the one in front

A wide plate makes side fins

Savage-looking teeth are two 1x1 plates with clips

SANDO AQUA MONSTER

OPEE SEA KILLER

Turn to page 129 to build the opee ▶

BONGO

RIDE WITH REY

Windshield made from clear slopes

Rey made her speeder from salvaged parts on the desert planet of Jakku. For this mini version, you can use salvaged parts, too – but from LEGO set 75099!

Sides attach to 1x2x2 brick with side studs

Weapon attaches to the side of the speeder

MINI SPEEDER

RAISE AN X-WING

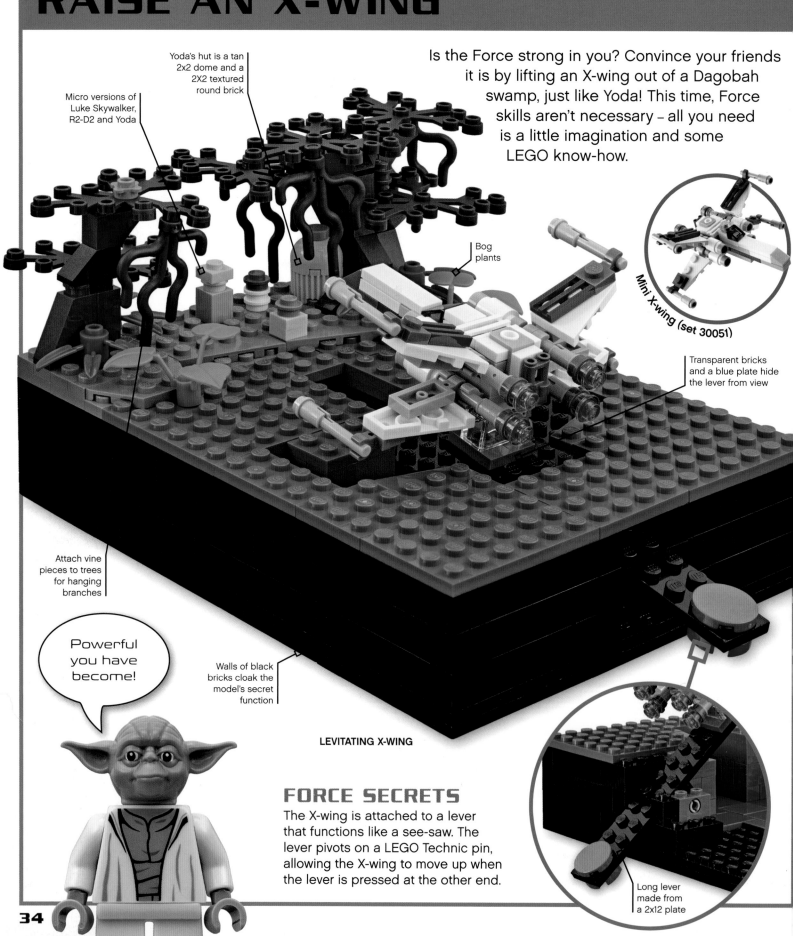

Yoda's hut is a tan 2x2 dome and a 2X2 textured round brick

Micro versions of Luke Skywalker, R2-D2 and Yoda

Is the Force strong in you? Convince your friends it is by lifting an X-wing out of a Dagobah swamp, just like Yoda! This time, Force skills aren't necessary – all you need is a little imagination and some LEGO know-how.

Bog plants

Mini X-wing (set 30051)

Transparent bricks and a blue plate hide the lever from view

Attach vine pieces to trees for hanging branches

Powerful you have become!

Walls of black bricks cloak the model's secret function

LEVITATING X-WING

FORCE SECRETS

The X-wing is attached to a lever that functions like a see-saw. The lever pivots on a LEGO Technic pin, allowing the X-wing to move up when the lever is pressed at the other end.

Long lever made from a 2x12 plate

34

MEASURE UP

When you are making the swamp surface from blue plates, use your mini X-wing model as a guide to create a sunken area in the surface that's exactly the right size and shape for the ship to emerge from.

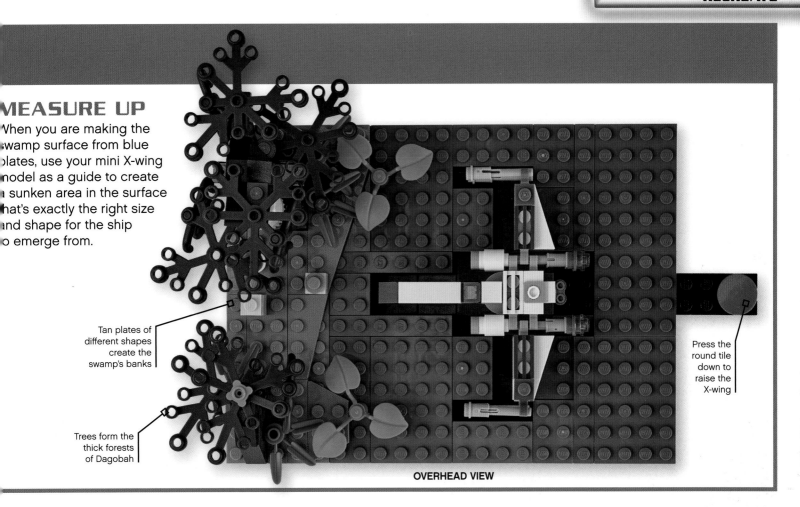

Tan plates of different shapes create the swamp's banks

Trees form the thick forests of Dagobah

Press the round tile down to raise the X-wing

OVERHEAD VIEW

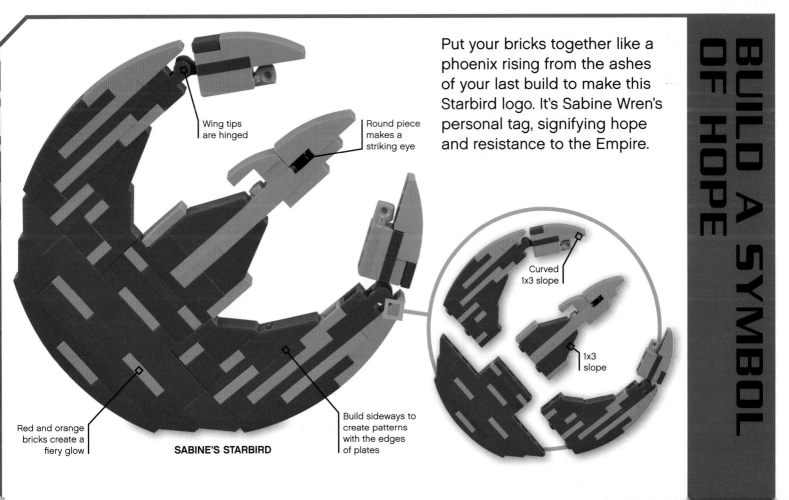

Put your bricks together like a phoenix rising from the ashes of your last build to make this Starbird logo. It's Sabine Wren's personal tag, signifying hope and resistance to the Empire.

BUILD A SYMBOL OF HOPE

Wing tips are hinged

Round piece makes a striking eye

Curved 1x3 slope

1x3 slope

Red and orange bricks create a fiery glow

SABINE'S STARBIRD

Build sideways to create patterns with the edges of plates

CREATE A GALAXY OF PLANETS

For a planet-sized challenge, try your hand at building LEGO globes! Choose colours to match existing *Star Wars* worlds, or invent new ones of your own. Building a sphere takes time and patience, so stick with it!

Frozen Hoth is almost completely white!

HOTH

Red and brown define this fiery lava planet

MUSTAFAR

The base of this planet is two 1x2 plates and a 2x4 plate

Naboo is a lush world of many oceans

NABOO

Luke Skywalker's home planet is just formed of sand and rocks with no seas at all

TATOOINE

This build starts with lots of criss-crossing 1x2 plates

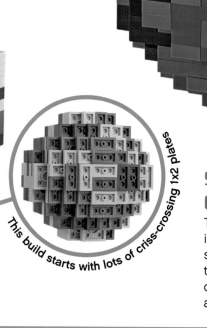

STACK YOUR CIRCLES

To create a LEGO sphere, think of it as building a stack of flat, round shapes. Make each round layer larger than the last until you get to the middle of the sphere, then make them smaller again until you reach the top.

Turn to page 60 to go into orbit with your planets ▶

PREPARE FOR LANDING

Building landing platforms for your favourite LEGO *Star Wars* Microfighters not only boosts their play potential, it also creates a great way to display them. Match the landing pad to the style of the ship that will land on it – or to the kind of planet it is landing on. The Wookiees of Kashyyyk, for example, might use wooden landing bays.

BUILDER'S TIP

Use a variety of shapes to add interest to single-colour builds. This landing pad's legs use two types of round brick, sideways slopes and exposed jumper plates.

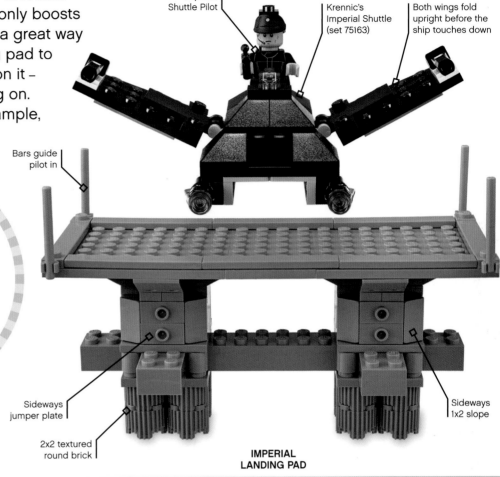

Imperial Shuttle Pilot

Krennic's Imperial Shuttle (set 75163)

Both wings fold upright before the ship touches down

Bars guide pilot in

Sideways jumper plate

2x2 textured round brick

Sideways 1x2 slope

IMPERIAL LANDING PAD

The galaxy is packed full of cute and cuddly critters that would make great pets – although some might need a little housebreaking! This friendly Loth-cat from the planet Lothal, for example, is just longing for an owner to adopt her. Will it be you?

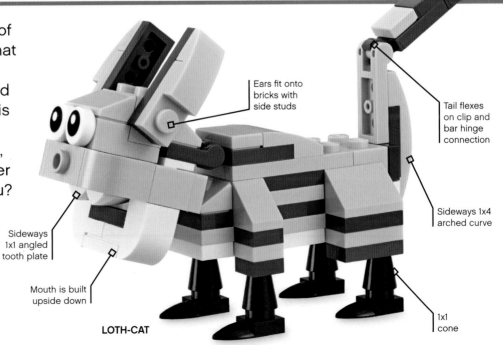

Ears fit onto bricks with side studs

Tail flexes on clip and bar hinge connection

Sideways 1x4 arched curve

Sideways 1x1 angled tooth plate

Mouth is built upside down

1x1 cone

LOTH-CAT

Ever fancied yourself as one of the Empire's best pilots? Get your hands on these replica TIE starfighter controls by making them out of LEGO bricks. First build a sturdy stand with a platform in front and then add control sticks, a screen and a cockpit canopy.

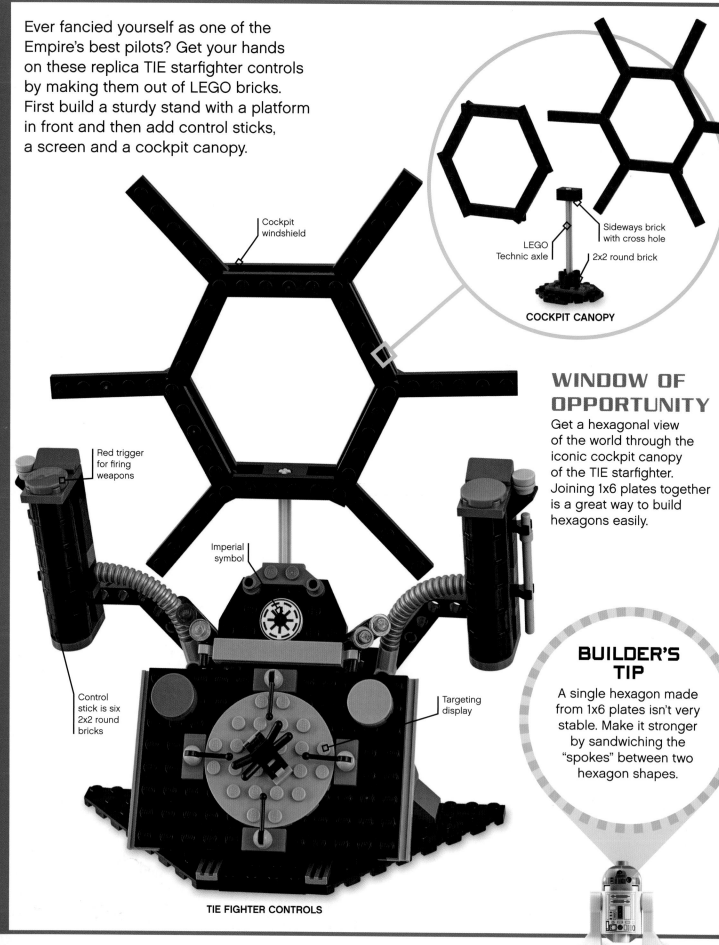

Cockpit windshield

Sideways brick with cross hole

LEGO Technic axle

2x2 round brick

COCKPIT CANOPY

Red trigger for firing weapons

Imperial symbol

Control stick is six 2x2 round bricks

Targeting display

TIE FIGHTER CONTROLS

WINDOW OF OPPORTUNITY

Get a hexagonal view of the world through the iconic cockpit canopy of the TIE starfighter. Joining 1x6 plates together is a great way to build hexagons easily.

BUILDER'S TIP

A single hexagon made from 1x6 plates isn't very stable. Make it stronger by sandwiching the "spokes" between two hexagon shapes.

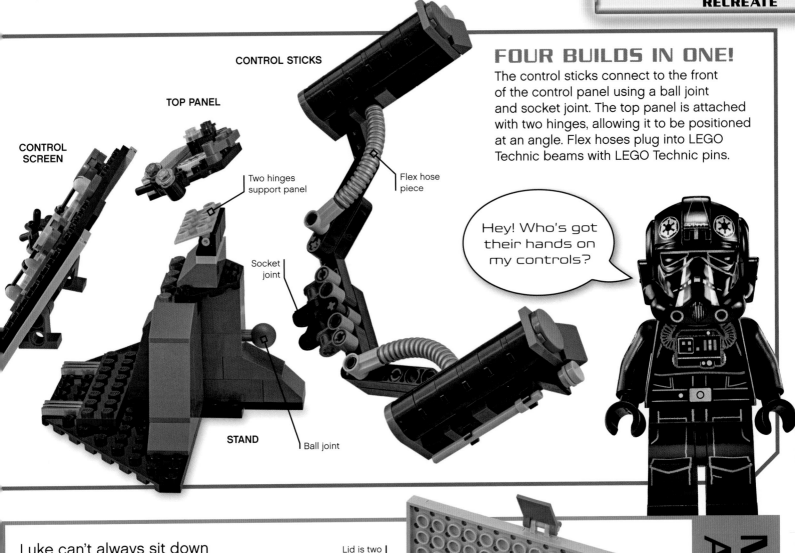

CONTROL STICKS

TOP PANEL

CONTROL SCREEN

Two hinges support panel

Flex hose piece

Socket joint

STAND

Ball joint

FOUR BUILDS IN ONE!

The control sticks connect to the front of the control panel using a ball joint and socket joint. The top panel is attached with two hinges, allowing it to be positioned at an angle. Flex hoses plug into LEGO Technic beams with LEGO Technic pins.

Hey! Who's got their hands on my controls?

Luke can't always sit down for a meal when he's out and about in the galaxy, so build him a ration pack. This one is filled with delicacies from Dagobah, inspired by Luke's stay on the lush, swampy planet.

Lid is two plates deep

Plates with side clips form the middle part of the hinge

Sohli bark

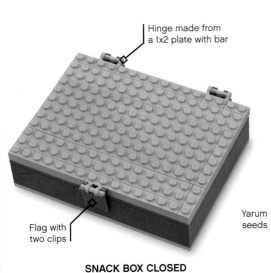

Hinge made from a 1x2 plate with bar

Flag with two clips

Mushroom spores

Yarum seeds

Galla seeds

Jedi energy capsules

SNACK BOX CLOSED

SNACK BOX OPEN

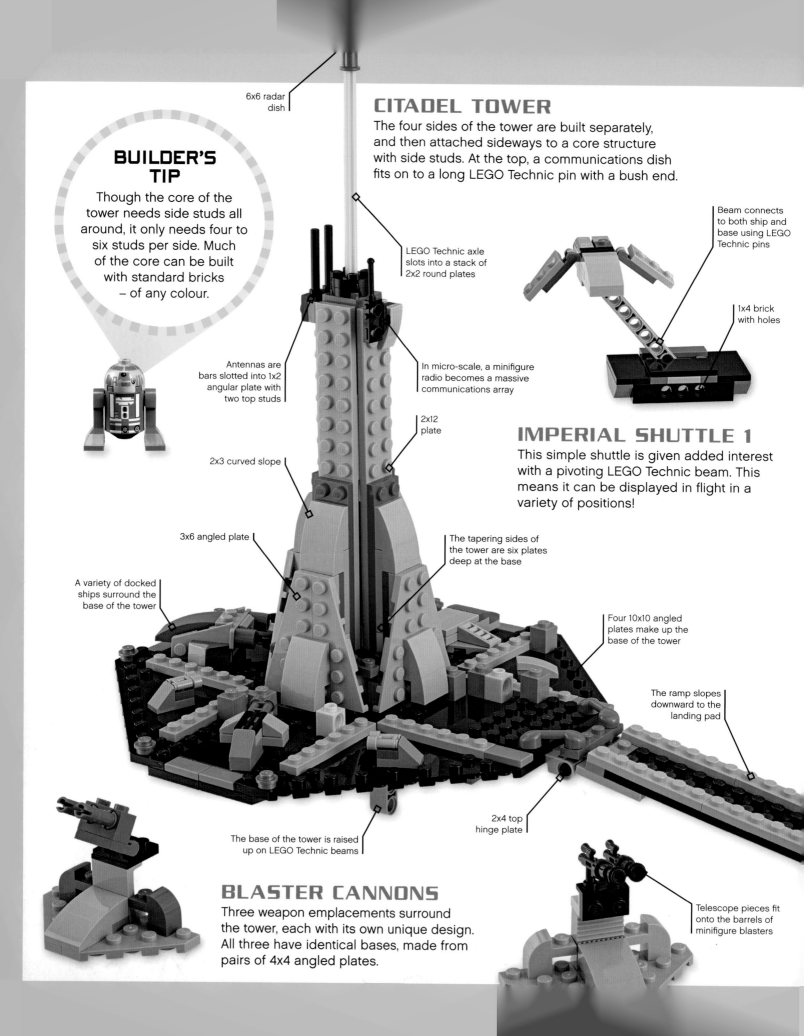

6x6 radar dish

CITADEL TOWER

The four sides of the tower are built separately, and then attached sideways to a core structure with side studs. At the top, a communications dish fits on to a long LEGO Technic pin with a bush end.

BUILDER'S TIP

Though the core of the tower needs side studs all around, it only needs four to six studs per side. Much of the core can be built with standard bricks – of any colour.

LEGO Technic axle slots into a stack of 2x2 round plates

Antennas are bars slotted into 1x2 angular plate with two top studs

In micro-scale, a minifigure radio becomes a massive communications array

2x3 curved slope

2x12 plate

3x6 angled plate

The tapering sides of the tower are six plates deep at the base

A variety of docked ships surround the base of the tower

Beam connects to both ship and base using LEGO Technic pins

1x4 brick with holes

IMPERIAL SHUTTLE 1

This simple shuttle is given added interest with a pivoting LEGO Technic beam. This means it can be displayed in flight in a variety of positions!

Four 10x10 angled plates make up the base of the tower

The ramp slopes downward to the landing pad

2x4 top hinge plate

The base of the tower is raised up on LEGO Technic beams

BLASTER CANNONS

Three weapon emplacements surround the tower, each with its own unique design. All three have identical bases, made from pairs of 4x4 angled plates.

Telescope pieces fit onto the barrels of minifigure blasters

RADICAL REBUILD

TIE STRIKER™

When rebels try to steal the Death Star plans from the Imperial base on Scarif, a squadron of fearsome TIE Strikers is on hand to defend the planet's soaring Citadel Tower. The LEGO *Star Wars* TIE striker set includes all the pieces you need to make a micro-scale version of the Citadel Tower, complete with a fleet of Imperial shuttles!

DATA FILE

SET NUMBER
75154

LAUNCH DATE
October 2016

PIECE COUNT
543

Cannon barrels are long LEGO Technic pins in an upside-down 1x2 brick with two holes

2x4 hinge plates connect the ramp to the landing pad

IMPERIAL SHUTTLE 2

This sleek Imperial ship may be small, but it is armed with two spring-shooter missile launchers! Echoing the shape of the much larger Imperial Star Destroyer, it is built using just 24 pieces.

2x3 curved slope

The centre of the landing pad has just a few studs, so the shuttle is only lightly secured

Using a TIE to make a tower – that's recycling!

The colours red, blue, and yellow take on a whole new significance when you're an Imperial officer. These coloured bars are worn on Imperial uniforms to distinguish officers' ranks – and in the Empire, status is everything. Recreate the different plaques using tiles. Which will you wear?

NAVAL CADET

Grey base is two plates thick

ENSIGN FIRST CLASS

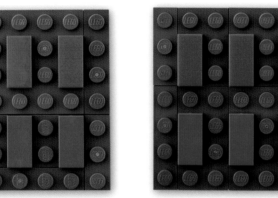

SUB-LIEUTENANT

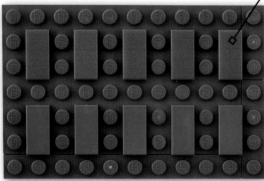

WING COMMANDER

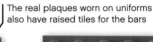

COMMODORE

The real plaques worn on uniforms also have raised tiles for the bars

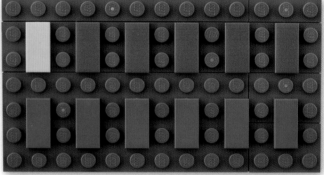

ADMIRAL

GRAND ADMIRAL

The title of High Admiral is given to the chief of the Imperial naval force

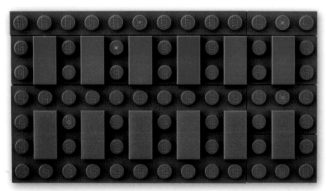

FLEET ADMIRAL

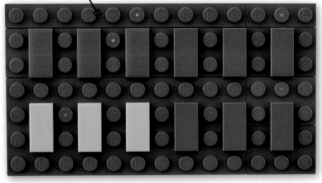

HIGH ADMIRAL

STORE THE DEATH STAR PLANS

People and droids have risked everything to get their hands on this cartridge containing secret plans (code-named "Stardust" by Galen Erso) to the first Death Star. Once you build it, keep it in a safe place – it is quite literally a matter of life and death!

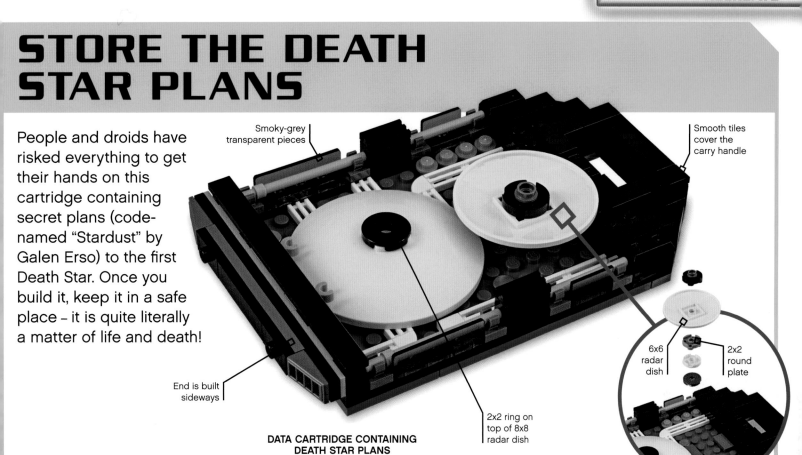

Smoky-grey transparent pieces

Smooth tiles cover the carry handle

End is built sideways

2x2 ring on top of 8x8 radar dish

6x6 radar dish

2x2 round plate

DATA CARTRIDGE CONTAINING DEATH STAR PLANS

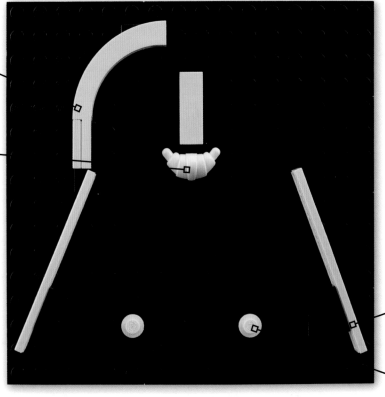

Use white bricks to show highlights on the helmet

Croissant piece is attached to a jumper plate

Smooth tiles on their sides attach to angle plates on jumper plates, creating straight lines

Round plates suggest the corners of the mouthpiece

MINIMALIST PORTRAIT OF DARTH VADER

Unleash your inner artist and build a 2-D character in a minimalist style. Minimalist art expresses something without copying exactly what it looks like. Try out your creative skills and see how few bricks you can use to build a *Star Wars* character that your friends can recognize!

CREATE SOME MINIMALIST ART

CUT THE SITH DOWN TO SIZE!

Make your bricks go further by building in micro-scale. These recreations of classic Sith ships are made with just a handful of pieces each, but still manage to capture the look of the movie originals.

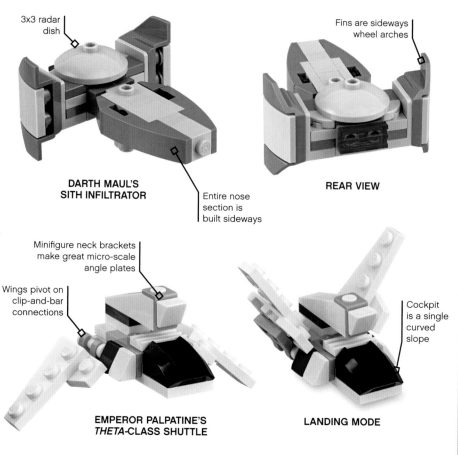

3x3 radar dish

DARTH MAUL'S SITH INFILTRATOR

Entire nose section is built sideways

Fins are sideways wheel arches

REAR VIEW

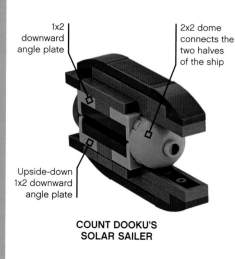

1x2 downward angle plate

2x2 dome connects the two halves of the ship

Upside-down 1x2 downward angle plate

COUNT DOOKU'S SOLAR SAILER

Minifigure neck brackets make great micro-scale angle plates

Wings pivot on clip-and-bar connections

EMPEROR PALPATINE'S *THETA*-CLASS SHUTTLE

Cockpit is a single curved slope

LANDING MODE

CREATE YOUR OWN KYBER CRYSTAL

Kyber crystals not only give power to lightsabers and the Death Star – they are also very beautiful. Rebel hero Jyn Erso treasures the small kyber crystal pendant given to her by her mother. Now you can make one of your very own!

Upside-down 1x1 ring plate

Main crystal is a stack of 14 transparent 1x2 plates

My crystal reminds me to trust the Force!

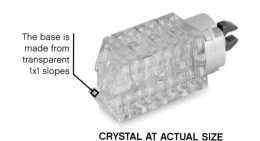

The base is made from transparent 1x1 slopes

CRYSTAL AT ACTUAL SIZE

The entire build is displayed upside-down when finished

KYBER CRYSTAL

STYLE A STANDEE

A standee is a flat decoration that can be positioned upright. They make interesting room displays that don't take up much space. You could build an entire figure like this Jawa, or a head-and-shoulders bust, such as this close-to-lifesize Greedo.

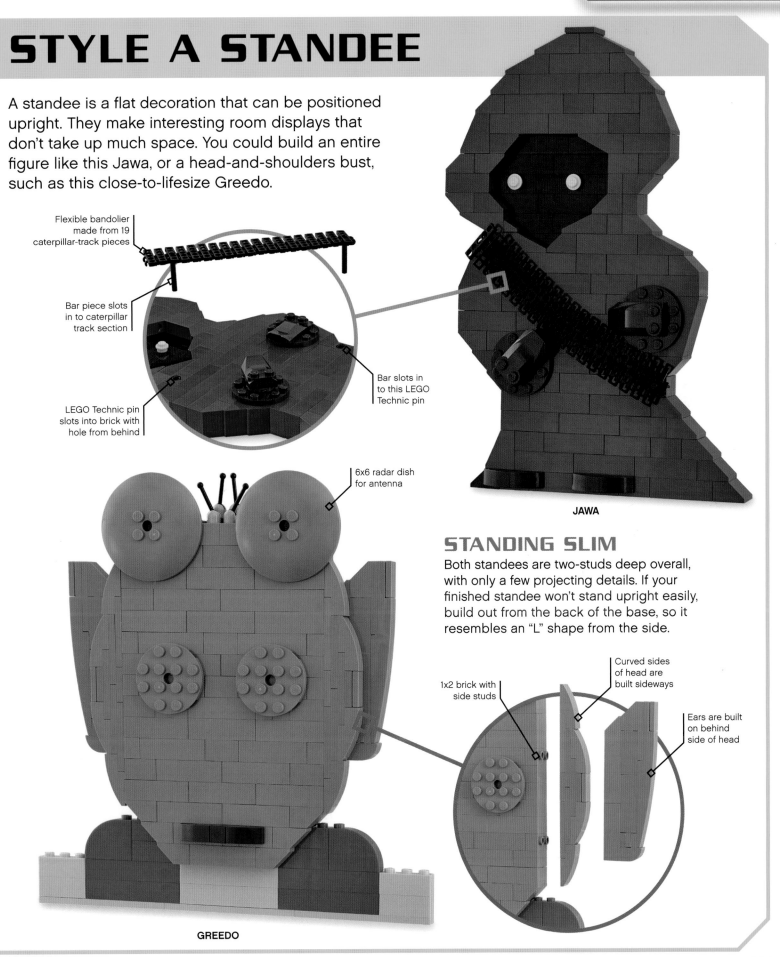

Flexible bandolier made from 19 caterpillar-track pieces

Bar piece slots in to caterpillar track section

LEGO Technic pin slots into brick with hole from behind

Bar slots in to this LEGO Technic pin

6x6 radar dish for antenna

JAWA

GREEDO

STANDING SLIM

Both standees are two-studs deep overall, with only a few projecting details. If your finished standee won't stand upright easily, build out from the back of the base, so it resembles an "L" shape from the side.

1x2 brick with side studs

Curved sides of head are built sideways

Ears are built on behind side of head

PROJECT A HOLOGRAPHIC MESSAGE

Do you have something vital to say? Perhaps the future of the galaxy depends on it? Why not create a holographic message, just like R2-D2 and Leia did? You could also make R2-D2. Blue transparent bricks will make the perfect projection.

SPECIAL BRICK
Transparent blue bricks are ideal for recreating the glow of an intergalactic holographic message. A 2x2 round brick makes a good head for your virtual character.

Slopes create R2's dome-shaped astromech head

Hologram represents Leia crouching down and reaching out

LEGO Technic pin allows the droid's body to tilt

FRONT VIEW

Transparent bricks built into the base so light can shine up through them

VIEW FROM BELOW

LIGHT UP YOUR MESSAGE

When your build is ready, slide a phone underneath to light up the blue bricks. As well as using a phone as a light, you could use it to record a voice message. Hit record and then pause for a few moments before speaking, to give you time to put the phone in position before the message plays.

Use the torch on a phone to light up your message!

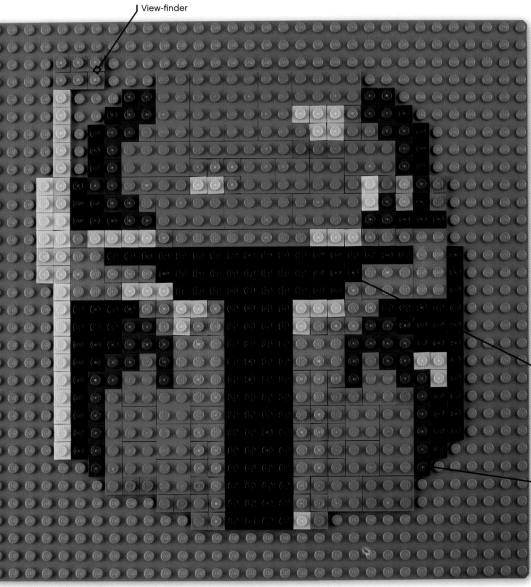

View-finder

Iconic
T-shaped
visor

Darker bricks are
used for areas in
shadow and paler
bricks for highlights

BOBA FETT

MAKE A MOSAIC

Despite its simplicity,
it's easy to recognize
that this is an image
of Boba Fett in his
Mandalorian helmet.
Bring together lots
of little LEGO pieces
to create a mosaic
of your own. To work
out how to build
your character out
of bricks, you could
draw the character
on squared paper or
pixelate the image
on a computer first.

BUILDER'S TIP

Every character has
a feature that sums up their
identity, so be sure to include
it in your build. For Boba Fett,
it's his T-shaped visor
that makes him instantly
recognizable.

Who's that
good-looking
guy?

47

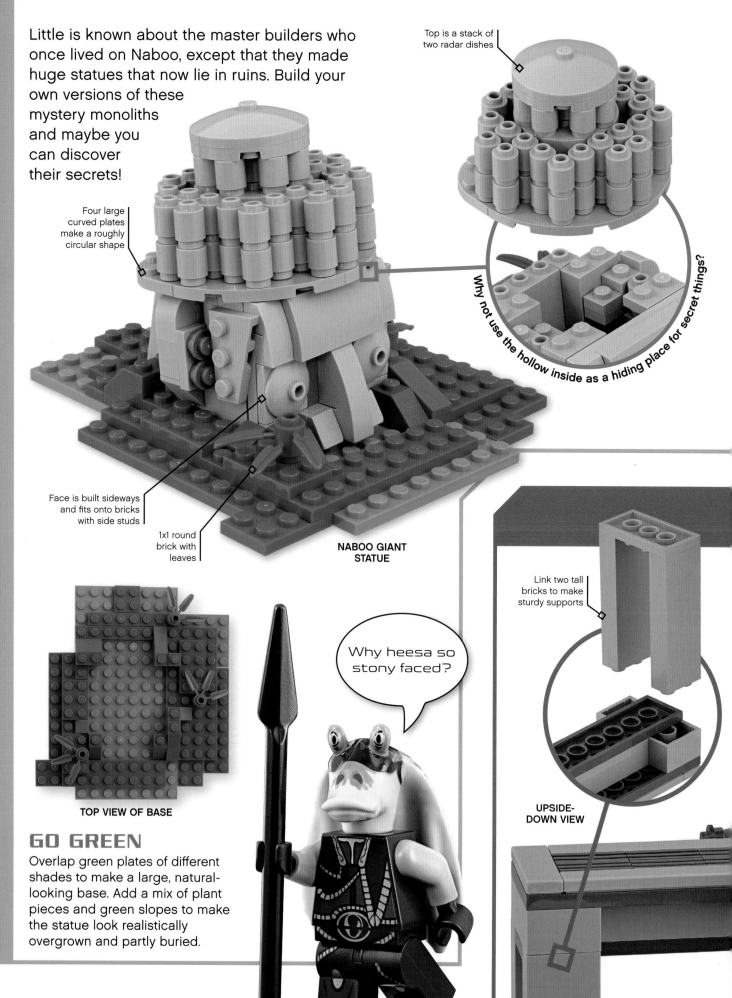

Little is known about the master builders who once lived on Naboo, except that they made huge statues that now lie in ruins. Build your own versions of these mystery monoliths and maybe you can discover their secrets!

Top is a stack of two radar dishes

Four large curved plates make a roughly circular shape

Why not use the hollow inside as a hiding place for secret things?

Face is built sideways and fits onto bricks with side studs

1x1 round brick with leaves

NABOO GIANT STATUE

Link two tall bricks to make sturdy supports

Why heesa so stony faced?

UPSIDE-DOWN VIEW

TOP VIEW OF BASE

GO GREEN

Overlap green plates of different shades to make a large, natural-looking base. Add a mix of plant pieces and green slopes to make the statue look realistically overgrown and partly buried.

SCALE UP A STORMTROOPER

Around the world, LEGOLAND® Parks are home to incredible LEGO *Star Wars* scenes, recreated at a size known as Miniland scale. Miniland figures have more realistic body shapes than minifigures, and allow for greater detail. Bring Miniland to your own home by building this stormtrooper, or by scaling up another of your favourite LEGO *Star Wars* minifigures.

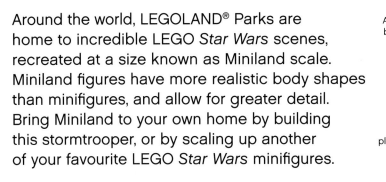

BUILDER'S TIP

Most Miniland-scale figures have hips made from a 2x3 plate or a 2x3 brick. Start with this piece when building the body, then add the arms, legs and head last.

Angled hinge brick creates chin shape

Shoulder rotates on a LEGO Technic half pin in a brick with a hole

Hinge plates for arms

Plate-with-clip hand can hold a weapon

Middle of torso is centred on jumper plates

2x3 plate

Knee armour is a 1x1 tile on a headlight brick

MINILAND STORMTROOPER

BUILD THE LONGEST BRIDGE

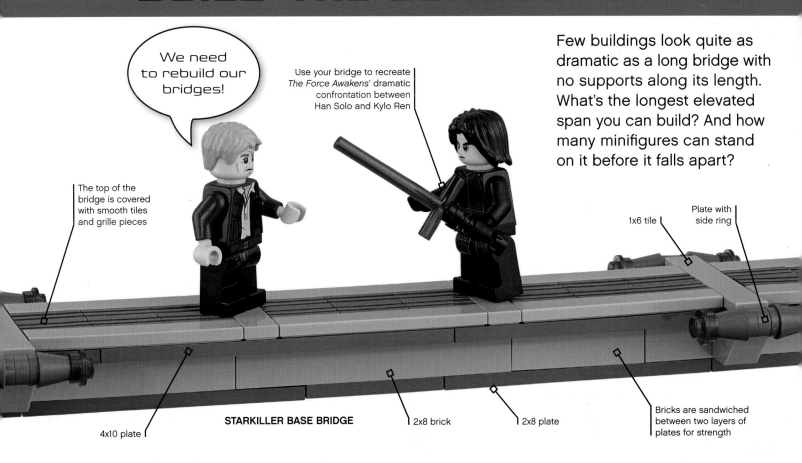

We need to rebuild our bridges!

Use your bridge to recreate *The Force Awakens*' dramatic confrontation between Han Solo and Kylo Ren

Few buildings look quite as dramatic as a long bridge with no supports along its length. What's the longest elevated span you can build? And how many minifigures can stand on it before it falls apart?

The top of the bridge is covered with smooth tiles and grille pieces

1x6 tile

Plate with side ring

STARKILLER BASE BRIDGE

4x10 plate

2x8 brick

2x8 plate

Bricks are sandwiched between two layers of plates for strength

RELEASE THE RATHTAR!

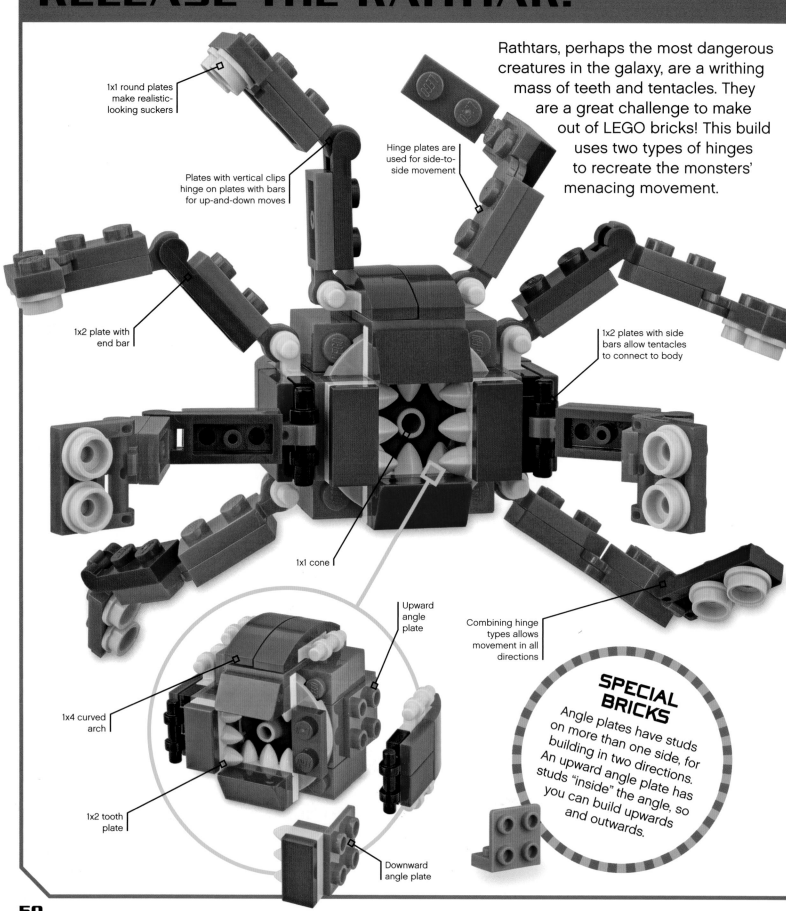

Rathtars, perhaps the most dangerous creatures in the galaxy, are a writhing mass of teeth and tentacles. They are a great challenge to make out of LEGO bricks! This build uses two types of hinges to recreate the monsters' menacing movement.

1x1 round plates make realistic-looking suckers

Plates with vertical clips hinge on plates with bars for up-and-down moves

Hinge plates are used for side-to-side movement

1x2 plate with end bar

1x2 plates with side bars allow tentacles to connect to body

1x1 cone

Combining hinge types allows movement in all directions

Upward angle plate

1x4 curved arch

1x2 tooth plate

Downward angle plate

SPECIAL BRICKS

Angle plates have studs on more than one side, for building in two directions. An upward angle plate has studs "inside" the angle, so you can build upwards and outwards.

50

These classic characters are built in the style of 8-bit video games from the 1980s. Their blocky appearance makes them easy to build, but also presents a challenge in terms of making them look like who they're supposed to be! Focus on getting the hair and clothes right to make your 8-bit creations recognizable.

Grey plates suggest areas of shadow

Each build is only one-stud deep

Model stands on a 10x4 base

STORMTROOPER

Padded shoulder

Ankle-length dress

PRINCESS LEIA

Blaster holster

HAN SOLO

Stripes for Luke's puttee leg wraps

8-bit builds use no curved or slope bricks

LUKE SKYWALKER

BUILDER'S TIP

Find a character's key features by looking at a picture of them with your eyes half closed. The colours and shapes that stand out are what defines them visually.

51

RADICAL REBUILD

When Han Solo and Chewie meet new friends Rey and Finn on board the *Millennium Falcon*, they also cross paths with some old enemies! The gangsters of Kanjiklub are ruthless pirates, and this Radical Rebuild imagines what their base might be like. It also equips Chewbacca with a powerful defensive walker in which to face them!

DATA FILE

SET NUMBER
75105

LAUNCH DATE
September 2015

PIECE COUNT
1,329

Turn to pages 104-105 for more ways to radically rebuild the *Millennium Falcon* ▶

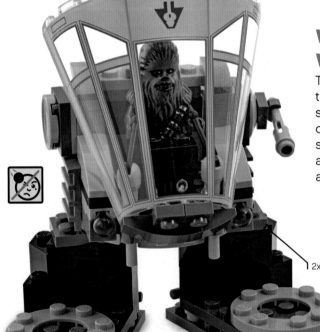

WOOKIEE WALKER

The large cockpit piece from the *Falcon* set keeps Chewie safe from enemy attack in this chunky walker. It is armed with spring-shooter missiles, and a pair of 2x2 turntable pieces allow its huge feet to move.

Chewbacca stands behind the controls

Each joystick fits onto a LEGO Technic half pin with a bar

Hinge made from 1x2 plates with end bars and 1x2 plates with clips

2x2 turntable

MILLENNIUM FALCON™

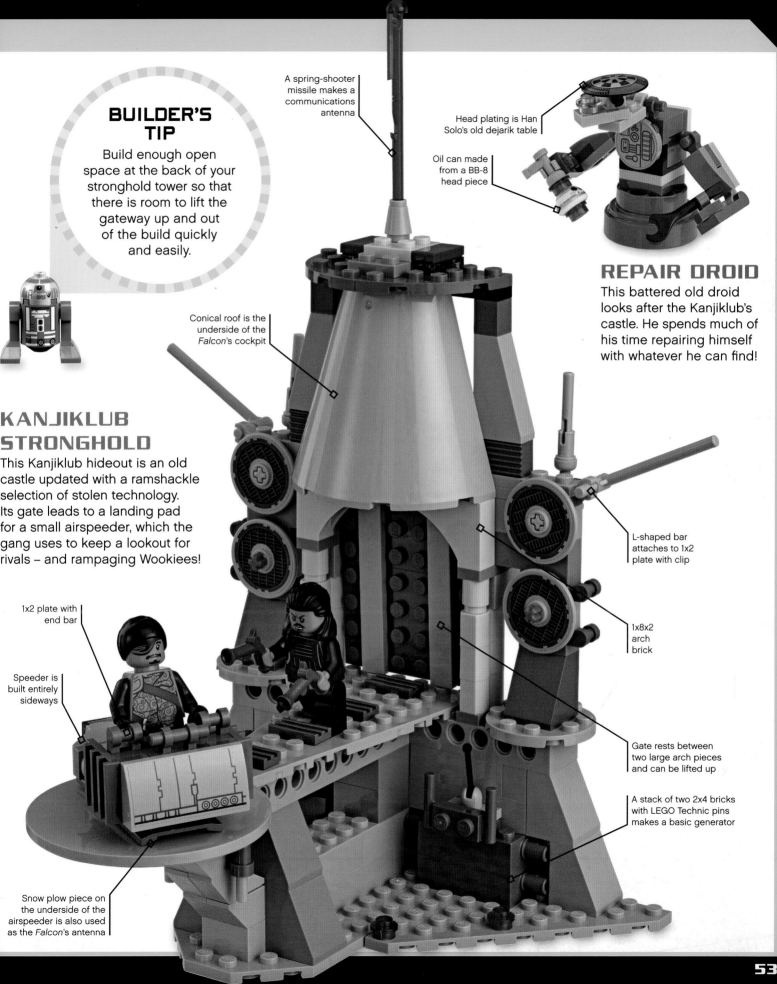

A spring-shooter missile makes a communications antenna

Head plating is Han Solo's old dejarik table

Oil can made from a BB-8 head piece

REPAIR DROID

This battered old droid looks after the Kanjiklub's castle. He spends much of his time repairing himself with whatever he can find!

Conical roof is the underside of the *Falcon*'s cockpit

KANJIKLUB STRONGHOLD

This Kanjiklub hideout is an old castle updated with a ramshackle selection of stolen technology. Its gate leads to a landing pad for a small airspeeder, which the gang uses to keep a lookout for rivals – and rampaging Wookiees!

L-shaped bar attaches to 1x2 plate with clip

1x8x2 arch brick

1x2 plate with end bar

Speeder is built entirely sideways

Gate rests between two large arch pieces and can be lifted up

A stack of two 2x4 bricks with LEGO Technic pins makes a basic generator

Snow plow piece on the underside of the airspeeder is also used as the *Falcon*'s antenna

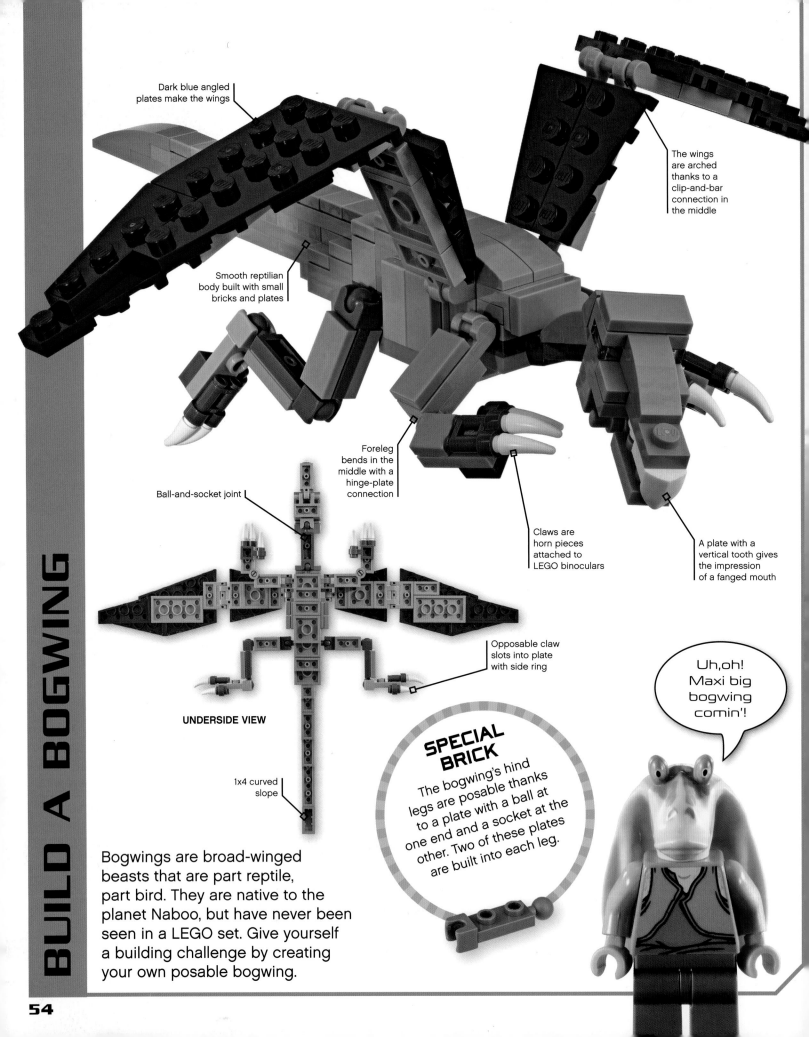

Dark blue angled plates make the wings

The wings are arched thanks to a clip-and-bar connection in the middle

Smooth reptilian body built with small bricks and plates

Foreleg bends in the middle with a hinge-plate connection

Claws are horn pieces attached to LEGO binoculars

A plate with a vertical tooth gives the impression of a fanged mouth

Ball-and-socket joint

Opposable claw slots into plate with side ring

UNDERSIDE VIEW

1x4 curved slope

Uh,oh! Maxi big bogwing comin'!

SPECIAL BRICK
The bogwing's hind legs are posable thanks to a plate with a ball at one end and a socket at the other. Two of these plates are built into each leg.

BUILD A BOGWING

Bogwings are broad-winged beasts that are part reptile, part bird. They are native to the planet Naboo, but have never been seen in a LEGO set. Give yourself a building challenge by creating your own posable bogwing.

SPELL OUT THE AUREBESH ALPHABET

Do you speak Galactic Basic? Give yourself a head start and learn the letters of the Aurebesh alphabet by spelling them out in LEGO pieces. You could use them to decorate your LEGO models or write secret coded messages to your friends!

Use one-stud-wide plates and corner plates to create the letters

A (AUREK) **B** (BESH) **C** (CRESH) **D** (DORN) **E** (ESK) **F** (FORN) **G** (GREK)

A base plate in a contrasting colour helps the letters stand out

H (HERF) **I** (ISK) **J** (JENTH) **K** (KRILL) **L** (LETH) **M** (MERN) **N** (NERN)

O (OSK) **P** (PETH) **Q** (QEK) **R** (RESH) **S** (SENTH) **T** (TRILL) **U** (USK)

V (VEV) **W** (WESK) **X** (XESH) **Y** (YIRT) **Z** (ZEREK) **CH** (CHEREK) **AE** (ENTH)

EO (ONITH) **KH** (KRENTH) **NG** (NEN) **OO** (ORENTH) **SH** (SHEN) **TH** (THESH)

FLY YOUR FLAG

Fly a flag to support your favourite podracer at Tatooine's galaxy-famous circuit! The base and flagpole are the same for all – just add your hero's colours, design and pennants. Then get ready… set… GO!

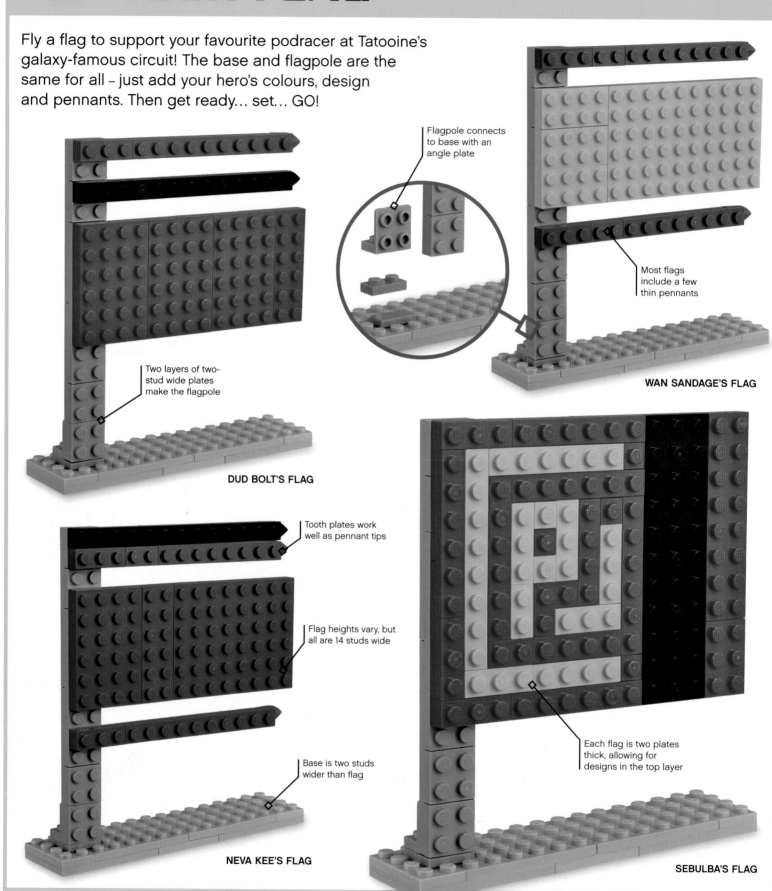

Flagpole connects to base with an angle plate

Most flags include a few thin pennants

WAN SANDAGE'S FLAG

Two layers of two-stud wide plates make the flagpole

DUD BOLT'S FLAG

Tooth plates work well as pennant tips

Flag heights vary, but all are 14 studs wide

Base is two studs wider than flag

NEVA KEE'S FLAG

Each flag is two plates thick, allowing for designs in the top layer

SEBULBA'S FLAG

MAKE ANAKIN'S GOGGLES

Goggles like these helped young Anakin focus on the perilous Boonta Eve Classic podrace course. Make your own set using curved bricks with webbed radar dishes for flip-up lens covers.

LENS-UP VIEW

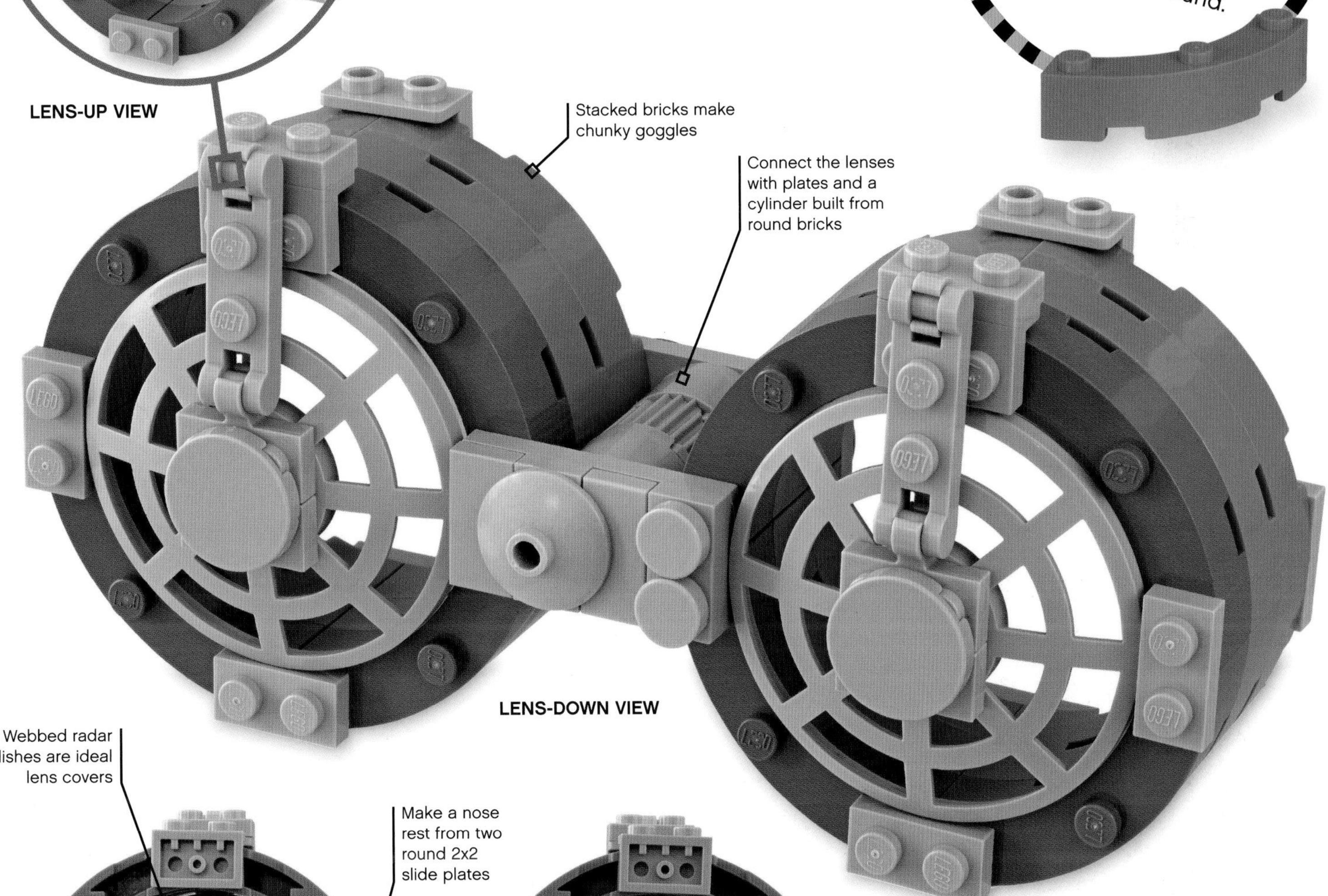

Stacked bricks make chunky goggles

Connect the lenses with plates and a cylinder built from round bricks

LENS-DOWN VIEW

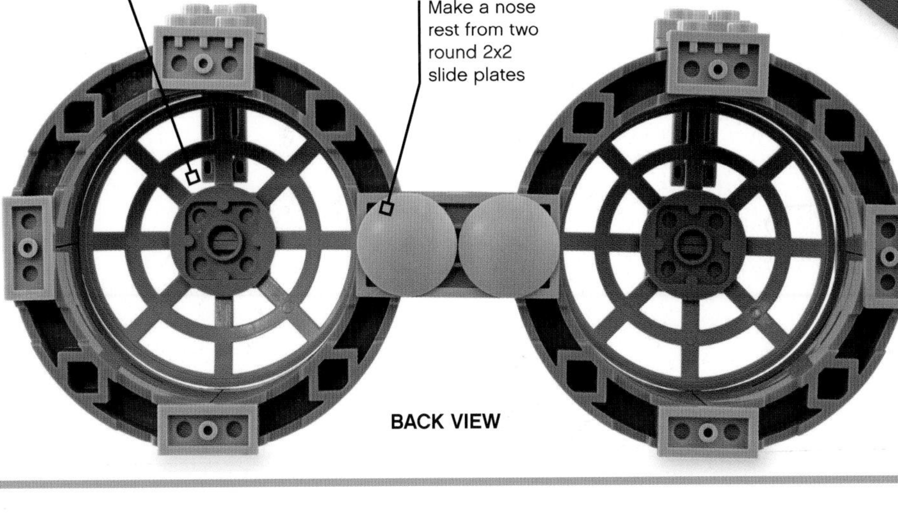

Webbed radar dishes are ideal lens covers

Make a nose rest from two round 2x2 slide plates

BACK VIEW

FLIP YOUR LIDS

Give your goggles flip-up lenses! Attach plates with clips to the lens cover and surround, then use a plate with a bar at each end to connect the cover to the goggles.

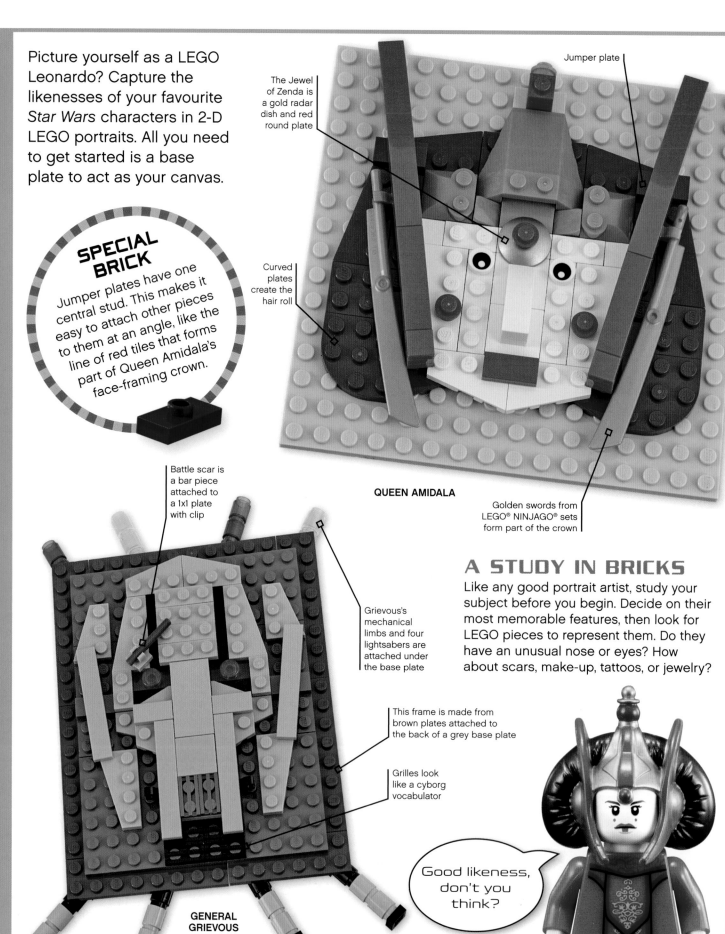

BE A LEGO PORTRAIT ARTIST

Picture yourself as a LEGO Leonardo? Capture the likenesses of your favourite *Star Wars* characters in 2-D LEGO portraits. All you need to get started is a base plate to act as your canvas.

SPECIAL BRICK

Jumper plates have one central stud. This makes it easy to attach other pieces to them at an angle, like the line of red tiles that forms part of Queen Amidala's face-framing crown.

Jumper plate

The Jewel of Zenda is a gold radar dish and red round plate

Curved plates create the hair roll

QUEEN AMIDALA

Golden swords from LEGO® NINJAGO® sets form part of the crown

Battle scar is a bar piece attached to a 1x1 plate with clip

Grievous's mechanical limbs and four lightsabers are attached under the base plate

A STUDY IN BRICKS

Like any good portrait artist, study your subject before you begin. Decide on their most memorable features, then look for LEGO pieces to represent them. Do they have an unusual nose or eyes? How about scars, make-up, tattoos, or jewelry?

This frame is made from brown plates attached to the back of a grey base plate

Grilles look like a cyborg vocabulator

GENERAL GRIEVOUS

Good likeness, don't you think?

GET IN SHAPE WITH SILHOUETTES

Star Wars is full of iconic shapes. For striking builds, create silhouettes of characters or vehicles. Without a shadow of a doubt, you'll recognize these characters a mile away!

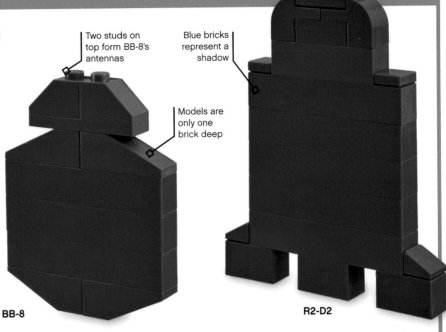

Two studs on top form BB-8's antennas

Blue bricks represent a shadow

Models are only one brick deep

BB-8

R2-D2

BUILDER'S TIP

To help you turn elements into simple shapes, try drawing them flat on paper first. Then work out which bricks to use to create their distinctive outlines.

SHRINK A PALACE

Simplifying complex shapes into micro builds is a fun way to use LEGO bricks. Here, Theed Royal Palace on Naboo has been recreated in micro-scale, with architecture combined with natural landscapes.

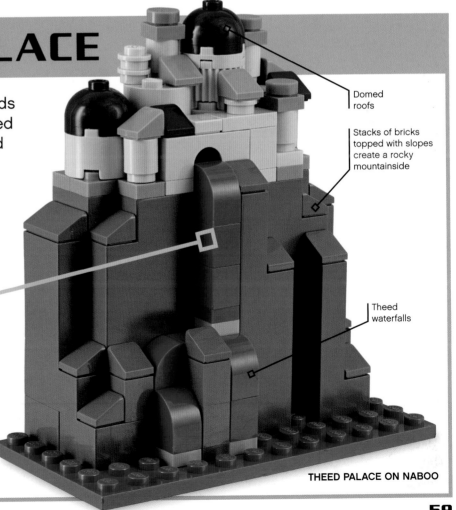

Domed roofs

Stacks of bricks topped with slopes create a rocky mountainside

Theed waterfalls

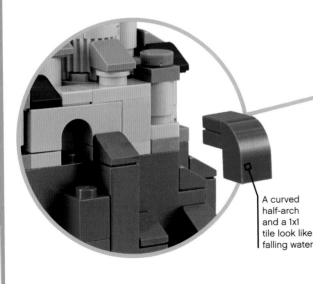

A curved half-arch and a 1x1 tile look like falling water

THEED PALACE ON NABOO

GO INTO ORBIT

Make your LEGO bricks dizzy with an armillary sphere based around a *Star Wars* planet. An armillary sphere is a model of objects in the sky that shows how they orbit on different paths. Here, the frozen planet Hoth, built from white and blue plates, spins in one direction. Around it, a mini TIE fighter chases a mini X-wing in the other direction.

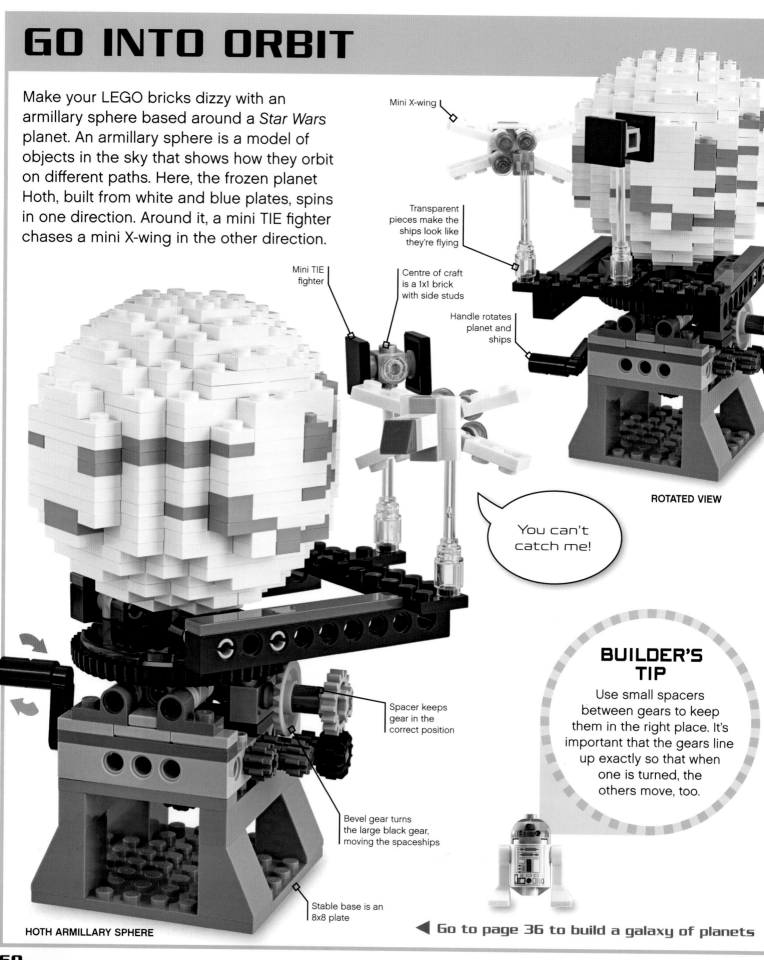

Mini X-wing

Transparent pieces make the ships look like they're flying

Mini TIE fighter

Centre of craft is a 1x1 brick with side studs

Handle rotates planet and ships

ROTATED VIEW

You can't catch me!

Spacer keeps gear in the correct position

Bevel gear turns the large black gear, moving the spaceships

Stable base is an 8x8 plate

BUILDER'S TIP

Use small spacers between gears to keep them in the right place. It's important that the gears line up exactly so that when one is turned, the others move, too.

HOTH ARMILLARY SPHERE

◄ Go to page 36 to build a galaxy of planets

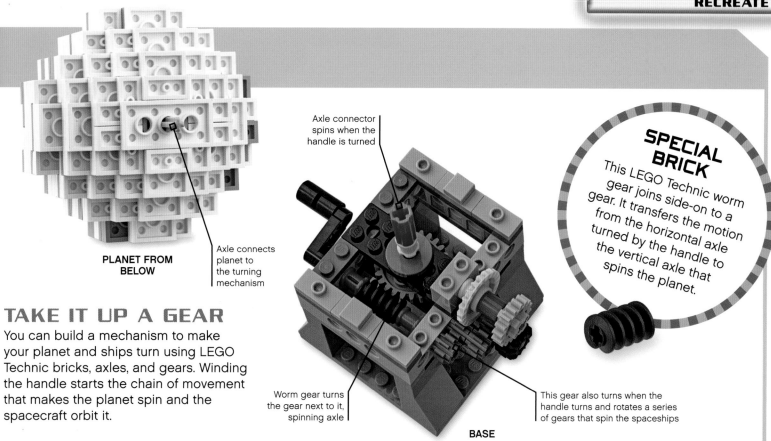

PLANET FROM BELOW

Axle connects planet to the turning mechanism

Axle connector spins when the handle is turned

TAKE IT UP A GEAR

You can build a mechanism to make your planet and ships turn using LEGO Technic bricks, axles, and gears. Winding the handle starts the chain of movement that makes the planet spin and the spacecraft orbit it.

Worm gear turns the gear next to it, spinning axle

This gear also turns when the handle turns and rotates a series of gears that spin the spaceships

BASE

SPECIAL BRICK

This LEGO Technic worm gear joins side-on to a gear. It transfers the motion from the horizontal axle turned by the handle to the vertical axle that spins the planet.

FLATTEN A TUSKEN FAMILY

Who's afraid of Tusken Raiders? They're fierce desert nomads who inhabit Tatooine. Since these savage humanoids are less imposing in 2-D, why not recreate a Tusken family in this flat building style?

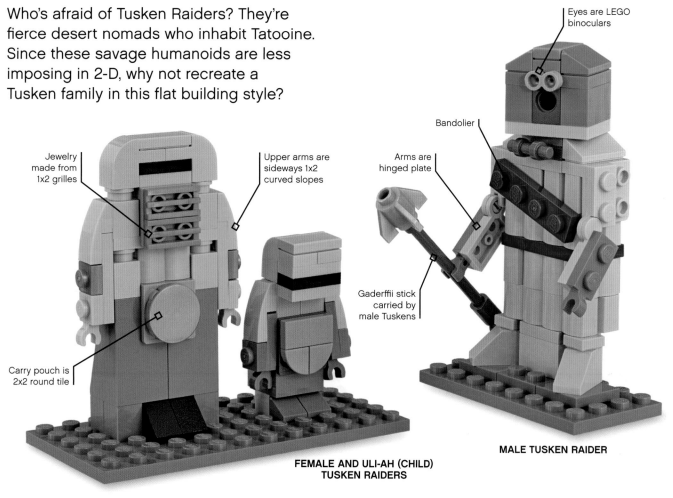

Jewelry made from 1x2 grilles

Upper arms are sideways 1x2 curved slopes

Carry pouch is 2x2 round tile

Eyes are LEGO binoculars

Bandolier

Arms are hinged plate

Gaderffii stick carried by male Tuskens

FEMALE AND ULI-AH (CHILD) TUSKEN RAIDERS

MALE TUSKEN RAIDER

Relive the amazing chase on Endor's moon with this spinning speeder bike build. But wait – is Princess Leia chasing the stormtrooper around the tree, or is he chasing her? You decide! However hard you spin them, the speeders will always stay the same distance apart. Use speeders from a set you have or build two of your own.

Speeder from Ewok Village (set 10236)

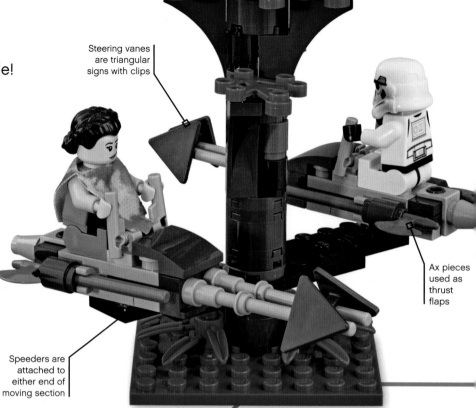

Steering vanes are triangular signs with clips

Ax pieces used as thrust flaps

Speeders are attached to either end of moving section

FORM A FOREST

Use round bricks for the tree trunk and sandwich a moving section, made from plates, between them. Add lush greenery to your tree. Don't forget – you're on a forest moon!

Whoa... feeling a little dizzy here!

A LEGO Technic axle links the two tree sections

Central black piece is a LEGO Technic plate with holes

A 2x2 ring stops the moving part from catching on the upper part of the tree

Another 2x2 ring makes a smooth base for the moving section above

BUILDER'S TIP

For the best effect, make skyscrapers different heights and leave gaps so you can see sky between them. Top some towers with cones to vary the skyline.

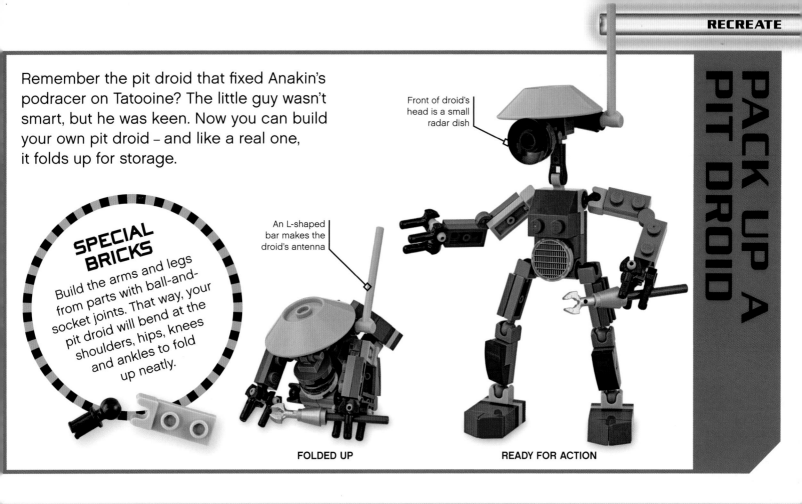

Remember the pit droid that fixed Anakin's podracer on Tatooine? The little guy wasn't smart, but he was keen. Now you can build your own pit droid – and like a real one, it folds up for storage.

PACK UP A PIT DROID

Front of droid's head is a small radar dish

An L-shaped bar makes the droid's antenna

SPECIAL BRICKS

Build the arms and legs from parts with ball-and-socket joints. That way, your pit droid will bend at the shoulders, hips, knees and ankles to fold up neatly.

FOLDED UP

READY FOR ACTION

MAKE A CITY SILHOUETTE

Use cones and antennas to add height to towers

Coruscant City's skyscrapers look even more dramatic by night. Recreate the city's famous skyline in silhouette, using black LEGO pieces. Build as high as you can – the sky's the limit!

Place low builds in front of higher builds to add depth to skyline

FRONT VIEW

BACK VIEW

Hide the bases of the tall buidings at the back

BUILD MICRO MOVIE SCENES

Shrink the biggest *Star Wars* scenes into micro moments! Select your smallest LEGO pieces and consider what they could be used for – in micro-scale, a horn piece could be a giant sarlacc beast's tentacle, and a flag piece makes a starship's wing.

BUILDER'S TIP

Building in micro-scale means anything smaller than minifigure scale. Decide what your scale is before you begin so you don't get a confusing-looking result!

DEATH STAR DIORAMAS

Some of the galaxy's most dramatic moments happen aboard or around the Death Star. Create grey, angled walls and smooth tiled floors to capture the battle station's cold, ordered environment.

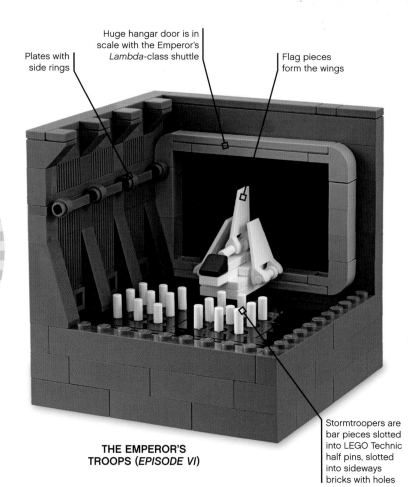

Plates with side rings

Huge hangar door is in scale with the Emperor's *Lambda*-class shuttle

Flag pieces form the wings

Stormtroopers are bar pieces slotted into LEGO Technic half pins, slotted into sideways bricks with holes

THE EMPEROR'S TROOPS (*EPISODE VI*)

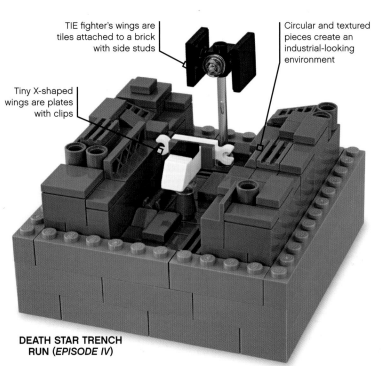

TIE fighter's wings are tiles attached to a brick with side studs

Circular and textured pieces create an industrial-looking environment

Tiny X-shaped wings are plates with clips

DEATH STAR TRENCH RUN (*EPISODE IV*)

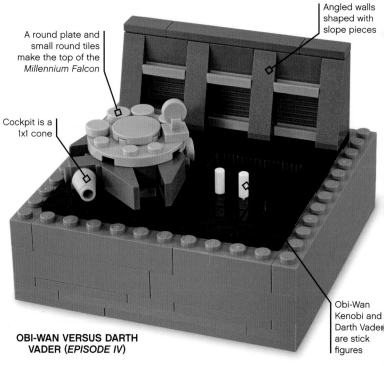

A round plate and small round tiles make the top of the *Millennium Falcon*

Angled walls shaped with slope pieces

Cockpit is a 1x1 cone

OBI-WAN VERSUS DARTH VADER (*EPISODE IV*)

Obi-Wan Kenobi and Darth Vader are stick figures

ENDOR ENDING

Technology plus dense woods create the forest moon of Endor, home to the Ewok village and an important shield generator.

Jabba's sail barge attaches to sideways bricks with side studs

Two upside-down flower stems make tree's foliage

Tiled platform provides a place for starship to land

Endor forest

Hose nozzles form the sides of the AT-AT's head

Rows of smooth tiles cover studs

Brown telescope piece is a tree trunk

Billowing sails are curved slopes

The desert is built sideways and rests inside the grey frame

Tentacles and beaked tongue of the carnivorous Sarlacc beast

BATTLE OF ENDOR
(*EPISODE VI*)

Upside-down 1x1 tiles attach to LEGO Technic half pins

The sandcrawler is built sideways

Short LEGO Technic half beams

A white dome and a tile stacked on a plate make the Lars' homestead

JABBA'S SAIL BARGE
(*EPISODE VI*)

TATOOINE SCENES

Gather tan pieces to make scenes from the desert planet Tatooine, featuring sand dunes, subterranean homes and scrap-metal vehicles.

SANDCRAWLER
(*EPISODE IV*)

White telescopes are moisture vaporators

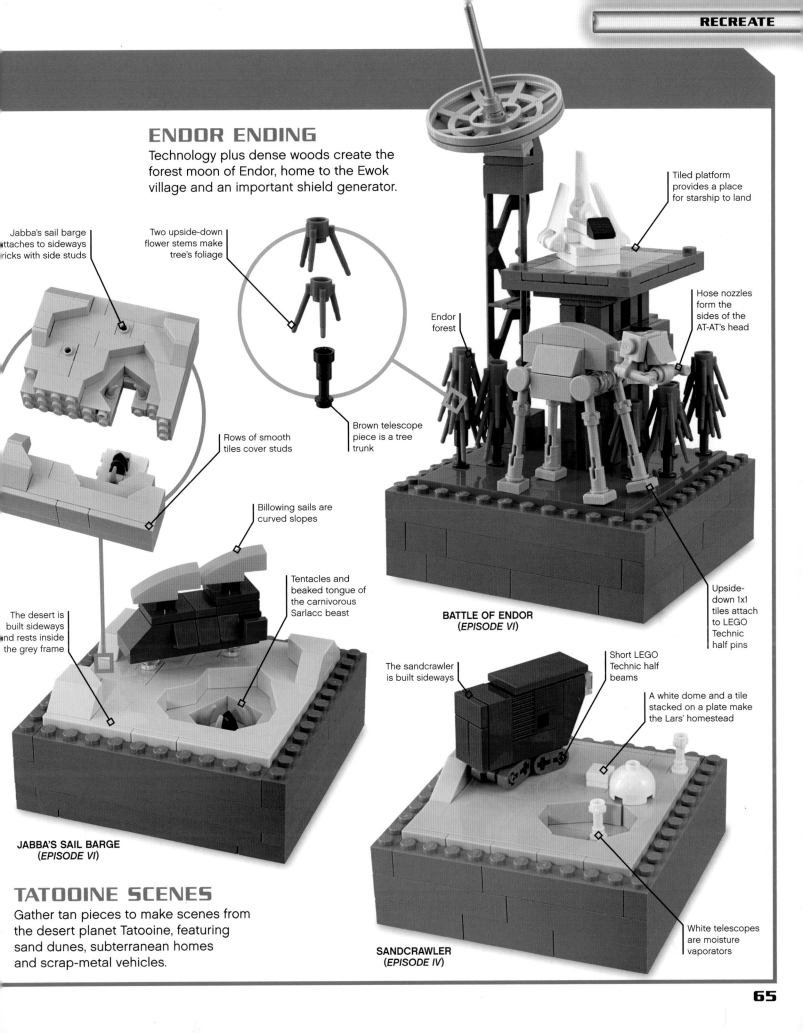

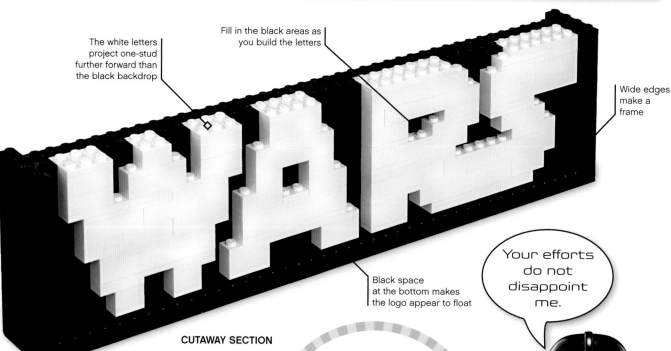

The white letters project one-stud further forward than the black backdrop

Fill in the black areas as you build the letters

Wide edges make a frame

Black space at the bottom makes the logo appear to float

CUTAWAY SECTION

Your efforts do not disappoint me.

BUILDER'S TIP

Start with the "W." All the other letters need black bricks to be built in as you go, making them harder to get right. Only the "W" can have its black parts added last.

It is one of the most famous logos in the world – but how well do you really know it? Challenge yourself to build a *Star Wars* sign and you might just find that its ins and outs have some surprises in store for you!

HOLD YOUR OWN HOLOCRON

Holocrons are powerful data cubes carried only by Force users – and by you, if you build one! This one is purely decorative, but you could make yours as a storage box, and keep a real data drive inside it.

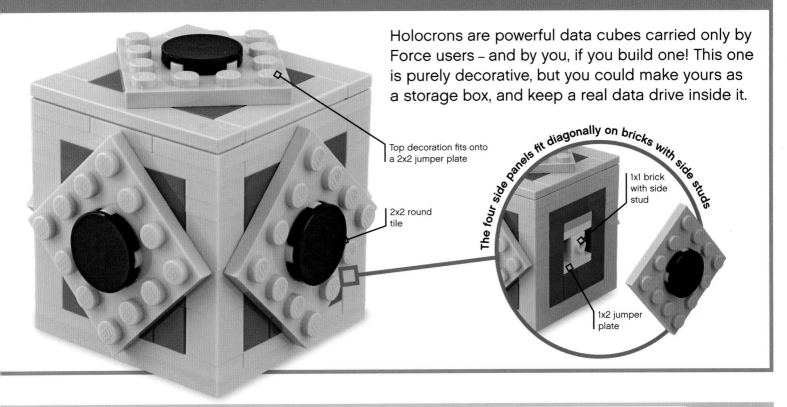

Top decoration fits onto a 2x2 jumper plate

2x2 round tile

The four side panels fit diagonally on bricks with side studs

1x1 brick with side stud

1x2 jumper plate

GO FISHING ON NABOO

The oceans of Naboo are home to many species of colourful scalefish. These examples are some of the smaller, friendlier ones, but you can make yours as big and beastly as you like!

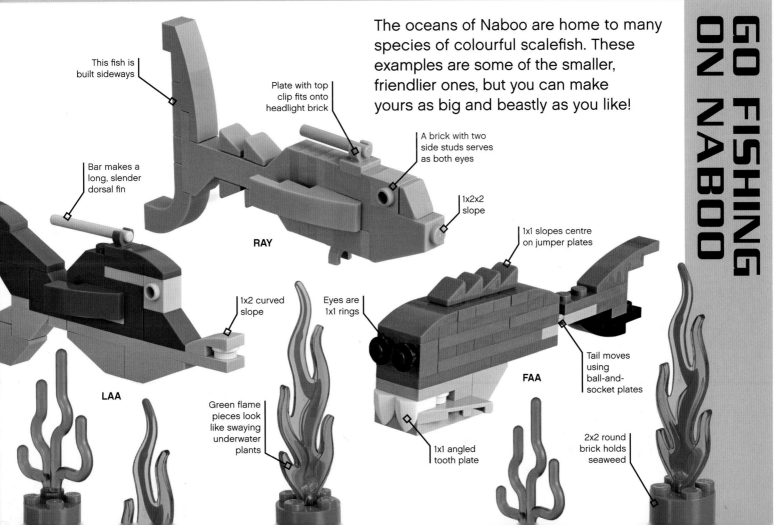

This fish is built sideways

Bar makes a long, slender dorsal fin

Plate with top clip fits onto headlight brick

A brick with two side studs serves as both eyes

1x2x2 slope

RAY

1x2 curved slope

1x1 slopes centre on jumper plates

Eyes are 1x1 rings

Tail moves using ball-and-socket plates

LAA

Green flame pieces look like swaying underwater plants

FAA

1x1 angled tooth plate

2x2 round brick holds seaweed

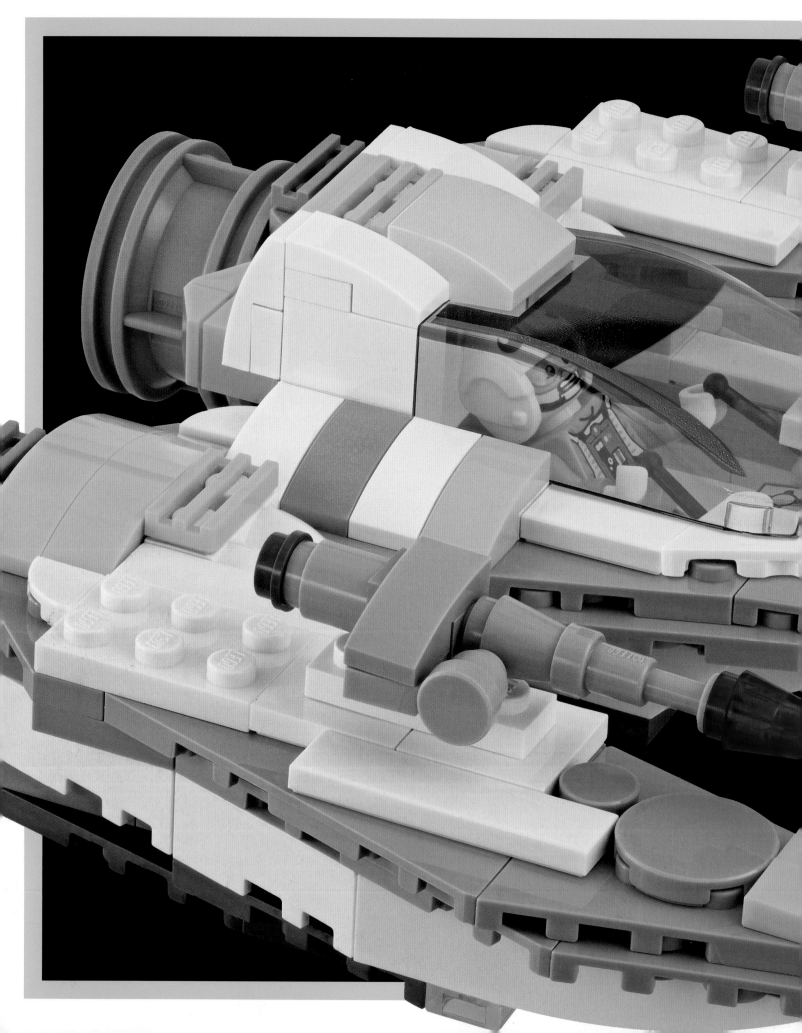

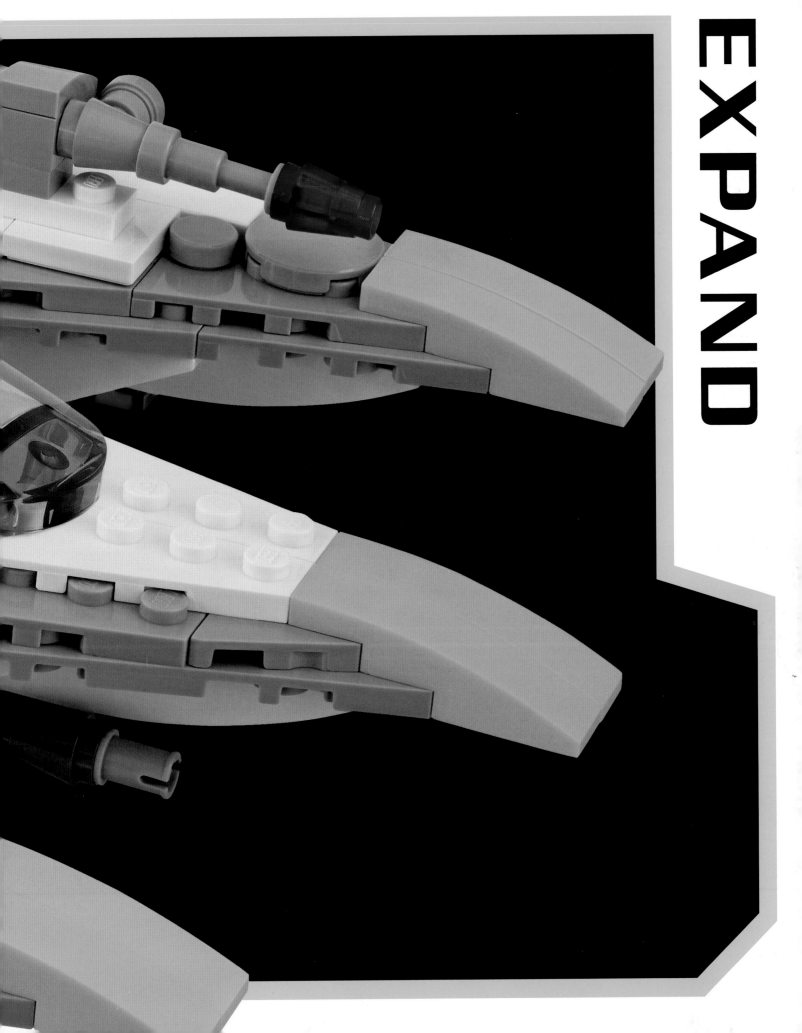

FORM A MARCHING BAND

It's not often that stormtroopers can express their creativity. Help them find their tune with an Imperial marching band. Create some crazy minifigure-scale musical instruments to liven up parades.

Palm tree top makes the horn's valves

Faucet piece

Mug piece

BASS HORN PLAYER

LEAD HORN PLAYER

DRUMMER

INVENT A CANTINA ALIEN

Species of every size, shape and colour inhabit the galaxy, and many of them frequent the slime pit that is the Mos Eisley cantina. Here you'll find an eye-popping array of characters and creatures. Why not create your own?

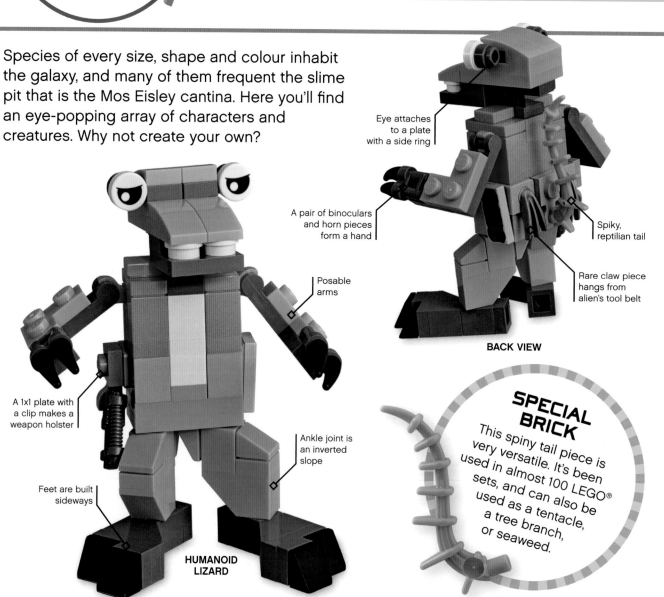

Eye attaches to a plate with a side ring

A pair of binoculars and horn pieces form a hand

Spiky, reptilian tail

Rare claw piece hangs from alien's tool belt

BACK VIEW

Posable arms

A 1x1 plate with a clip makes a weapon holster

Ankle joint is an inverted slope

Feet are built sideways

HUMANOID LIZARD

SPECIAL BRICK
This spiny tail piece is very versatile. It's been used in almost 100 LEGO® sets, and can also be used as a tentacle, a tree branch, or seaweed.

ROCK AND ROLL WITH BARQUIN AND R2-A5

Dig that crazy beat, guys!

TENOR HORN PLAYER

Bith musician Barquin D'an rocks out with the Max Rebo band in Jabba the Hutt's palace, so why not make him actually rock, by building him on a curved base? Use the same technique to build any character and make them shake, rattle and roll!

Turntable piece moves the head

Minifigure lasso makes the kloo horn's mouthpiece

A half arch curves the arm to help hold the kloo horn

LEGO® Technic pins connect the round bricks of the legs back to back, allowing the base to be attached upside down.

SPECIAL BRICK

The 1x1 plate with a side ring is usually used for holding small elements at right angles, but a pair of them also make good hands for a figure.

1x1 plate fits onto LEGO Technic half pin in a brick with a hole.

R2-A5

Astromech droid R2-A5 takes a break from collecting data to rock out with the band. Instead of moving side-to-side like Barquin, R2-A5 rocks forwards and backwards on two smaller curved pieces.

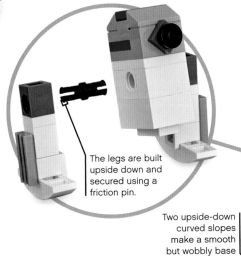

The legs are built upside down and secured using a friction pin.

Two upside-down curved slopes make a smooth but wobbly base

MAKE AN ALPHABET OF STARFIGHTERS

Many starfighters are named for their resemblance to letters of the alphabet. There are A-wings, B-wings, U-wings, V-wings, and X-wings! But what about the other letters of the alphabet? Can you come up with a starfighter shape for every letter in your name?

SPECIAL BRICK
Huge LEGO Technic wheel rims feature in many of the largest LEGO vehicles. Without tyres, they are perfect as starship engines.

G-WING STARFIGHTER
The G-wing is almost all engine, with a small passenger pod on one side. Its chunky, curving shape is created using quarter-dome pieces and big curved half-arch bricks. The engines themselves are wheel rim pieces.

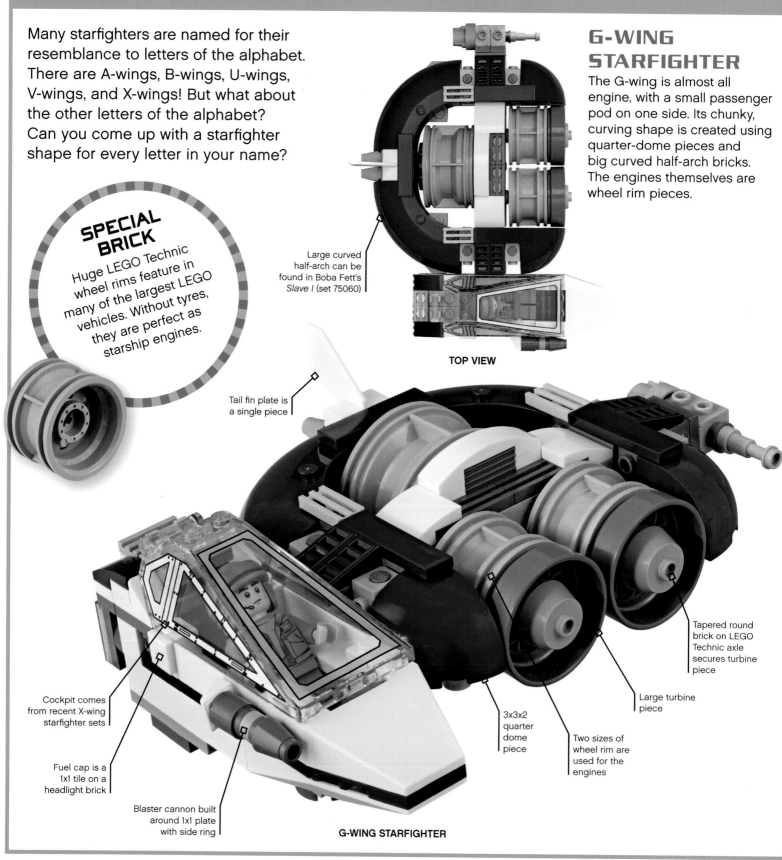

Large curved half-arch can be found in Boba Fett's *Slave I* (set 75060)

TOP VIEW

Tail fin plate is a single piece

Tapered round brick on LEGO Technic axle secures turbine piece

Large turbine piece

Cockpit comes from recent X-wing starfighter sets

3x3x2 quarter dome piece

Two sizes of wheel rim are used for the engines

Fuel cap is a 1x1 tile on a headlight brick

Blaster cannon built around 1x1 plate with side ring

G-WING STARFIGHTER

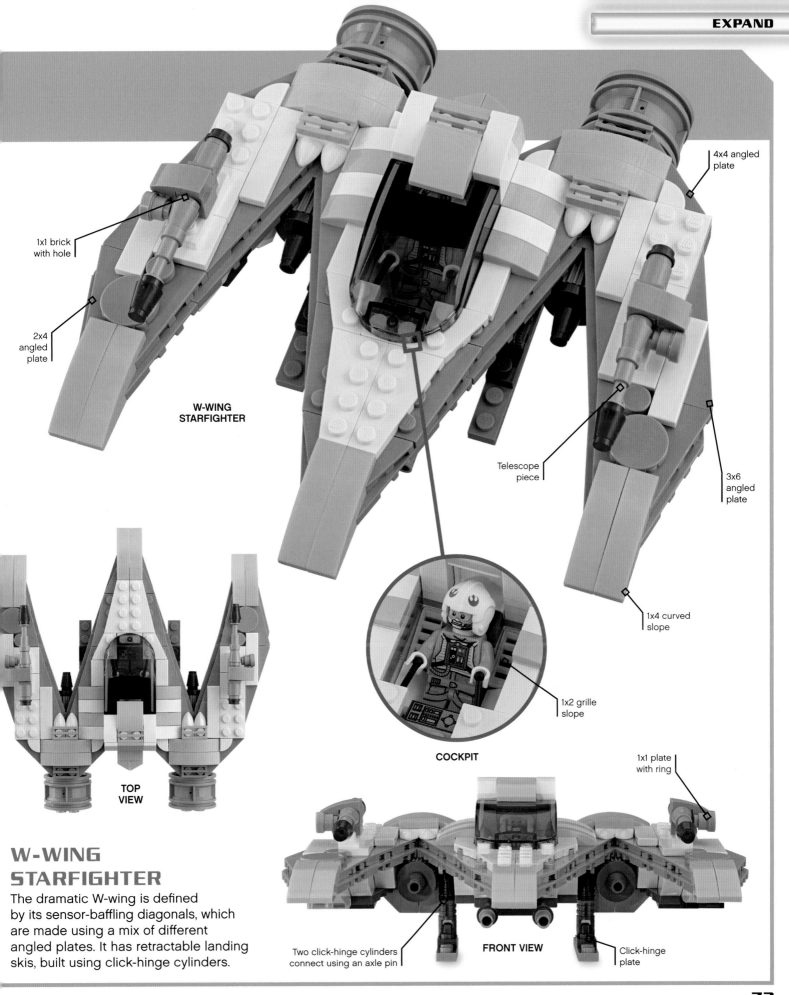

1x1 brick
with hole

2x4
angled
plate

W-WING
STARFIGHTER

4x4 angled
plate

Telescope
piece

3x6
angled
plate

1x4 curved
slope

1x2 grille
slope

COCKPIT

1x1 plate
with ring

TOP
VIEW

FRONT VIEW

Two click-hinge cylinders
connect using an axle pin

Click-hinge
plate

W-WING
STARFIGHTER

The dramatic W-wing is defined
by its sensor-baffling diagonals, which
are made using a mix of different
angled plates. It has retractable landing
skis, built using click-hinge cylinders.

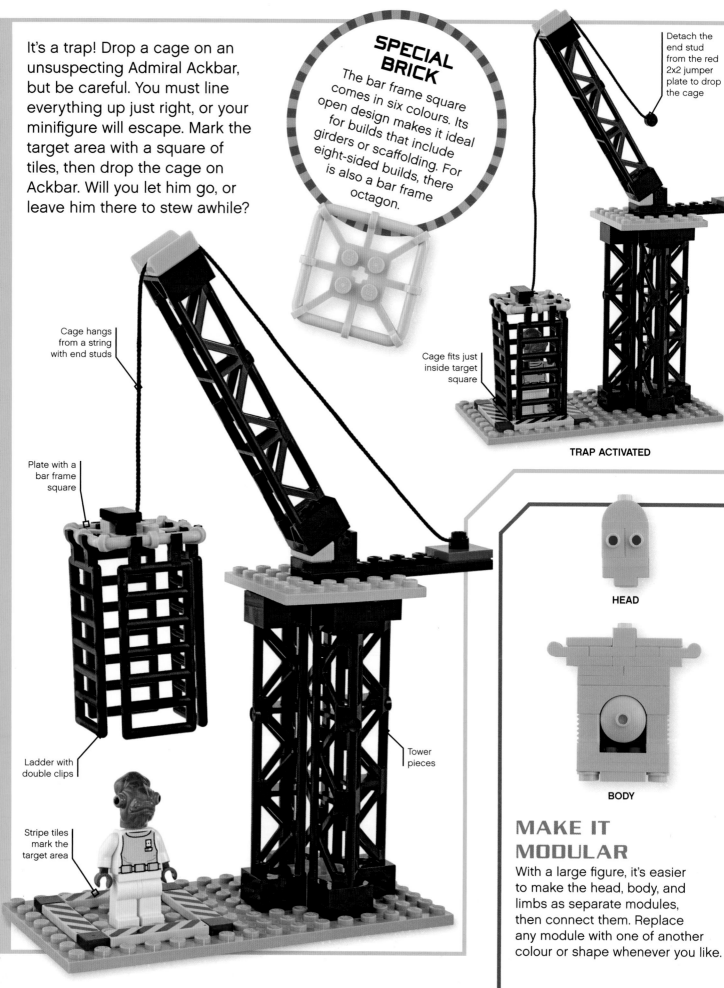

SET A TRAP FOR ACKBAR

It's a trap! Drop a cage on an unsuspecting Admiral Ackbar, but be careful. You must line everything up just right, or your minifigure will escape. Mark the target area with a square of tiles, then drop the cage on Ackbar. Will you let him go, or leave him there to stew awhile?

SPECIAL BRICK

The bar frame square comes in six colours. Its open design makes it ideal for builds that include girders or scaffolding. For eight-sided builds, there is also a bar frame octagon.

Detach the end stud from the red 2x2 jumper plate to drop the cage

Cage fits just inside target square

TRAP ACTIVATED

Cage hangs from a string with end studs

Plate with a bar frame square

Ladder with double clips

Stripe tiles mark the target area

Tower pieces

HEAD

BODY

MAKE IT MODULAR

With a large figure, it's easier to make the head, body, and limbs as separate modules, then connect them. Replace any module with one of another colour or shape whenever you like.

BUILD EZRA A SKATE PARK

Even rebels need to kick back. Build a park so Ezra can practise his skateboard tricks and forget about the Empire for a while. You could make him some especially difficult elements – remember, this kid is powered by the Force!

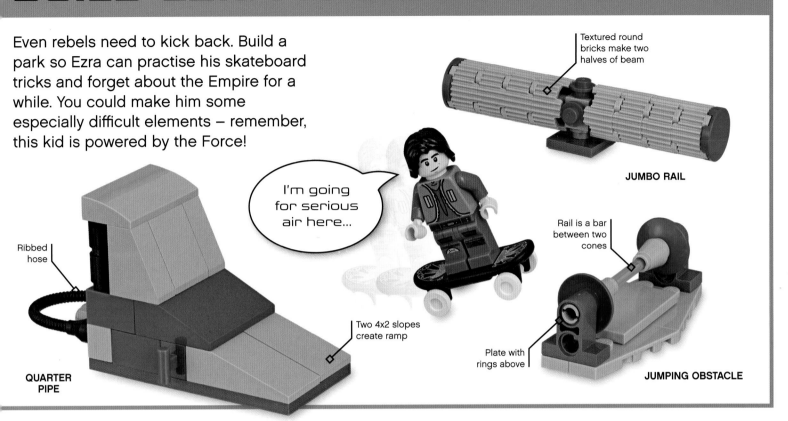

Textured round bricks make two halves of beam

JUMBO RAIL

I'm going for serious air here...

Rail is a bar between two cones

Ribbed hose

Two 4x2 slopes create ramp

QUARTER PIPE

Plate with rings above

JUMPING OBSTACLE

Don't worry if you run out of yellow bricks when making a maxi C-3PO. Droids get patched up all the time, so be like Watto and use what you have to finish yours. You could make up a story about how your droid lost his original part!

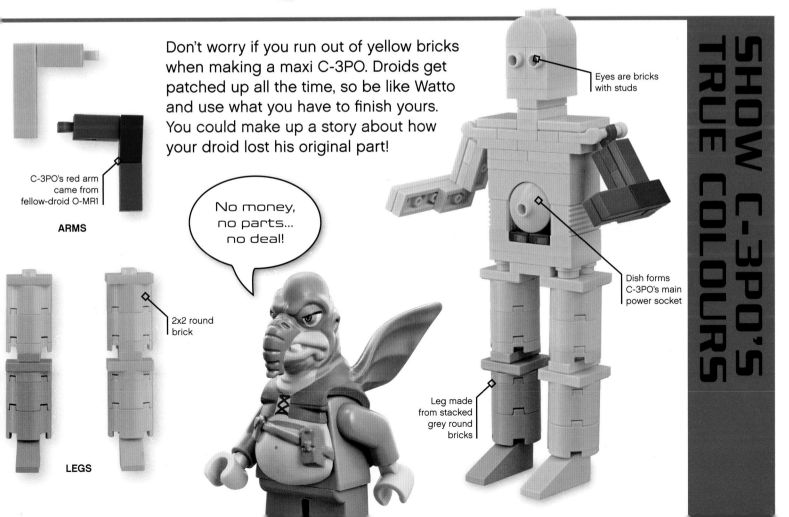

Eyes are bricks with studs

C-3PO's red arm came from fellow-droid O-MR1

ARMS

No money, no parts... no deal!

2x2 round brick

Dish forms C-3PO's main power socket

Leg made from stacked grey round bricks

LEGS

SHOW C-3PO'S TRUE COLOURS

BUILD A REBEL BASE

Home is wherever a rebel lays their helmet. The Rebel Alliance is always on the run from the Empire, having to move on every time they're discovered. They are always on the lookout for their next base, so why not build them one?

BUILDER'S TIP
Use tiles for the floor, to give a smooth look. Jumper plates allow you to easily move the minifigures around or rearrange the furniture.

Private Kappehl

Corporal Tonc

General Rieekan

Mon Mothma

Hey! You moved bases without telling me!

AT HOME WITH THE REBELS
A Rebellion requires a nerve centre. Build machinery for a technical advantage over the enemy, but remember, an army marches on its stomach – so perhaps you should squeeze in a food station, too?

DESIGN YOUR OWN LANDSPEEDER

Can you imagine owning a landspeeder like Luke's and zipping around, just above the ground? Make it a reality by building the landspeeder of your dreams out of LEGO bricks. Will yours have an open top or closed cockpit? Will it be small and nimble or big enough for a family? The sky's the limit!

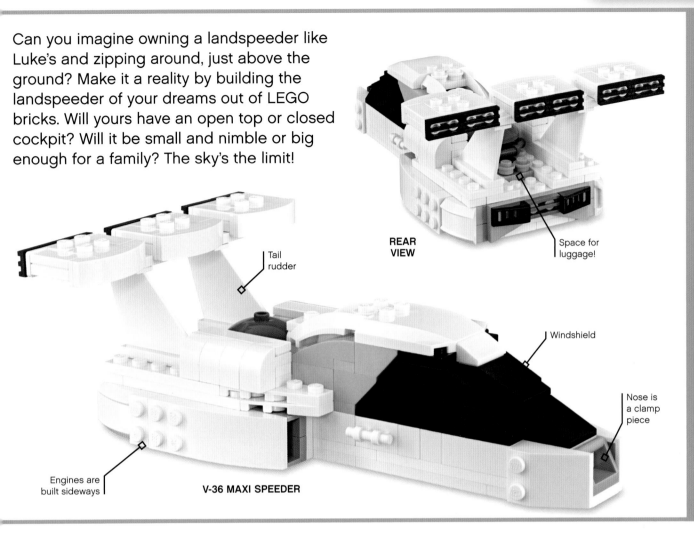

REAR VIEW

Space for luggage!

Tail rudder

Windshield

Nose is a clamp piece

Engines are built sideways

V-36 MAXI SPEEDER

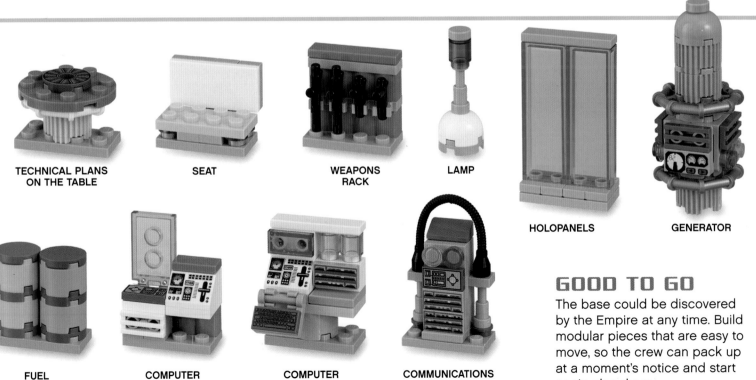

TECHNICAL PLANS ON THE TABLE

SEAT

WEAPONS RACK

LAMP

HOLOPANELS

GENERATOR

FUEL CELLS

COMPUTER CONTROLS

COMPUTER INTERFACE

COMMUNICATIONS STATION

GOOD TO GO

The base could be discovered by the Empire at any time. Build modular pieces that are easy to move, so the crew can pack up at a moment's notice and start again elsewhere.

LET YOUR EMOJIS SHOW

Happy, sad, angry, confused, shocked, or serene – *Star Wars* heroes experience a whole galaxy of emotions on their adventures. Why not build *Star Wars* emojis? You could start with a surprised Leia, a calm Yoda and a determined podracer Anakin.

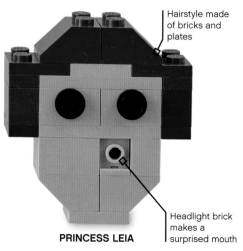

Hairstyle made of bricks and plates

Headlight brick makes a surprised mouth

PRINCESS LEIA

Round plates built onto headlight bricks

Upside-down 3x1 slopes make ears

YODA

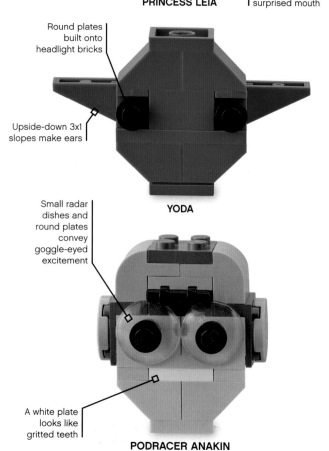

Small radar dishes and round plates convey goggle-eyed excitement

A white plate looks like gritted teeth

PODRACER ANAKIN

Turn your minifigures into tiny actors! This stage is specially built for Obi-Wan Kenobi and Darth Vader to act out their epic duel scene on the Death Star. Attach the minifigures to bars so you can make them interact.

BUILDER'S TIP

Give your minifigure actors plenty of room – the duel will look more exciting if they move around a lot. Two 16x16 plates are ideal to create the stage floor.

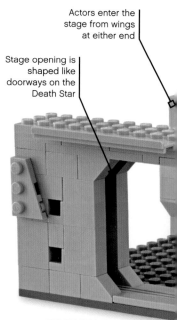

Actors enter the stage from wings at either end

Stage opening is shaped like doorways on the Death Star

STAGE READY

STAGE A SPACE DRAMA

ACTION VIEW

Long bars with stud ends

> Hey Darth, who are you calling "old man"?

Sideways plates create detail on the wall

PLAY IT YOUR WAY

Remember, you are the director of this play, so you can change the ending if you like. You might want to make Obi-Wan win the duel, or have some other minifigures rush onstage in a dramatic rescue!

RADICAL REBUILD

Jedi Master Yoda's Eta-2 *Actis*-class light interceptor has been modified to suit his diminutive stature. With R2-D2 as his companion, he flies it on missions to the mysterious world of Dagobah and elsewhere during the Clone Wars. But it doesn't take Yoda's Force powers to modify it even further and transform it into something completely different!

YODA'S JEDI STARFIGHTER™

DATA FILE

SET NUMBER
75168

LAUNCH DATE
January 2017

PIECE COUNT
262

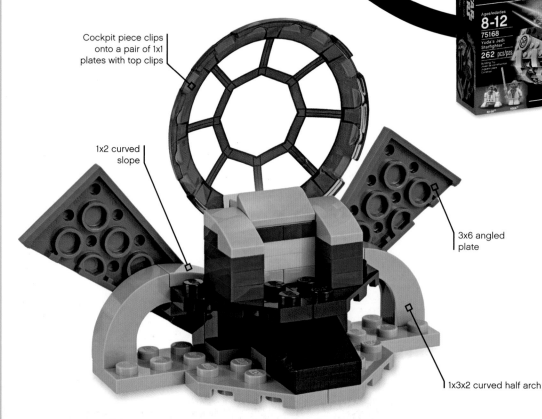

Cockpit piece clips onto a pair of 1x1 plates with top clips

1x2 curved slope

3x6 angled plate

1x3x2 curved half arch

GRAND MASTER'S THRONE

As its oldest and wisest member, Yoda holds the title of Grand Master of the Jedi Order. Though he shuns most ceremony in favour of a simple life, he occasionally meditates on the Grand Master's throne, in the hope of communing with its former occupants through the Force.

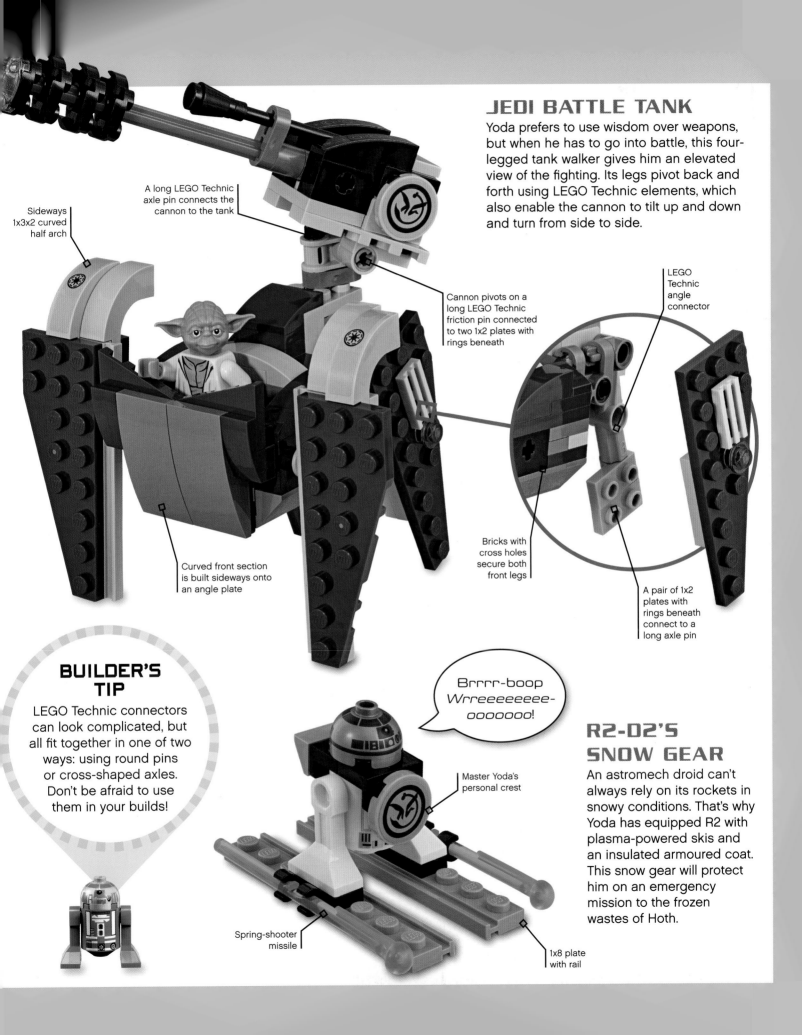

JEDI BATTLE TANK

Yoda prefers to use wisdom over weapons, but when he has to go into battle, this four-legged tank walker gives him an elevated view of the fighting. Its legs pivot back and forth using LEGO Technic elements, which also enable the cannon to tilt up and down and turn from side to side.

A long LEGO Technic axle pin connects the cannon to the tank

Sideways 1x3x2 curved half arch

Cannon pivots on a long LEGO Technic friction pin connected to two 1x2 plates with rings beneath

LEGO Technic angle connector

Curved front section is built sideways onto an angle plate

Bricks with cross holes secure both front legs

A pair of 1x2 plates with rings beneath connect to a long axle pin

BUILDER'S TIP

LEGO Technic connectors can look complicated, but all fit together in one of two ways: using round pins or cross-shaped axles. Don't be afraid to use them in your builds!

Brrrr-boop Wrreeeeeeee-oooooo!

Master Yoda's personal crest

Spring-shooter missile

1x8 plate with rail

R2-D2'S SNOW GEAR

An astromech droid can't always rely on its rockets in snowy conditions. That's why Yoda has equipped R2 with plasma-powered skis and an insulated armoured coat. This snow gear will protect him on an emergency mission to the frozen wastes of Hoth.

TRANSFORM YOUR DROIDS

If you could create a droid, what would it be like?
Why not try experimenting with modular building.
Modular builds have mix-and-match parts so
you can keep changing your mind!

MIX AND MATCH

A basic torso can be
fitted with different
arms, legs and heads
to customize your
droid for the mission
it has been assigned.

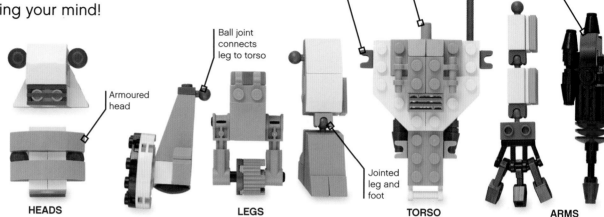

Armoured head

Ball joint connects leg to torso

Socket joint for modular arm

Pin for head to build onto

Laser arm

Jointed leg and foot

HEADS

LEGS

TORSO

ARMS

BUILD A BATTLE DROID FACTORY

Factories on Geonosis are a hive of activity.
Geonosian workers have a lot to do during the
Clone Wars, producing huge numbers of super
battle droids for the Separatist army.

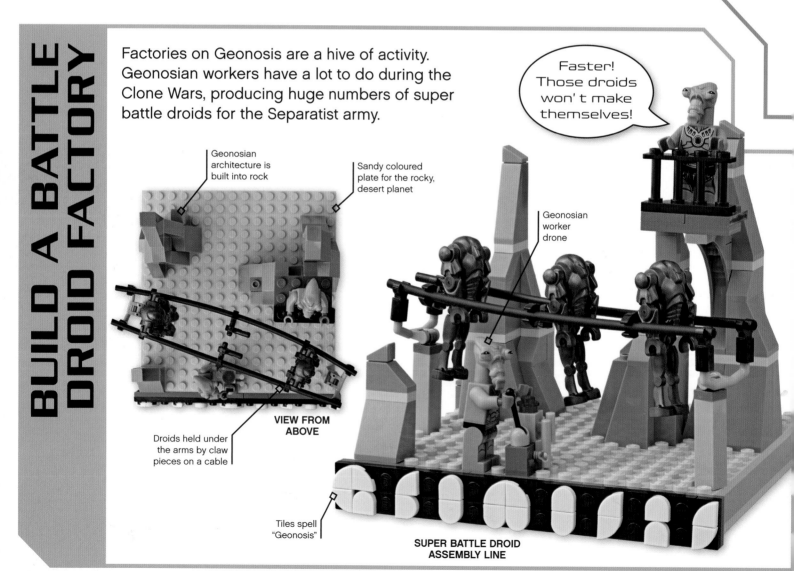

Faster! Those droids won't make themselves!

Geonosian architecture is built into rock

Sandy coloured plate for the rocky, desert planet

Geonosian worker drone

Droids held under the arms by claw pieces on a cable

VIEW FROM ABOVE

Tiles spell "Geonosis"

SUPER BATTLE DROID ASSEMBLY LINE

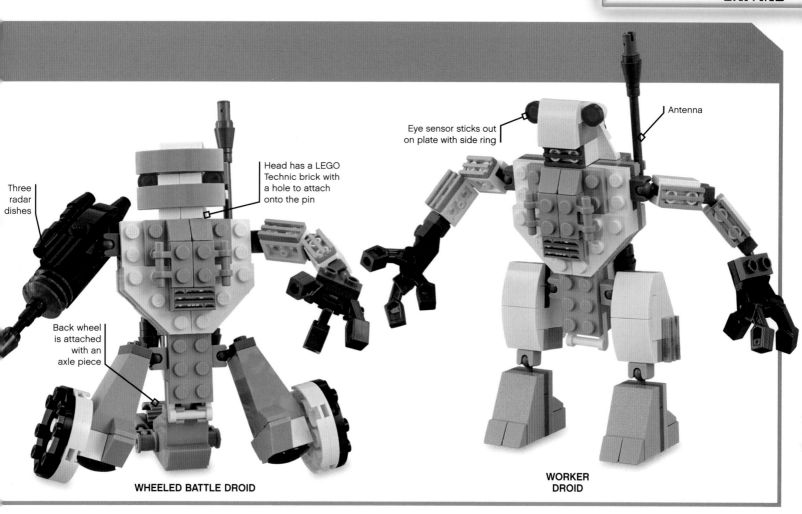

Three radar dishes

Head has a LEGO Technic brick with a hole to attach onto the pin

Back wheel is attached with an axle piece

WHEELED BATTLE DROID

Eye sensor sticks out on plate with side ring

Antenna

WORKER DROID

MAKE A DROID RAINBOW

Red and yellow and pink and green, orange and purple and blue... you can build a droid rainbow! A rainbow may be a common sight on Earth, but have you ever seen one in the *Star Wars* universe? Find bricks in all the colours of the rainbow and use them to make droids of all shapes and sizes.

SPECIAL BRICK
The 2x2 dome brick was created to be R2-D2's head piece! His is a special printed version, but the dome is now a versatile LEGO piece.

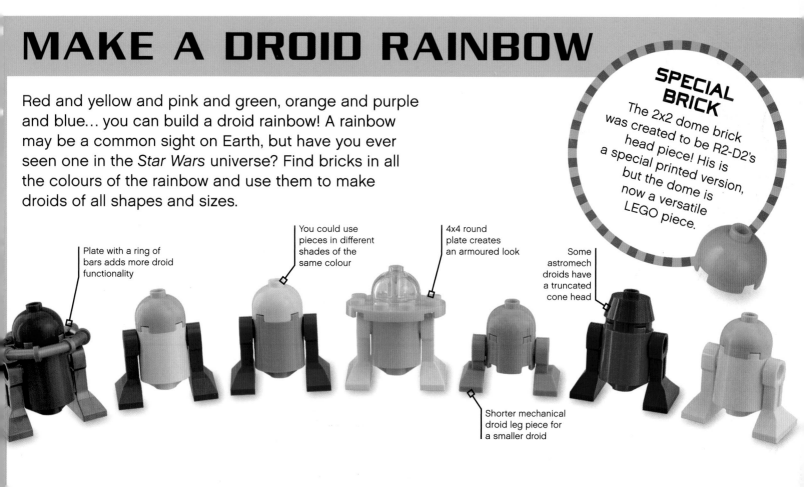

Plate with a ring of bars adds more droid functionality

You could use pieces in different shades of the same colour

4x4 round plate creates an armoured look

Some astromech droids have a truncated cone head

Shorter mechanical droid leg piece for a smaller droid

MIX UP SOME STARFIGHTERS

With these cool modular builds you can mix and match *Star Wars* starfighter sections in an instant! Each build is made with detachable wings that connect using the same LEGO Technic axle fitting. This way, all the wings and bodies are interchangable.

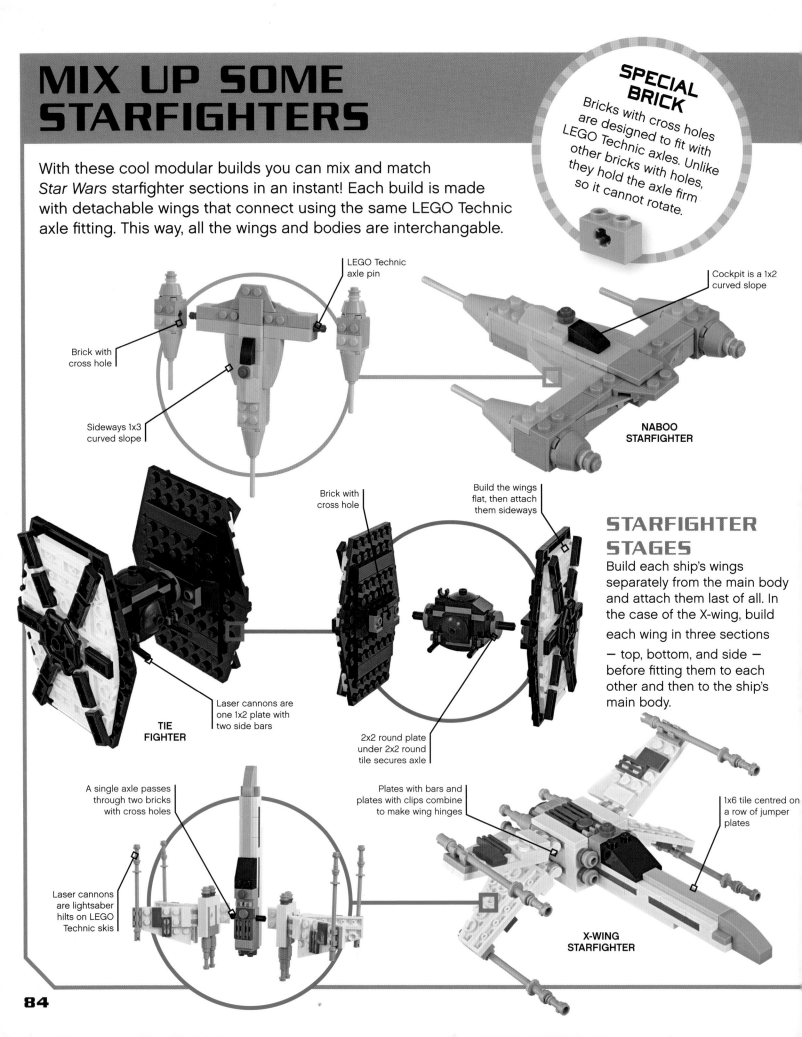

LEGO Technic axle pin

Brick with cross hole

Sideways 1x3 curved slope

Cockpit is a 1x2 curved slope

NABOO STARFIGHTER

Brick with cross hole

Build the wings flat, then attach them sideways

STARFIGHTER STAGES

Build each ship's wings separately from the main body and attach them last of all. In the case of the X-wing, build each wing in three sections — top, bottom, and side — before fitting them to each other and then to the ship's main body.

Laser cannons are one 1x2 plate with two side bars

TIE FIGHTER

2x2 round plate under 2x2 round tile secures axle

A single axle passes through two bricks with cross holes

Plates with bars and plates with clips combine to make wing hinges

1x6 tile centred on a row of jumper plates

Laser cannons are lightsaber hilts on LEGO Technic skis

X-WING STARFIGHTER

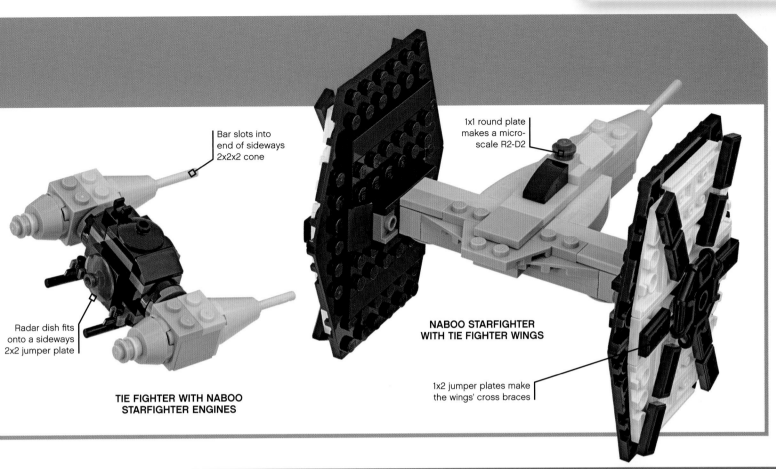

Bar slots into end of sideways 2x2x2 cone

1x1 round plate makes a micro-scale R2-D2

Radar dish fits onto a sideways 2x2 jumper plate

NABOO STARFIGHTER WITH TIE FIGHTER WINGS

1x2 jumper plates make the wings' cross braces

TIE FIGHTER WITH NABOO STARFIGHTER ENGINES

GIVE A MINIFIGURE A LIFT

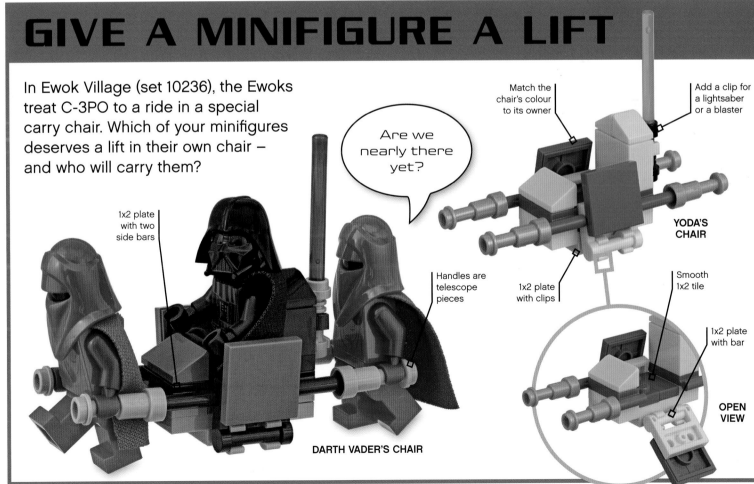

In Ewok Village (set 10236), the Ewoks treat C-3PO to a ride in a special carry chair. Which of your minifigures deserves a lift in their own chair – and who will carry them?

Are we nearly there yet?

Match the chair's colour to its owner

Add a clip for a lightsaber or a blaster

1x2 plate with two side bars

Handles are telescope pieces

YODA'S CHAIR

1x2 plate with clips

Smooth 1x2 tile

1x2 plate with bar

DARTH VADER'S CHAIR

OPEN VIEW

MAKE A MEAL FIT FOR A HUTT

Gruesome gangster Jabba the Hutt takes greed to a whole new level. He demands nine meals a day, and even gobbles creatures up whole. Make Jabba some snacks – then decide whether to feed them to him or set them free!

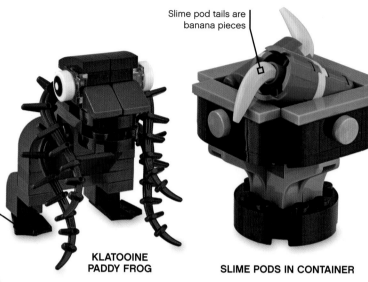

Slime pod tails are banana pieces

Minifigure flippers make webbed feet

KLATOOINE PADDY FROG

SLIME PODS IN CONTAINER

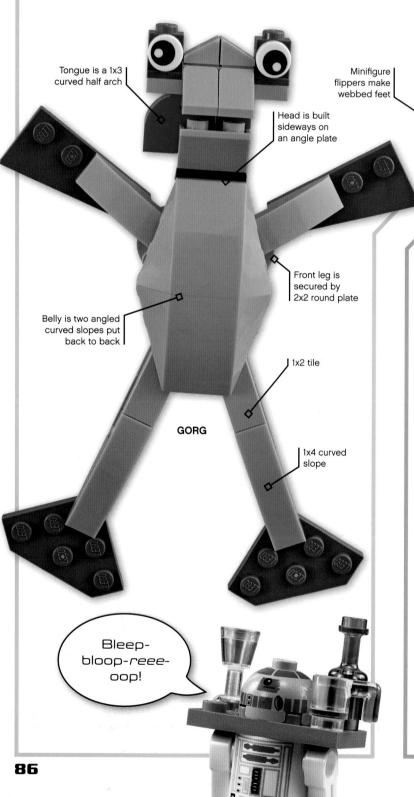

Tongue is a 1x3 curved half arch

Head is built sideways on an angle plate

Front leg is secured by 2x2 round plate

Belly is two angled curved slopes put back to back

1x2 tile

GORG

1x4 curved slope

Bleep-bloop-*reee*-oop!

AROUND THE ARENA

The upper level of the training arena is supported by stacks of bricks and sturdy tower pieces. The corner where the two walls meet is made from two large, strong diagonal panel pieces.

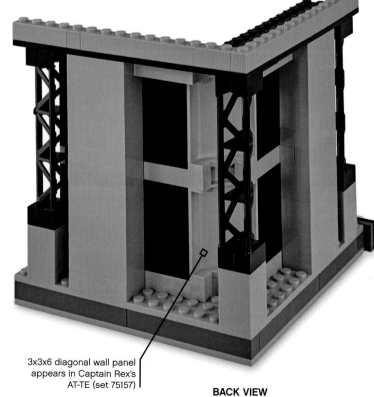

3x3x6 diagonal wall panel appears in Captain Rex's AT-TE (set 75157)

BACK VIEW

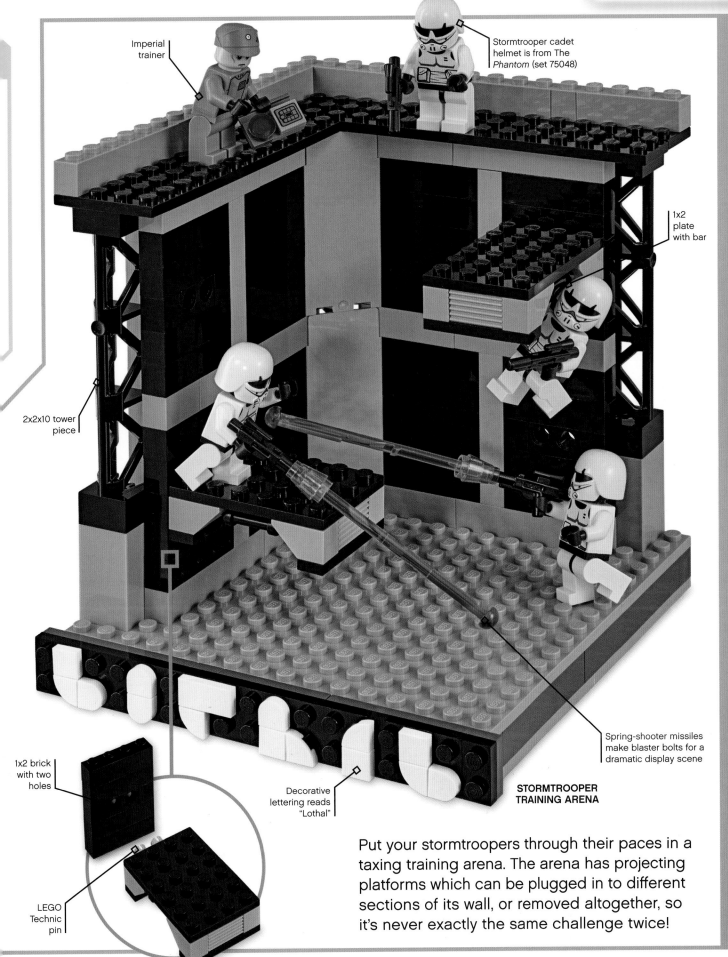

Imperial trainer

Stormtrooper cadet helmet is from The *Phantom* (set 75048)

1x2 plate with bar

2x2x10 tower piece

Spring-shooter missiles make blaster bolts for a dramatic display scene

1x2 brick with two holes

LEGO Technic pin

Decorative lettering reads "Lothal"

STORMTROOPER TRAINING ARENA

TRAIN YOUR TROOPERS

Put your stormtroopers through their paces in a taxing training arena. The arena has projecting platforms which can be plugged in to different sections of its wall, or removed altogether, so it's never exactly the same challenge twice!

Is your minifigure in a tight spot? Don't leave them high and dry – string a line between two columns and have them zipping to safety in no time. Minifigures can be attached to the line with a harness, or you can transport smaller figures like Ewoks in a barrel or basket.

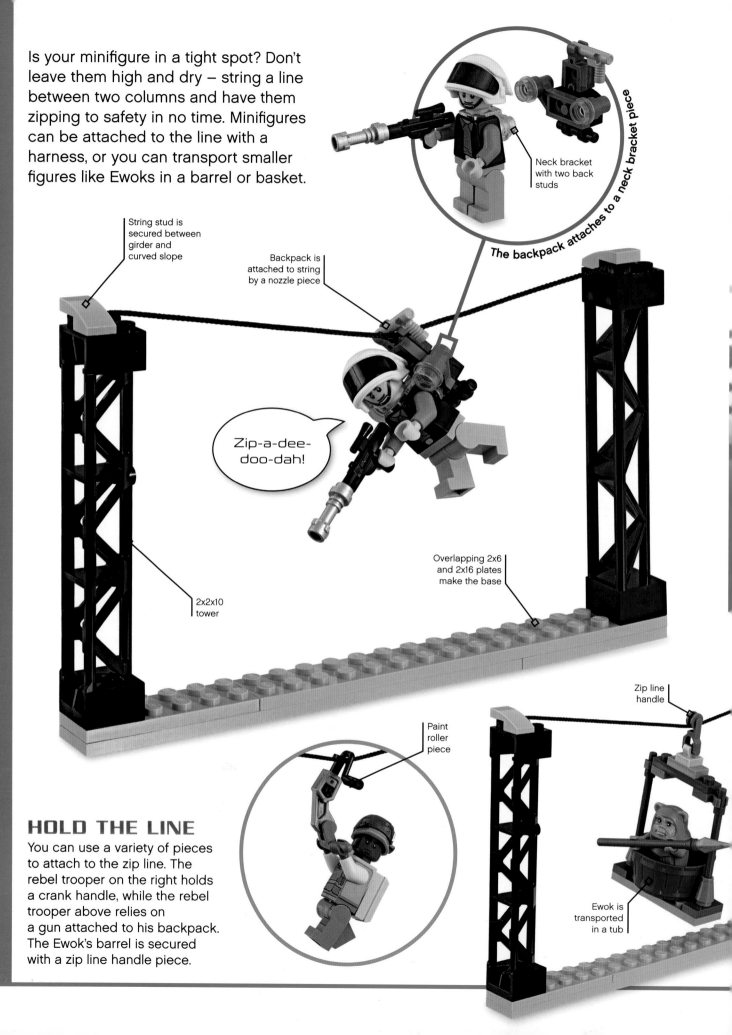

Neck bracket with two back studs

The backpack attaches to a neck bracket piece

String stud is secured between girder and curved slope

Backpack is attached to string by a nozzle piece

Zip-a-dee-doo-dah!

2x2x10 tower

Overlapping 2x6 and 2x16 plates make the base

Zip line handle

Paint roller piece

HOLD THE LINE

You can use a variety of pieces to attach to the zip line. The rebel trooper on the right holds a crank handle, while the rebel trooper above relies on a gun attached to his backpack. The Ewok's barrel is secured with a zip line handle piece.

Ewok is transported in a tub

On the forest moon of Endor, the Ewoks keep a constant lookout for danger. It's a challenge, since the trees are tall and the Ewoks are short! Give your furry friends a boost by building them a watchtower, built from different-coloured, Ewok-shaped pods, each facing a different direction.

Crow's nest built with plates and 1x4 log bricks

Tiles, round plates and slopes are used to make the pod look like an Ewok's head

FACING NORTH

The pods attach to 2x2 bricks

FACING WEST

Leafy branches between the lookout pods

Er... what's that rustling up in the trees?

FACING SOUTH

FACING EAST

BUILD A LOOKOUT FOR EWOKS

BUILD MIGHTY MECHS

A mech is a large mechanized suit designed for fighting. Think of a *Star Wars* character and build a mech based on their personality, allegiance, or fighting style. Add shields, weapons and gadgets of your choice... then prepare for battle!

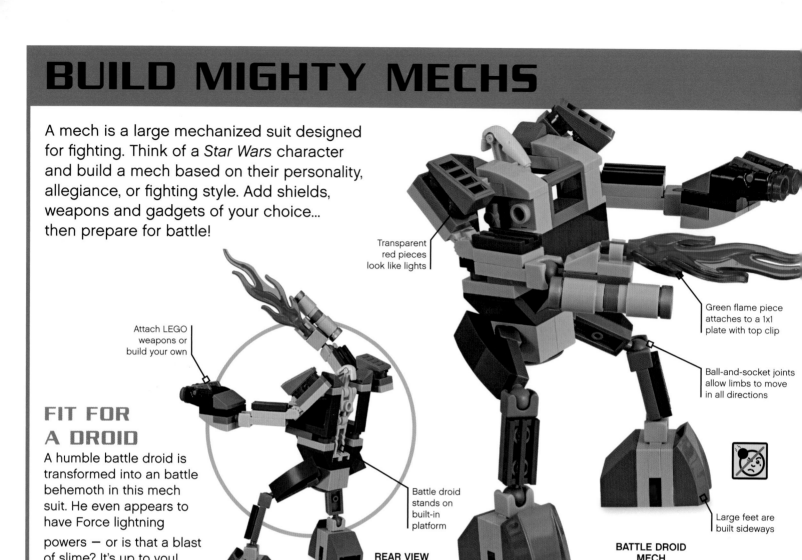

Transparent red pieces look like lights

Green flame piece attaches to a 1x1 plate with top clip

Ball-and-socket joints allow limbs to move in all directions

Large feet are built sideways

BATTLE DROID MECH

Attach LEGO weapons or build your own

FIT FOR A DROID

A humble battle droid is transformed into an battle behemoth in this mech suit. He even appears to have Force lightning powers — or is that a blast of slime? It's up to you!

Battle droid stands on built-in platform

REAR VIEW

CUSTOMIZE A STORMTROOPER

The Republic's clone troopers are all genetically identical, but the Empire's stormtroopers are a more varied bunch, with different personalities and hobbies. What if they took on part-time jobs to earn some extra cash? Give them outfits and accessories to kit them out for their roles.

Standard-issue stormtrooper helmet

Do you want fries with that?

Roast leg of nuna

Grappling hook

Flippers for speed

Overalls from the Decorator Minifigure

AT-AT driver's armour

DEEP-SEA DIVER TROOPER

HANDYMAN TROOPER

CHEF TROOPER

ESCAPED PRISONER RECAPTURE TROOPER

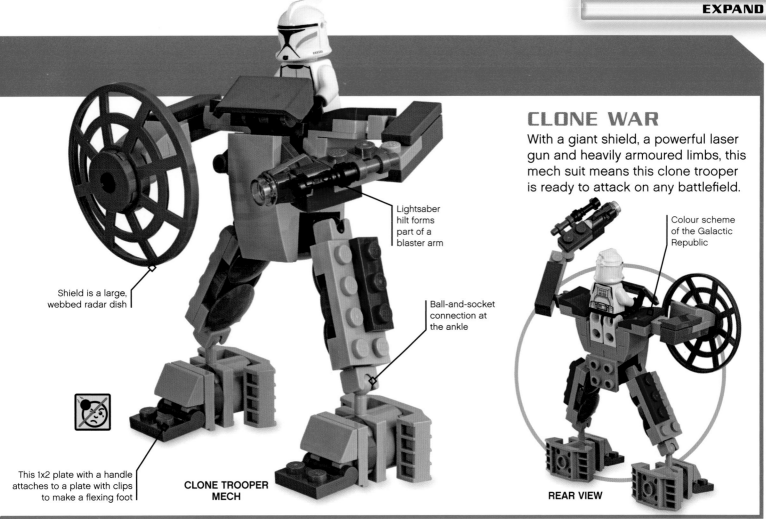

CLONE WAR

With a giant shield, a powerful laser gun and heavily armoured limbs, this mech suit means this clone trooper is ready to attack on any battlefield.

Shield is a large, webbed radar dish

Lightsaber hilt forms part of a blaster arm

Ball-and-socket connection at the ankle

This 1x2 plate with a handle attaches to a plate with clips to make a flexing foot

CLONE TROOPER MECH

Colour scheme of the Galactic Republic

REAR VIEW

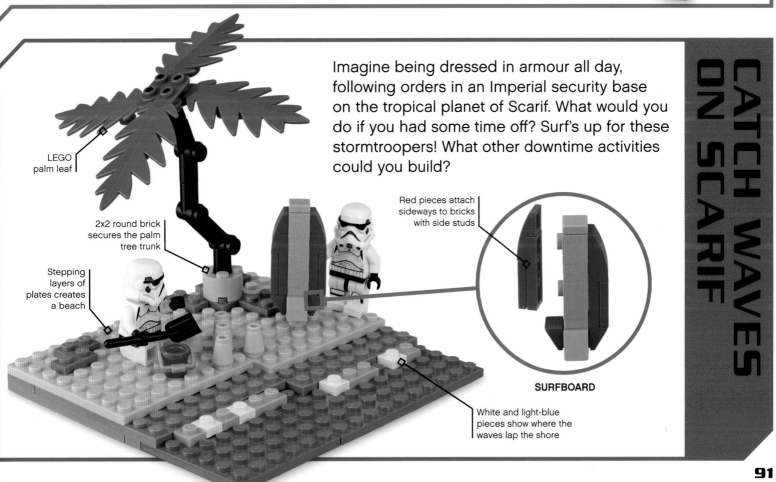

Imagine being dressed in armour all day, following orders in an Imperial security base on the tropical planet of Scarif. What would you do if you had some time off? Surf's up for these stormtroopers! What other downtime activities could you build?

LEGO palm leaf

2x2 round brick secures the palm tree trunk

Stepping layers of plates creates a beach

Red pieces attach sideways to bricks with side studs

SURFBOARD

White and light-blue pieces show where the waves lap the shore

CATCH WAVES ON SCARIF

CASSIAN'S SUPERCAR

Brave rebel spy Cassian Andor drives this car when he is undercover on worlds where wheels are still the primary mode of transportation. It is big enough for a passenger to travel in the back.

Large cockpit piece comes from underside of U-wing

Wheels built on using LEGO Technic parts

Spoiler made from 4x4 plates with four studs

Small cockpit piece from top of U-wing

Angled plate fitted to hidden LEGO Technic beam using LEGO Technic half pins

LEGO Technic axle with end stud

Tilted sides angled on LEGO Technic pins

LEGO Technic angle beam

LEGO Technic friction pin

BUILDER'S TIP

Use black LEGO Technic friction pins to anchor the base of the crane and it will stay up when you raise it. Use grey pins wherever you want a looser connection.

Smooth areas around the cab enable the crane arm to swivel

1x1 cone secures stack of three wheel rims on LEGO Technic axle

PLASMA DRILL PLATFORM

Rebel fighter Bistan is using this heavy-duty drill to search for precious plasma, which the rebels can use to power their weapons. The drill arm rotates and moves up and down.

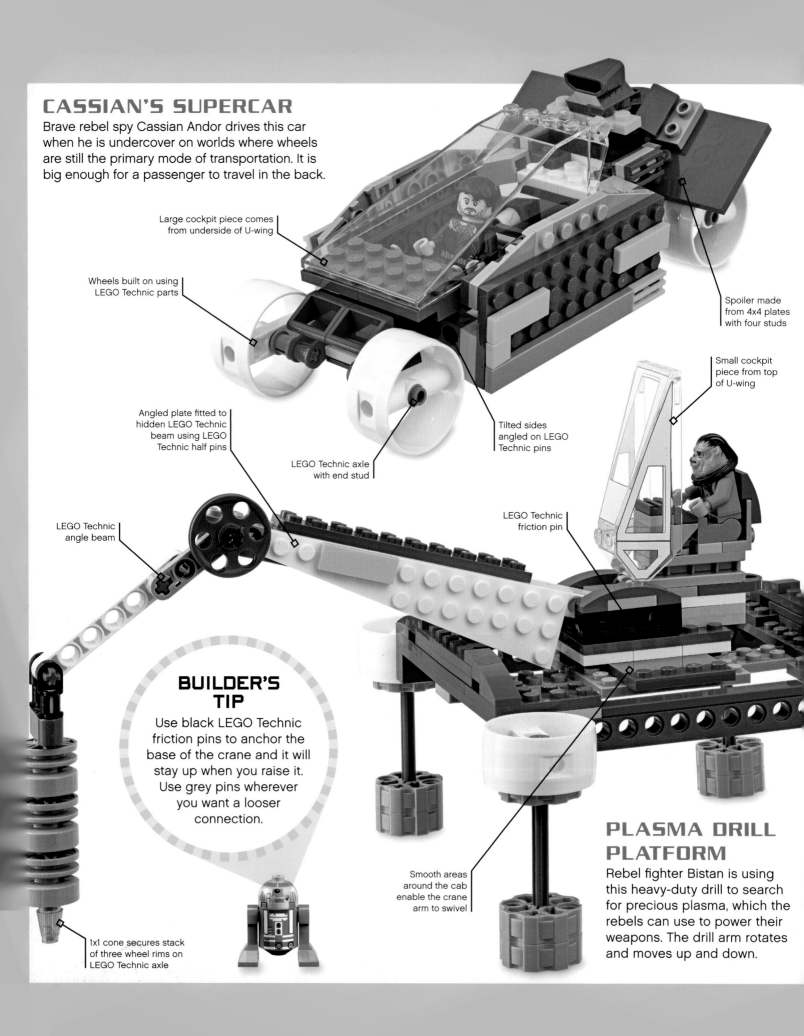

RADICAL REBUILD

The UT-60D U-wing starfighter is noted for its ability to dramatically change shape in flight – folding its wings forward or backward as its mission requires. It's certainly an impressive trick, but it can't compare to the incredible range of U-wing transformations that are on display right here!

REBEL U-WING FIGHTER™

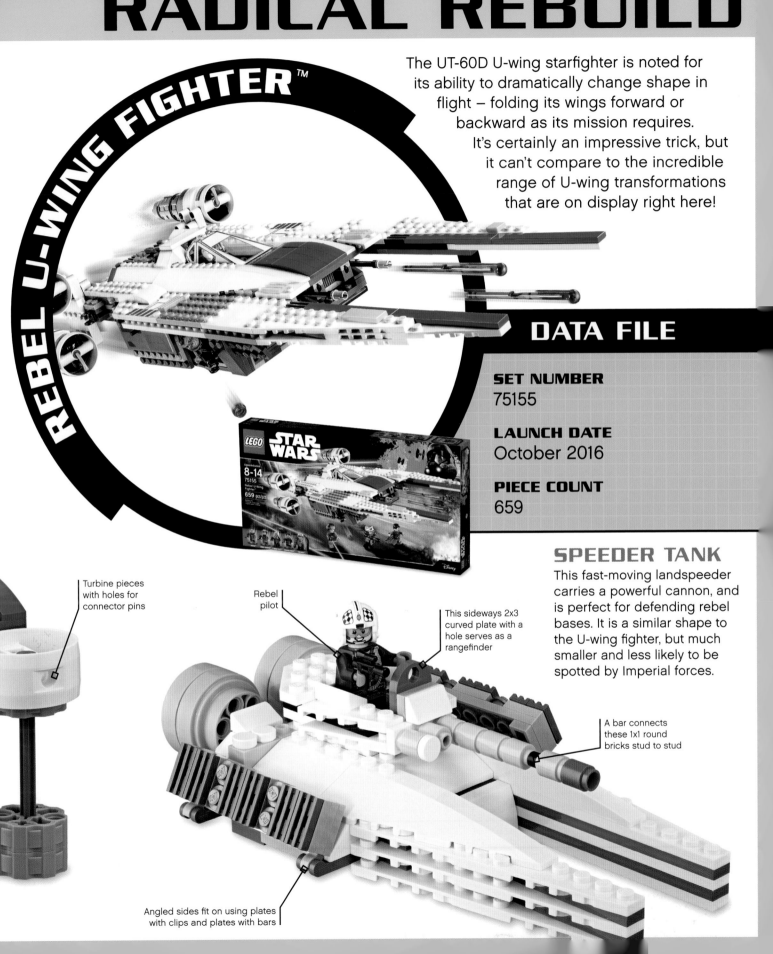

DATA FILE

SET NUMBER
75155

LAUNCH DATE
October 2016

PIECE COUNT
659

SPEEDER TANK

This fast-moving landspeeder carries a powerful cannon, and is perfect for defending rebel bases. It is a similar shape to the U-wing fighter, but much smaller and less likely to be spotted by Imperial forces.

Turbine pieces with holes for connector pins

Rebel pilot

This sideways 2x3 curved plate with a hole serves as a rangefinder

A bar connects these 1x1 round bricks stud to stud

Angled sides fit on using plates with clips and plates with bars

Need to whizz across a planet's rough terrain? Speeder bikes are hover vehicles that are both fast and manoeuvrable. Build LEGO speeders for an Imperial death trooper and a rebel trooper for an exciting chase.

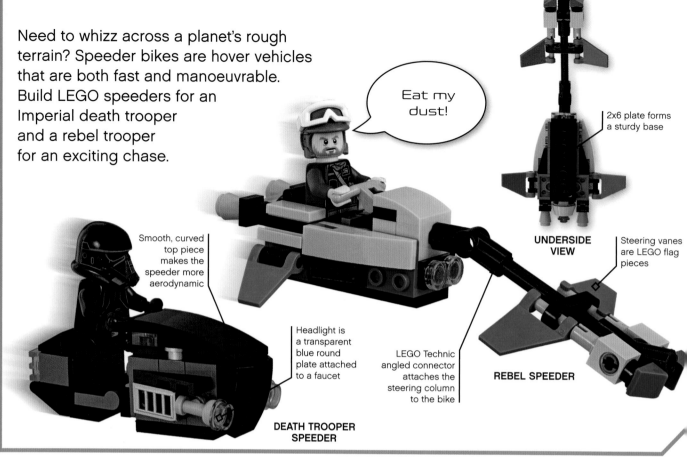

Eat my dust!

2x6 plate forms a sturdy base

UNDERSIDE VIEW

Steering vanes are LEGO flag pieces

Smooth, curved top piece makes the speeder more aerodynamic

Headlight is a transparent blue round plate attached to a faucet

LEGO Technic angled connector attaches the steering column to the bike

REBEL SPEEDER

DEATH TROOPER SPEEDER

SELL OR SWAP ON JAKKU

Shop till you drop on Jakku with these market stalls at the Niima trading post. Niima is the scruffy desert settlement where Rey exchanges her scavenged parts for food from Unkar Plutt, and where Teedo, mounted on a luggabeast, chases BB-8.

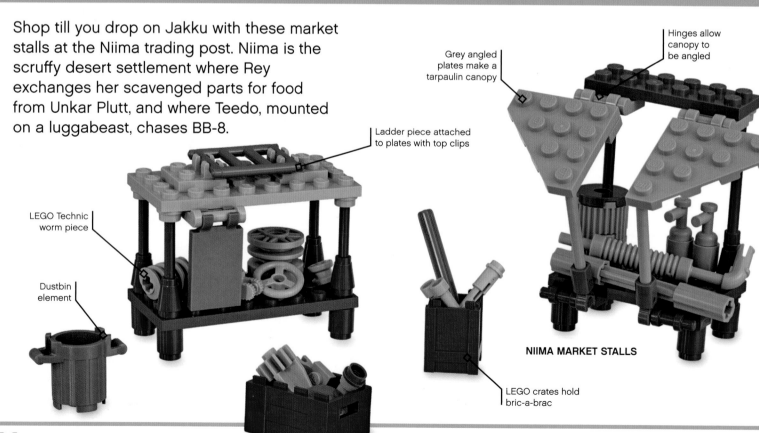

Hinges allow canopy to be angled

Grey angled plates make a tarpaulin canopy

Ladder piece attached to plates with top clips

LEGO Technic worm piece

Dustbin element

NIIMA MARKET STALLS

LEGO crates hold bric-a-brac

CULTIVATE FANTASY FLOWERS

From kwazel candy on Rodia to umbrella trees on Balnab, the galaxy is full of fascinating flora. Copy them in LEGO bricks – or invent your own! Think about bright colours, unusual structures, and all the ways that plants could attract alien insects.

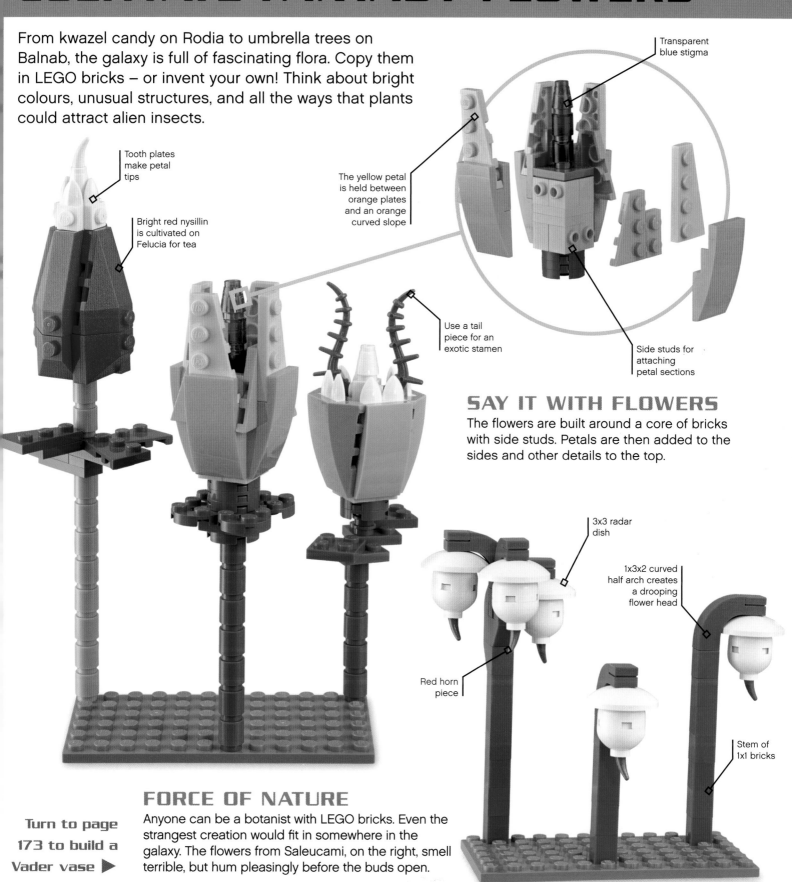

Transparent blue stigma

Tooth plates make petal tips

Bright red nysillin is cultivated on Felucia for tea

The yellow petal is held between orange plates and an orange curved slope

Use a tail piece for an exotic stamen

Side studs for attaching petal sections

SAY IT WITH FLOWERS

The flowers are built around a core of bricks with side studs. Petals are then added to the sides and other details to the top.

3x3 radar dish

1x3x2 curved half arch creates a drooping flower head

Red horn piece

Stem of 1x1 bricks

FORCE OF NATURE

Anyone can be a botanist with LEGO bricks. Even the strangest creation would fit in somewhere in the galaxy. The flowers from Saleucami, on the right, smell terrible, but hum pleasingly before the buds open.

Turn to page 173 to build a Vader vase ▶

Anyone willing to fight the Empire is welcome to join the Rebel Alliance, so its fleet is a rag-tag collection of different ship designs and colours. Build your own rebel fleet by making a mix of familiar ships, new versions of existing vessels and some craft that are all your own invention.

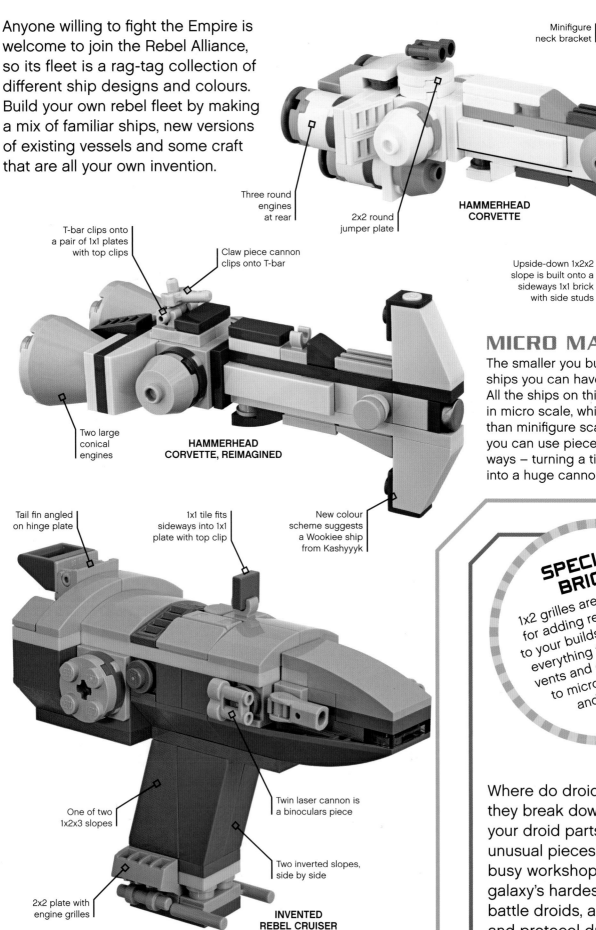

Minifigure neck bracket

Three round engines at rear

2x2 round jumper plate

HAMMERHEAD CORVETTE

Upside-down 1x2x2 slope is built onto a sideways 1x1 brick with side studs

T-bar clips onto a pair of 1x1 plates with top clips

Claw piece cannon clips onto T-bar

Two large conical engines

HAMMERHEAD CORVETTE, REIMAGINED

Tail fin angled on hinge plate

1x1 tile fits sideways into 1x1 plate with top clip

New colour scheme suggests a Wookiee ship from Kashyyyk

One of two 1x2x3 slopes

Twin laser cannon is a binoculars piece

Two inverted slopes, side by side

2x2 plate with engine grilles

INVENTED REBEL CRUISER

MICRO MAGIC

The smaller you build, the more ships you can have in your fleet! All the ships on this page are built in micro scale, which is far smaller than minifigure scale. This means you can use pieces in whole new ways – turning a tiny claw piece into a huge cannon, for example!

SPECIAL BRICK

1x2 grilles are very useful for adding realistic detail to your builds. They can be everything from machine vents and conveyor belts to micro-scale doors and windows!

Where do droids go when they break down? Gather your droid parts and other unusual pieces to build a busy workshop where the galaxy's hardest-working battle droids, astromechs and protocol droids can get a new lease of life!

CHECK OUT CHEWIE'S TOOLBOX

The *Millennium Falcon*'s copilot isn't just a pretty face! He's also a brilliant engineer. But Chewbacca can't fix the *Falcon* without his toolbox, and that's where you come in. Build the Wookiee a box with a lid where he can keep all his tools and gadgets.

Lid can lift and turn on box without being removed entirely

LID

LEGO Technic axle with end stud slots into plate with holes

2x4 plate with holes

1x2 panel

1x2 handle

1x2 corner panel

TOOLBOX CLOSED

TOOLBOX

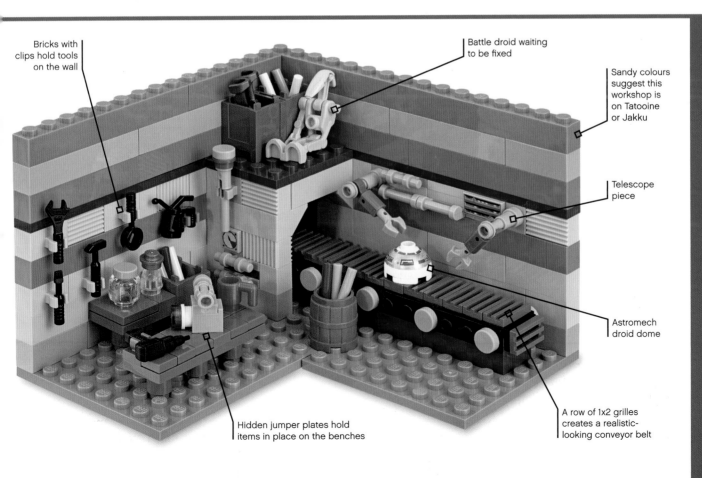

Bricks with clips hold tools on the wall

Battle droid waiting to be fixed

Sandy colours suggest this workshop is on Tatooine or Jakku

Telescope piece

Astromech droid dome

Hidden jumper plates hold items in place on the benches

A row of 1x2 grilles creates a realistic-looking conveyor belt

DESIGN A DROID WORKSHOP

A powerful crime lord like Jabba the Hutt needs a galaxy of minions to respond to his many demands. Dream up new droids and toys to keep Jabba happy – or at least, as happy as the humorless Hutt ever gets!

SPYBOT

BIB FORTUNA

SPYBOT

Spybot's camera is a round plate and a faucet piece

Ketchup and mustard are red and yellow faucet pieces

Roller-skate piece

Disco light is transparent green round plate and plate with top clip

Drinks tray is a 1x2 plate with handle

Sausages attach to plates with top clips

BB-Q DROID AND SAUCE-BOT

ROLLER-SKATING GAMORREAN GUARD

Droid leg piece forms leg of Dancetron

Mop is a hose nozzle piece

Curved slope feet glide over drool puddles

MOP-DROID

UNDERSIDE OF DANCETRON

DANCETRON

HUTT HELPERS

Create new jobs for minifigures, or build new droids. How about some spybots to help Bib Fortuna organize the staff, or roller-skating Gamorreans for speedier service? BB-Q and his partner Sauce-Bot are on hand to supply snacks, while a Dancetron provides emergency dancer deployment. The mop-droid is kept busy 24/7, wiping up drool spillage.

Extra mustard, Sauce-Bot!

GO BEHIND THE SCENES ON JABBA'S BARGE

Some of Jabba the Hutt's minions are well known, but many others toil behind the scenes. Go beyond the palace parties and barge banquets and imagine life working in the kitchen, preparing Jabba's endless, lavish meals.

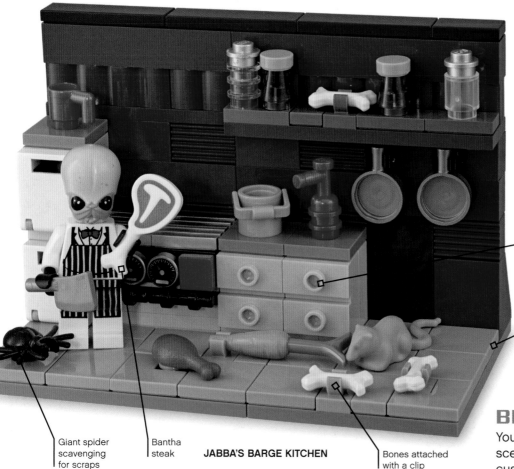

Jumper plate studs make drawer handles

Tiles of different shapes and sizes create the kitchen floor

Giant spider scavenging for scraps

Bantha steak

JABBA'S BARGE KITCHEN

Bones attached with a clip

BRICK WALL

You can add texture to a simple scene by using detailed bricks in a custom way. Textured bricks and log bricks give an everyday wall a more interesting look.

BUILDER'S TIP

When you are building a scene like this, it helps to keep a minifigure on hand to get a sense of scale and help ensure everything in the scene is the right size.

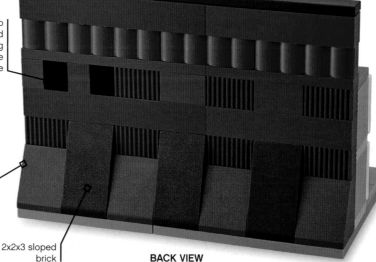

Black clip pieces hold the frying pans on the other side

2x2x2 sloped brick

2x2x3 sloped brick

BACK VIEW

TRAIN ON DAGOBAH

Give your minifigures a Jedi-style workout by building them a training ground. These three builds are inspired by Luke's Jedi training under Yoda on the swamp planet Dagobah. Can you think of more ways to test your minifigures' Force powers?

Roger, roger!

L-shaped bar slots into LEGO Technic half pin

TESTING TREE
Luke tests both his physical strength and Force strength by swinging from this tree. He hangs onto an L-shaped bar that swings.

Headlamp piece and 1x1 plate joins the two torsos

Droid can stand on back legs

Body shape is similar to the mythological centaur

CENTAUR BATTLE DROID

Half arch pieces form branches and roots

Leaf piece secured above and below

Stack flower plates to make different-sized plants for a wild look

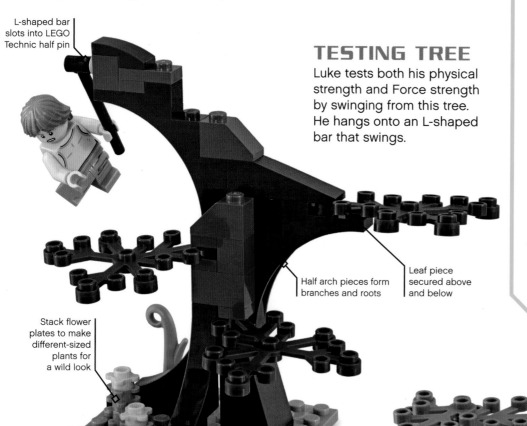

TREE SWING

Stack of three transparent 1x1 bricks

FORCE MOVEMENTS
Levitating is easy with LEGO bricks! Just stack up transparent pieces and place characters or objects on top. Recreate a classic Dagobah scene by levitating objects (including R2-D2!) while Luke performs a handstand.

LEVITATION PRACTICE

Luke holds the handle of a nozzle piece attached to a 1x1 stud

Tan base plate is the forest floor

ENGINEER NEW BATTLE DROIDS

Make the most of all the droid parts that come off the assembly lines of Geonosis by creating new battle droids. Build on the basic B1 battle droid model to create droids for different environments and tasks. Here are a few ideas to get you started with your own mash-ups.

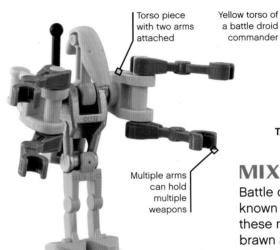

Blaster pistol

Upper and lower torsos join via a 1x1 plate with a side clip

Yellow torso of a battle droid commander

Extra height is useful to see over trenches or battlements

TALL SNIPER DROID

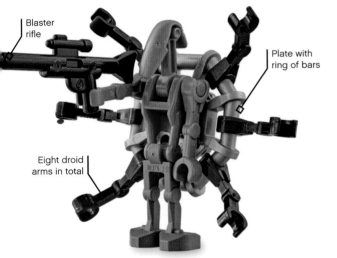

Blaster rifle

Plate with ring of bars

Eight droid arms in total

SPIDER BATTLE DROID

Torso piece with two arms attached

Multiple arms can hold multiple weapons

GRIEVOUS BATTLE DROID

MIX AND MATCH

Battle droid "clankers" aren't known for their brains, but these make up for it with their brawn and specialist functions. The sky's the limit for what you could create.

1x6 plate

Build foliage onto the walkway to make it more challenging

FOREST RUN

This zig-zagging, tree-top track tests Luke's agility and courage. Narrow plates span the tops of trees to form a challenging walkway.

Combine slope and half arch pieces to make natural-looking tree trunks

Look down, do not.

Dark green 1x1 plates for moss

CANOPY CATWALK

Direct your own LEGO® *Star Wars*™ storyline by setting up a changeable scene or stop-motion video. Build a simple set, such as the barren desert of the planet Jakku, then add LEGO characters and props.

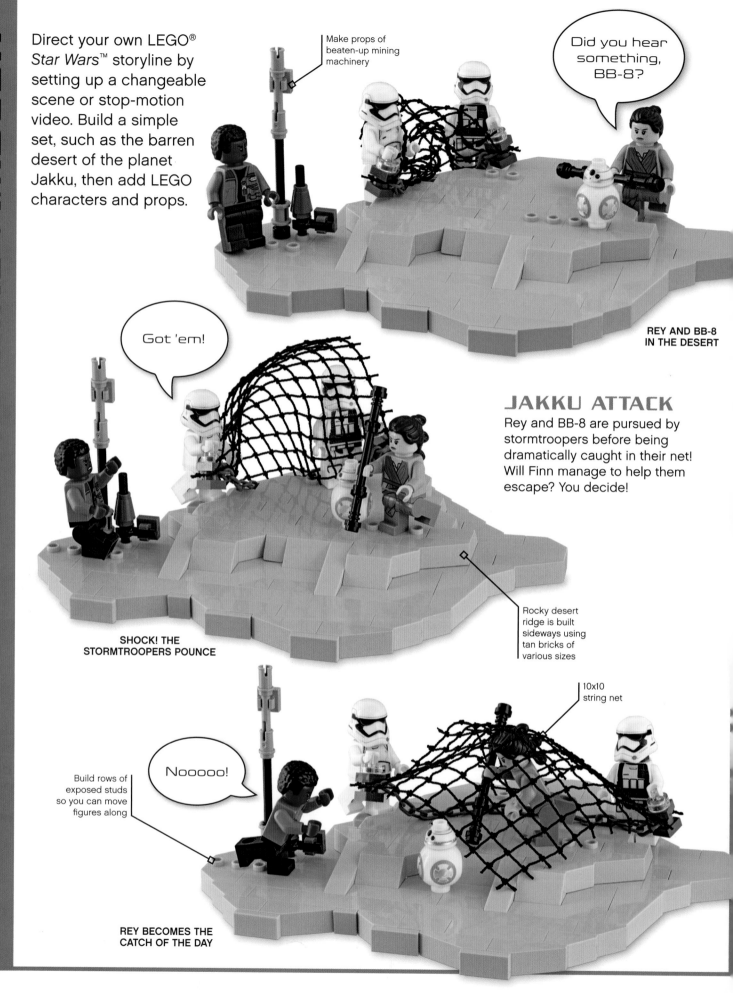

Make props of beaten-up mining machinery

Did you hear something, BB-8?

REY AND BB-8 IN THE DESERT

Got 'em!

SHOCK! THE STORMTROOPERS POUNCE

JAKKU ATTACK

Rey and BB-8 are pursued by stormtroopers before being dramatically caught in their net! Will Finn manage to help them escape? You decide!

Rocky desert ridge is built sideways using tan bricks of various sizes

10x10 string net

Build rows of exposed studs so you can move figures along

Nooooo!

REY BECOMES THE CATCH OF THE DAY

SABINE-IFY A SHIP

If you're not afraid to let the enemy see you coming, take a leaf out of Sabine Wren's artbook and blast your ship with colour. Sabine is a Mandalorian rebel who likes to brighten up the galaxy with her graffiti.

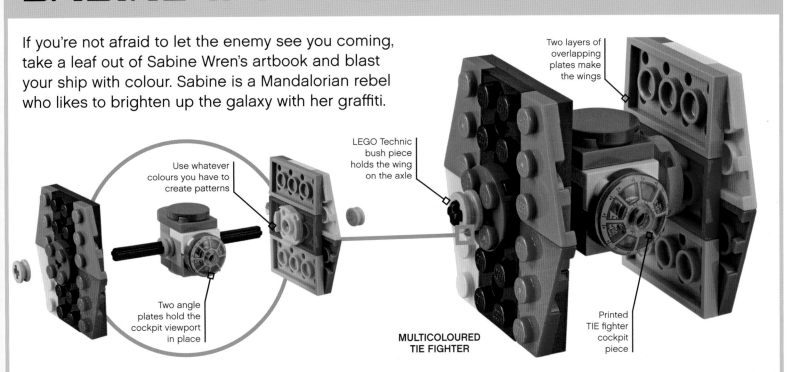

Use whatever colours you have to create patterns

Two angle plates hold the cockpit viewport in place

LEGO Technic bush piece holds the wing on the axle

Two layers of overlapping plates make the wings

Printed TIE fighter cockpit piece

MULTICOLOURED TIE FIGHTER

MAKE A REPLACEMENT RANCOR

Word on the street in Mos Eisley is that Jabba's looking for a new pet to replace his rancor. What wild creature can you come up with? The builder who created this sharp-clawed, colourful-headed dinosaur-bird has named him WooDoo.

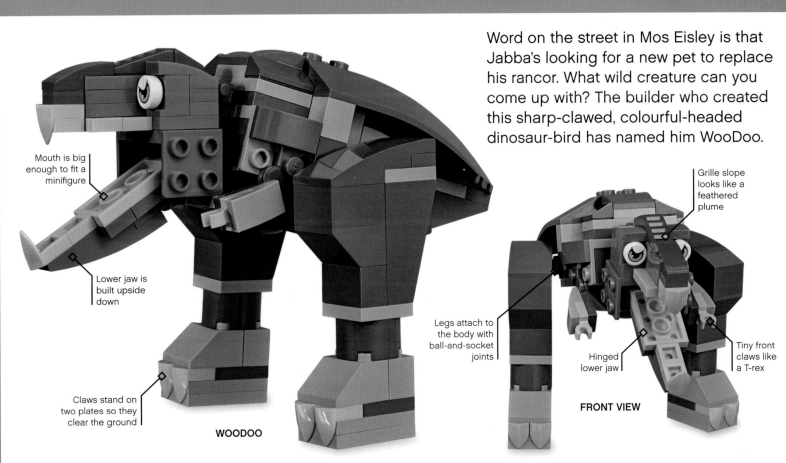

Mouth is big enough to fit a minifigure

Lower jaw is built upside down

Claws stand on two plates so they clear the ground

WOODOO

Legs attach to the body with ball-and-socket joints

Grille slope looks like a feathered plume

Hinged lower jaw

Tiny front claws like a T-rex

FRONT VIEW

RADICAL REBUILD

The *Millennium Falcon* might just be the most famous ship in the galaxy! With Han Solo at the helm, it played a vital part in the Rebellion against the Galactic Empire – and it is still fighting for freedom with Rey at the controls. What new adventures will it have when you take command and give it a nose-to-tail overhaul to beat all overhauls?

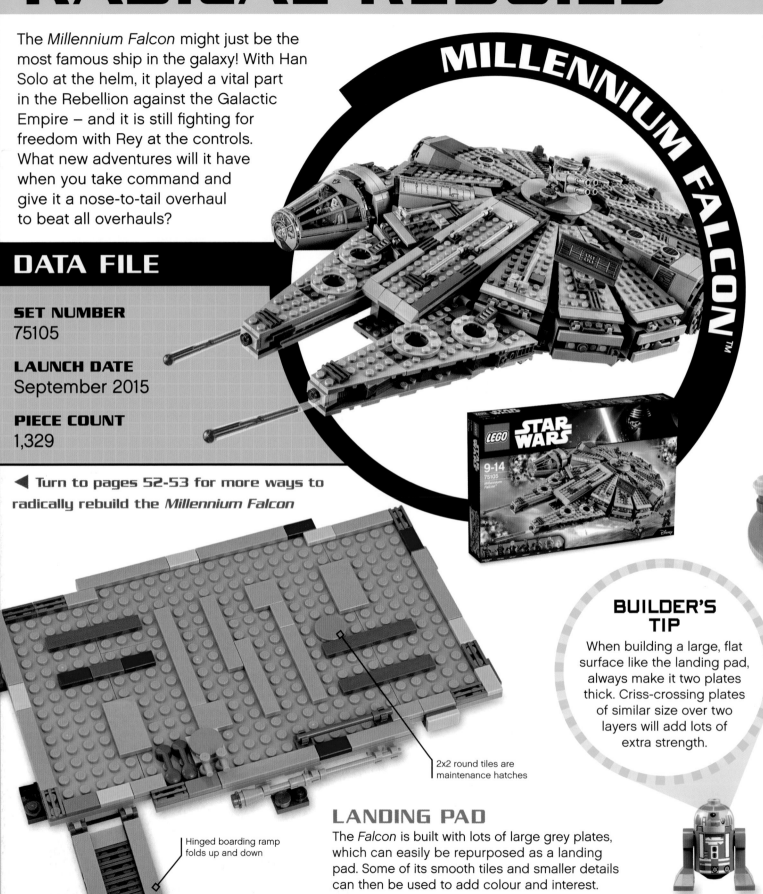

MILLENNIUM FALCON™

DATA FILE

SET NUMBER
75105

LAUNCH DATE
September 2015

PIECE COUNT
1,329

◀ Turn to pages 52-53 for more ways to radically rebuild the *Millennium Falcon*

STAR WARS
LEGO
9-14
75105
Millennium
Falcon™

BUILDER'S TIP

When building a large, flat surface like the landing pad, always make it two plates thick. Criss-crossing plates of similar size over two layers will add lots of extra strength.

2x2 round tiles are maintenance hatches

Hinged boarding ramp folds up and down

LANDING PAD

The *Falcon* is built with lots of large grey plates, which can easily be repurposed as a landing pad. Some of its smooth tiles and smaller details can then be used to add colour and interest.

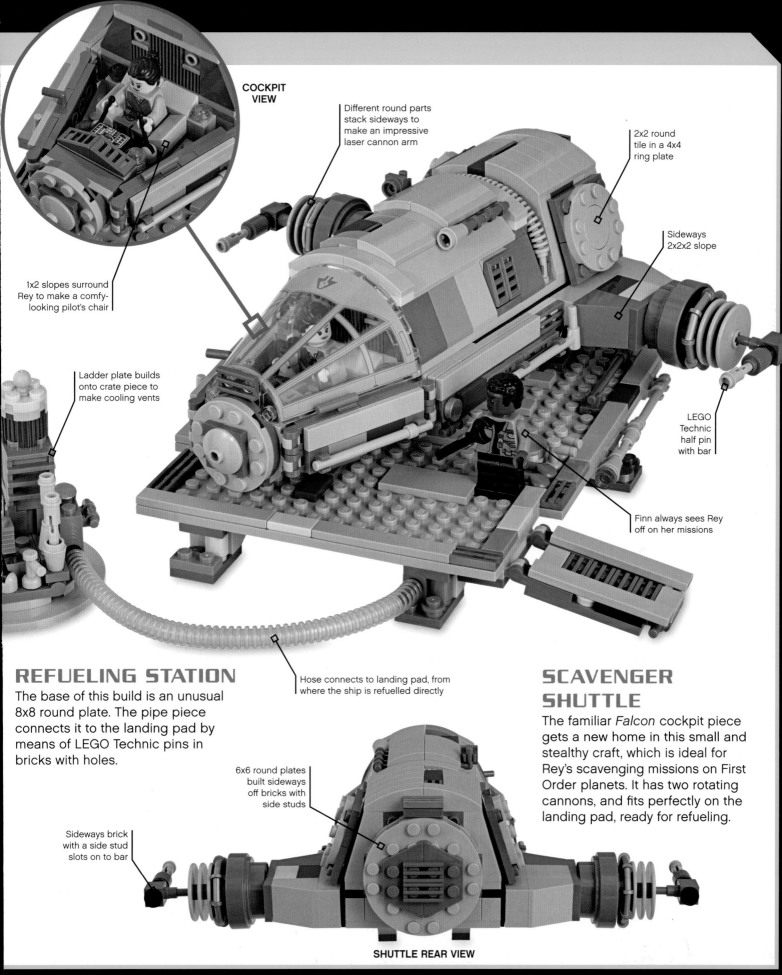

COCKPIT VIEW

Different round parts stack sideways to make an impressive laser cannon arm

2x2 round tile in a 4x4 ring plate

Sideways 2x2x2 slope

1x2 slopes surround Rey to make a comfy-looking pilot's chair

LEGO Technic half pin with bar

Ladder plate builds onto crate piece to make cooling vents

Finn always sees Rey off on her missions

REFUELING STATION

The base of this build is an unusual 8x8 round plate. The pipe piece connects it to the landing pad by means of LEGO Technic pins in bricks with holes.

Hose connects to landing pad, from where the ship is refuelled directly

6x6 round plates built sideways off bricks with side studs

Sideways brick with a side stud slots on to bar

SCAVENGER SHUTTLE

The familiar *Falcon* cockpit piece gets a new home in this small and stealthy craft, which is ideal for Rey's scavenging missions on First Order planets. It has two rotating cannons, and fits perfectly on the landing pad, ready for refueling.

SHUTTLE REAR VIEW

SEND GENERAL GRIEVOUS INTO A SPIN

Utapau landscape backdrop – the location of Grievous's duel with Obi-Wan Kenobi

There aren't many scarier sights than the cyborg General Grievous hurtling toward you on his wheel bike! Mimic its whizzing motion in a small-scale scene based on General Grievous's speedy getaway from Obi-Wan Kenobi in *Revenge of the Sith*.

Grille pieces look like wheel treads

A micro-scale General Grievous

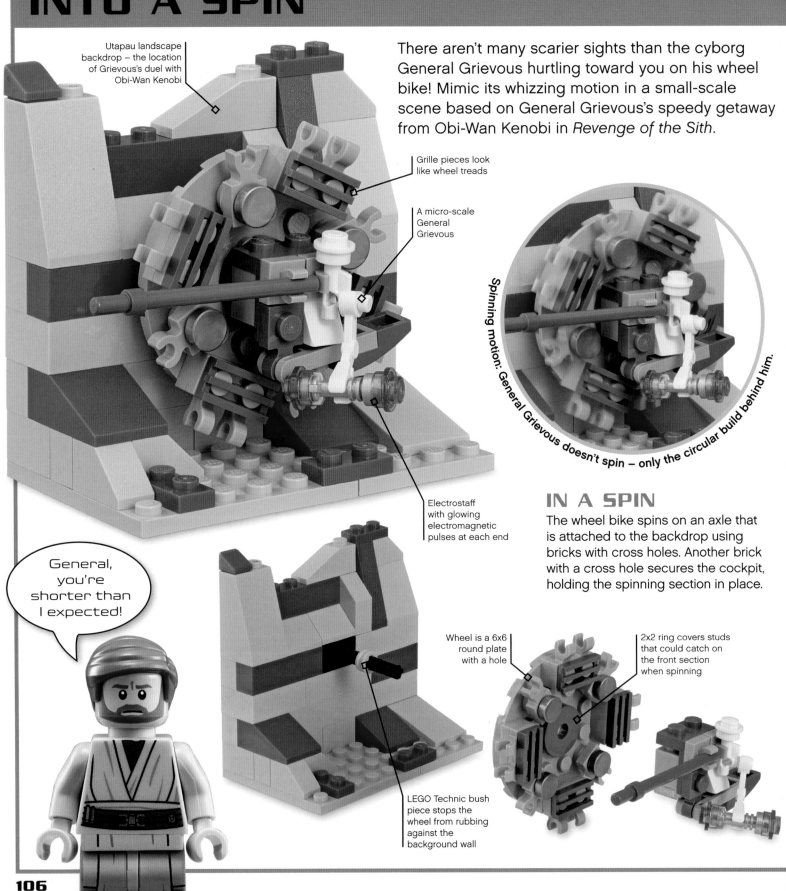

Spinning motion: General Grievous doesn't spin – only the circular build behind him.

General, you're shorter than I expected!

Electrostaff with glowing electromagnetic pulses at each end

IN A SPIN

The wheel bike spins on an axle that is attached to the backdrop using bricks with cross holes. Another brick with a cross hole secures the cockpit, holding the spinning section in place.

Wheel is a 6x6 round plate with a hole

2x2 ring covers studs that could catch on the front section when spinning

LEGO Technic bush piece stops the wheel from rubbing against the background wall

BUILDER'S TIP

To make sure the wheel whizzes around effectively, leave a small gap on both sides to allow it to spin smoothly.

The path to the Jedi Order is a long and arduous one. Padawans learn their craft in the field, but they must also train hard behind the scenes to hone their skills. Put your minifigures to the test and see if they have what it takes in a Padawan training arena.

Training remote for practising deflecting blaster bolts with lightsabers

Stud shooters for the Padawan to dodge

TRAINING ARENA

JEDI BOOT CAMP

Build a series of grueling drills and tests to help Padawan minifigures like Ahsoka develop their Force powers, fitness, physical strength, mental endurance and lightsaber combat.

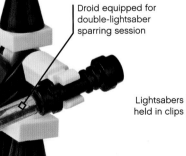

Droid equipped for double-lightsaber sparring session

Lightsabers held in clips

Teeth plate gives the droid stability

AHSOKA TANO

TRAINING DROID

STORAGE RACK

What would Ezra Bridger's room in the abandoned communications tower on Lothal look like? Would Ezra have a bed, a table, a stove? How about games? Where would he keep his prized stormtrooper helmets? Build whatever you imagine!

BUILDER'S TIP

The tower was not built as a home, so Ezra's room wouldn't have cosy comforts. Use grey, industrial-looking parts, security doors and viewports to create the hideout.

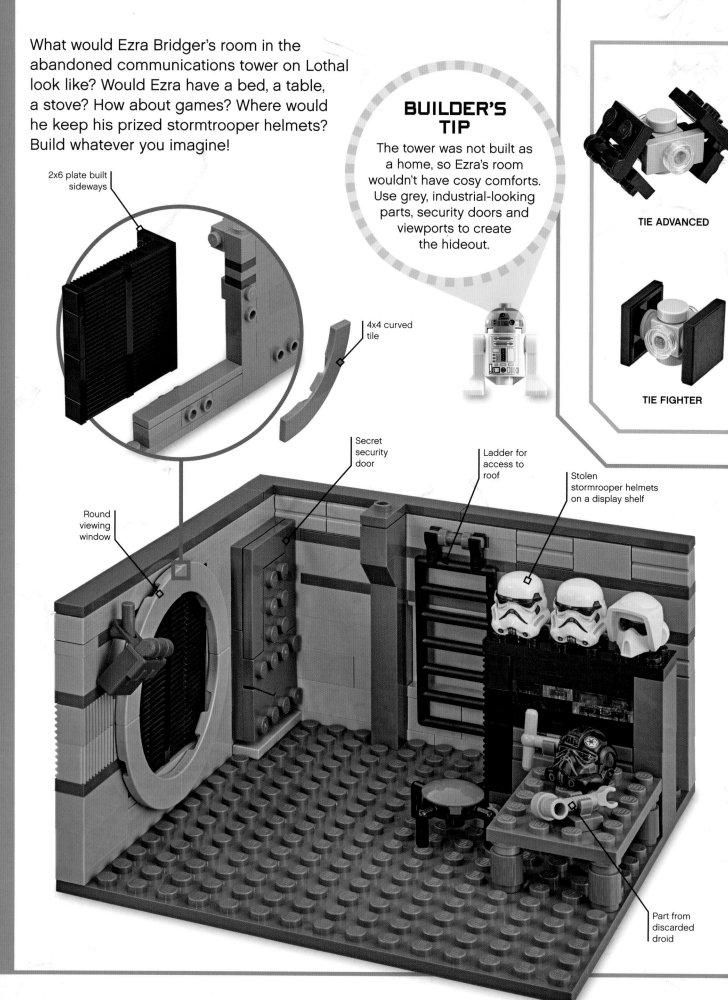

2x6 plate built sideways

4x4 curved tile

TIE ADVANCED

TIE FIGHTER

Round viewing window

Secret security door

Ladder for access to roof

Stolen stormrooper helmets on a display shelf

Part from discarded droid

MAKE TINY FAMILY TIES

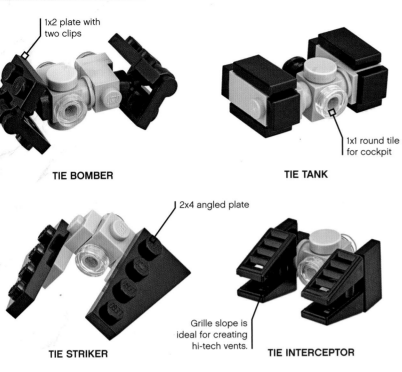

1x2 plate with two clips

TIE BOMBER

1x1 round tile for cockpit

TIE TANK

2x4 angled plate

TIE STRIKER

Grille slope is ideal for creating hi-tech vents.

TIE INTERCEPTOR

There are six members of this family of tiny TIE starfighters, and you won't need many parts to build them. All the TIEs have a 1x1 brick with side studs as their cockpit. The rest is up to you!

SPECIAL BRICK
The versatile 1x1 brick with four side studs forms the basis of all the tiny TIEs. It is the perfect size for the cockpit, and you can build out from it in all directions.

GIVE A LIFT TO A GEONOSIAN

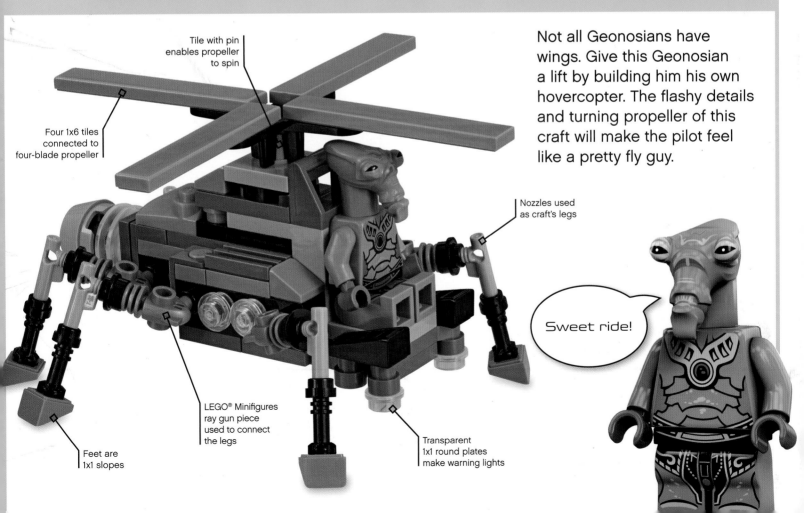

Tile with pin enables propeller to spin

Four 1x6 tiles connected to four-blade propeller

Nozzles used as craft's legs

Not all Geonosians have wings. Give this Geonosian a lift by building him his own hovercopter. The flashy details and turning propeller of this craft will make the pilot feel like a pretty fly guy.

Feet are 1x1 slopes

LEGO® Minifigures ray gun piece used to connect the legs

Transparent 1x1 round plates make warning lights

Sweet ride!

CREATE A GATEHOUSE FOR TATOOINE

Set yourself a challenge and restyle a popular LEGO set for the *Star Wars* galaxy. Here, the Gatehouse Raid set from the LEGO® Castle theme has been reworked to suit the desert planet of Tatooine. Instead of a raid from the Dragon Knight's forces, it's under attack from Imperial stormtroopers.

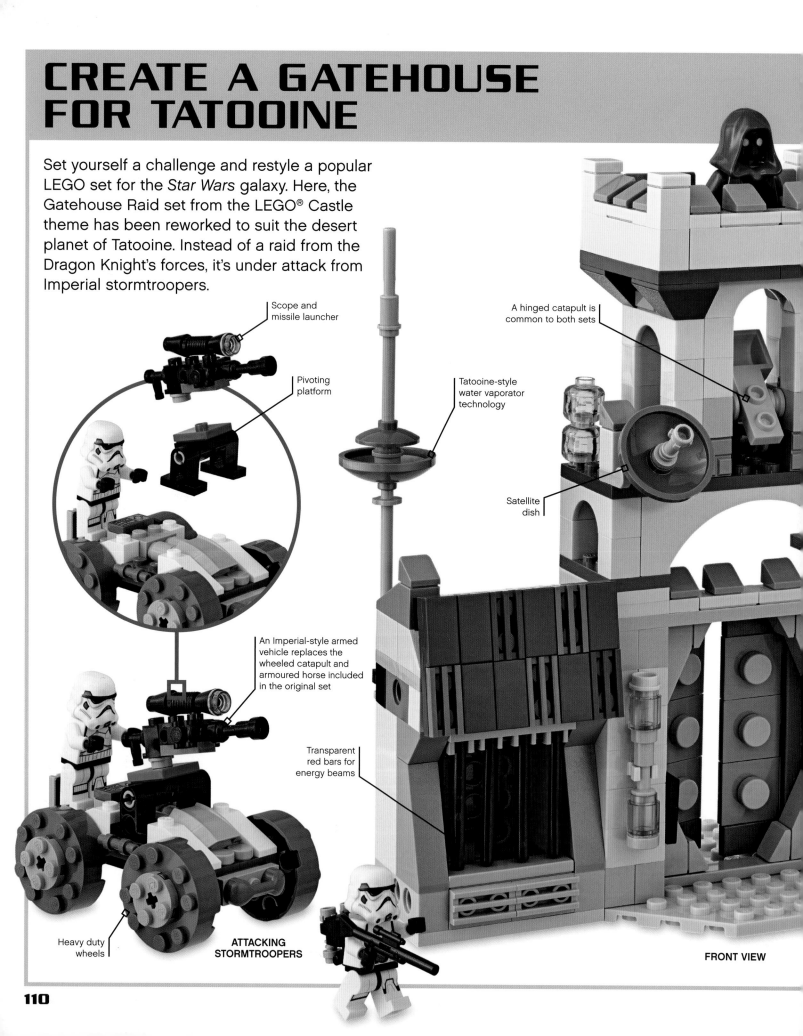

Scope and missile launcher

Pivoting platform

A hinged catapult is common to both sets

Tatooine-style water vaporator technology

Satellite dish

An Imperial-style armed vehicle replaces the wheeled catapult and armoured horse included in the original set

Transparent red bars for energy beams

Heavy duty wheels

ATTACKING STORMTROOPERS

FRONT VIEW

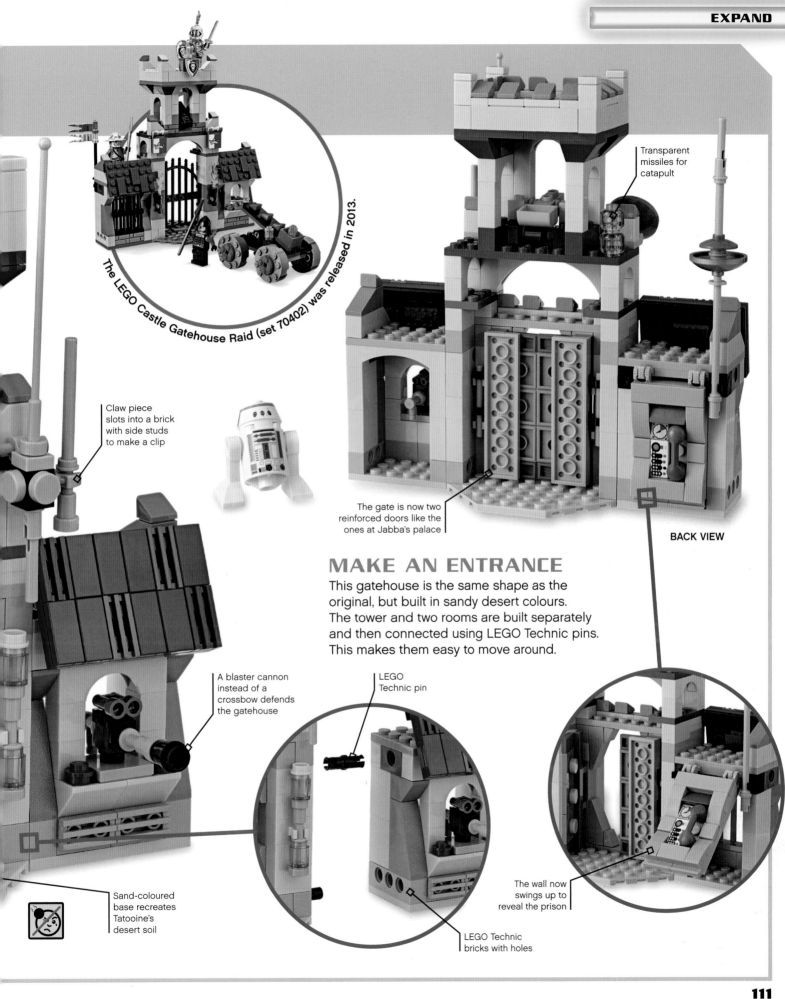

The LEGO Castle Gatehouse Raid (set 70402) was released in 2013.

Transparent missiles for catapult

Claw piece slots into a brick with side studs to make a clip

The gate is now two reinforced doors like the ones at Jabba's palace

BACK VIEW

MAKE AN ENTRANCE

This gatehouse is the same shape as the original, but built in sandy desert colours. The tower and two rooms are built separately and then connected using LEGO Technic pins. This makes them easy to move around.

A blaster cannon instead of a crossbow defends the gatehouse

LEGO Technic pin

Sand-coloured base recreates Tatooine's desert soil

LEGO Technic bricks with holes

The wall now swings up to reveal the prison

111

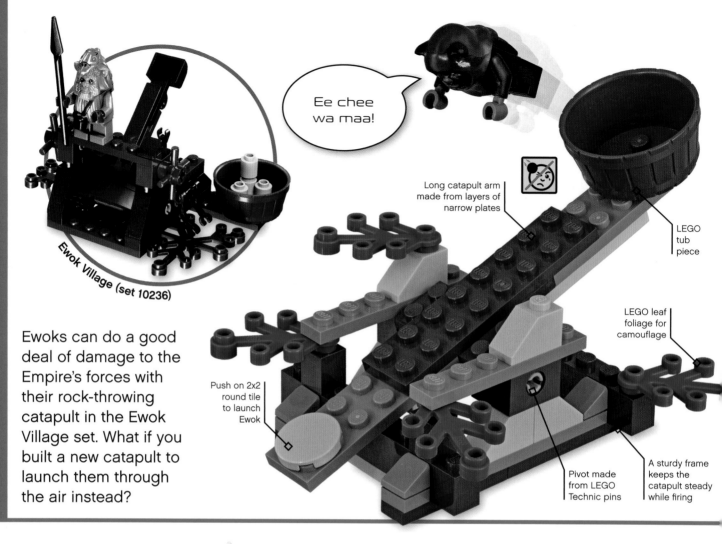

Ewok Village (set 10236)

Ewoks can do a good deal of damage to the Empire's forces with their rock-throwing catapult in the Ewok Village set. What if you built a new catapult to launch them through the air instead?

Ee chee wa maa!

Long catapult arm made from layers of narrow plates

LEGO tub piece

LEGO leaf foliage for camouflage

Push on 2x2 round tile to launch Ewok

Pivot made from LEGO Technic pins

A sturdy frame keeps the catapult steady while firing

BUILD A LIGHTSABER A DAY

Every lightsaber is unique – it is made by its owner to their personal design. Ezra Bridger's even incorporates a blaster. Build your own custom hilts for every day of the week!

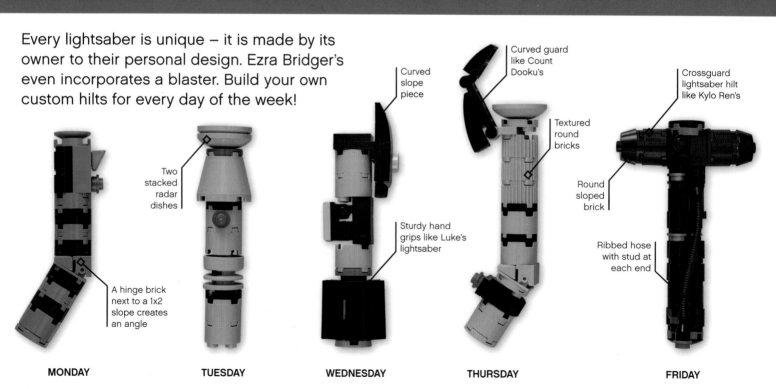

Curved slope piece

Curved guard like Count Dooku's

Crossguard lightsaber hilt like Kylo Ren's

Two stacked radar dishes

Textured round bricks

Round sloped brick

A hinge brick next to a 1x2 slope creates an angle

Sturdy hand grips like Luke's lightsaber

Ribbed hose with stud at each end

MONDAY   **TUESDAY**   **WEDNESDAY**   **THURSDAY**   **FRIDAY**

RECOLOUR A VEHICLE

Feeling a little blue from all the grey in the galaxy? Why not brighten things up? Take classic LEGO *Star Wars* builds and turn them technicolour! Swap the same shaped bricks for shades that wouldn't look out of place in the bright jungles of Felucia!

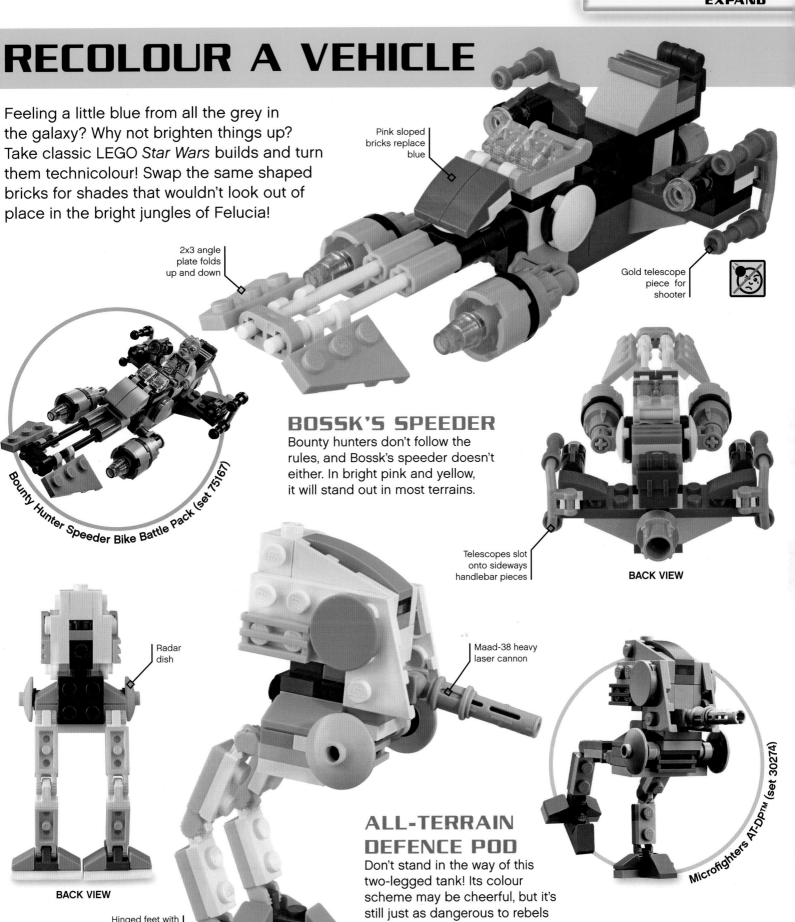

Pink sloped bricks replace blue

2x3 angle plate folds up and down

Gold telescope piece for shooter

Bounty Hunter Speeder Bike Battle Pack (set 75167)

BOSSK'S SPEEDER
Bounty hunters don't follow the rules, and Bossk's speeder doesn't either. In bright pink and yellow, it will stand out in most terrains.

Telescopes slot onto sideways handlebar pieces

BACK VIEW

Radar dish

BACK VIEW

Hinged feet with three lime-green "toes"

Maad-38 heavy laser cannon

ALL-TERRAIN DEFENCE POD
Don't stand in the way of this two-legged tank! Its colour scheme may be cheerful, but it's still just as dangerous to rebels trying to stop the Empire.

Microfighters AT-DP™ (set 30274A)

113

CUSTOMIZE PODRACERS

When it comes to podracers, one size does not fit all! Each racer builds their own unique machine in hope of winning at the Mos Espa Grand Arena. Why not create a basic base, then customize it for your favourite racer?

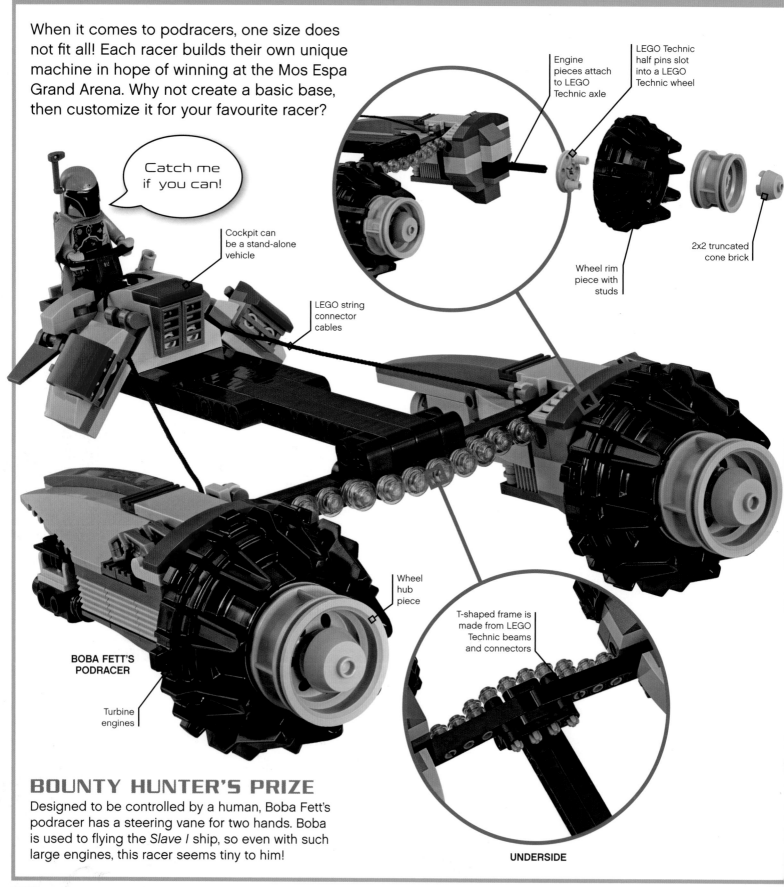

Catch me if you can!

Engine pieces attach to LEGO Technic axle

LEGO Technic half pins slot into a LEGO Technic wheel

2x2 truncated cone brick

Wheel rim piece with studs

Cockpit can be a stand-alone vehicle

LEGO string connector cables

Wheel hub piece

BOBA FETT'S PODRACER

Turbine engines

T-shaped frame is made from LEGO Technic beams and connectors

BOUNTY HUNTER'S PRIZE
Designed to be controlled by a human, Boba Fett's podracer has a steering vane for two hands. Boba is used to flying the *Slave I* ship, so even with such large engines, this racer seems tiny to him!

UNDERSIDE

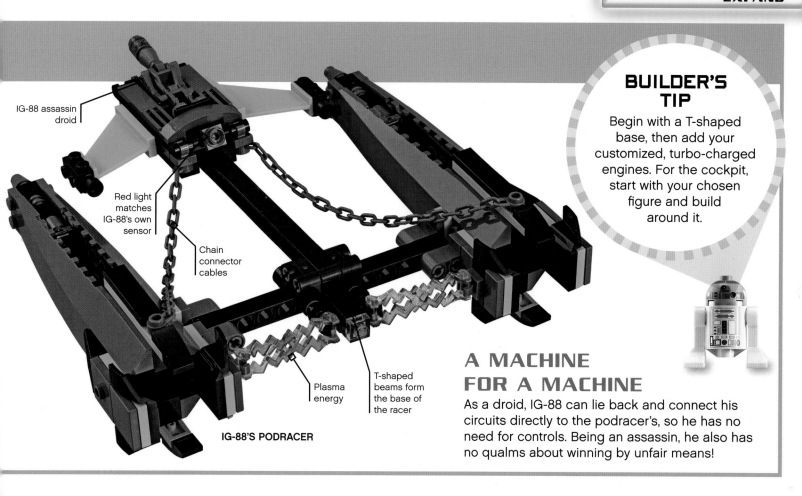

IG-88 assassin droid

Red light matches IG-88's own sensor

Chain connector cables

Plasma energy

T-shaped beams form the base of the racer

IG-88'S PODRACER

BUILDER'S TIP

Begin with a T-shaped base, then add your customized, turbo-charged engines. For the cockpit, start with your chosen figure and build around it.

A MACHINE FOR A MACHINE

As a droid, IG-88 can lie back and connect his circuits directly to the podracer's, so he has no need for controls. Being an assassin, he also has no qualms about winning by unfair means!

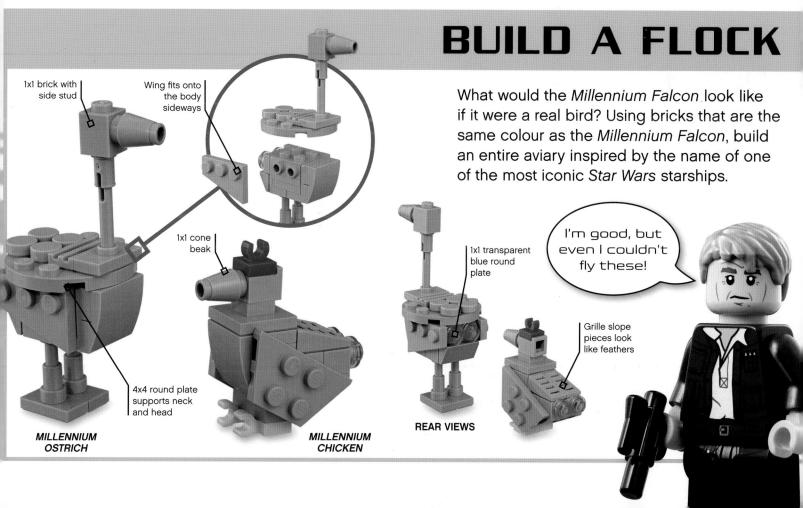

BUILD A FLOCK

What would the *Millennium Falcon* look like if it were a real bird? Using bricks that are the same colour as the *Millennium Falcon*, build an entire aviary inspired by the name of one of the most iconic *Star Wars* starships.

1x1 brick with side stud

Wing fits onto the body sideways

1x1 cone beak

1x1 transparent blue round plate

Grille slope pieces look like feathers

4x4 round plate supports neck and head

I'm good, but even I couldn't fly these!

MILLENNIUM OSTRICH

MILLENNIUM CHICKEN

REAR VIEWS

Fierce wampas are known for ripping limbs off things, rather than putting them on! But in this game you help a wampa out by trying to attach its arm. The catch? Your veterinary skills are hampered by not being able to see!

> Take my advice — never drop in on a wampa!

Angled plates fashion the wampa's shaggy mane

1x3 tooth plate makes spiky fur

1x1 plate with top clip holds the horn in place

Arm attaches to the board with a 1x1 round plate

PLAYABLE ARM

Base is two 6x14 plates held together by the wampa's body

Plates with side clips make perfect claws

WAMPA BOARD READY FOR PLAY

HOW TO PLAY

1 With their eyes covered, each player takes it in turn to place the loose arm on the picture.

2 The winner is whoever gets the arm closest to the correct position – without peeking!

HELPING HAND

A flat picture built from plates makes a great base for this game. Why not try building different game boards? You could pin the leg on a spider droid, or add the ears to an Ewok!

SPECIAL BRICK

Sausages aren't just for dinner! The sausage piece that makes the Wampa's horns is also useful for antennas, fingers or even engine parts!

Varying the angles of eye pieces makes expressive faces

WAMPA BOARD AFTER PLAY

RACE TO THE TOP OF MUSTAFAR

As if the fiery volcanic world of Mustafar wasn't dangerous enough, Obi-Wan is battling Anakin there. Build a hazardous obstacle course with stepping stones over molten lava pits and rivers, then play to see who will reach the control tower first.

HOW TO PLAY

1 Each player has a brick-built figure, which starts on the black square.

2 Players take turns to roll a die and move the corresponding number of places.

3 If you land on a red lava square, you must return to the start. If you land on another player, they go back to the start.

4 The winner is the first player to reach the control tower at the top of the volcano.

VOLATILE VOLCANO

Your volcano can be any size. This one has 17 steps up from the bottom. Cool grey bricks form volcanic rocks, with flowing bright-red lava. Lava-field hopping isn't just for Obi-Wan and Anakin – you can add more characters to race at once.

Curved half-arches look like liquid lava

Land on a red-hot lava tile and you have to start again!

Simple pieces create a mini-Anakin

Brick is the colour of Obi-Wan's Jedi robes

Players start on this black jumper plate

MUSTAFAR VOLCANO PLAYING BOARD

Ever thought those ranks of stormtroopers looked a little like rows of skittles, waiting to be knocked down? Well, here's a game that turns a corridor of the Death Star into your own bowling alley. Use skill and Force power to send a ball flying at these bucketheads.

Why do I always have to be at the front?

Walls are two bricks high

Smooth tiles for the ball to roll over

Adjust the height of the legs to get the pefect slope

Aim the launcher and release the ball

ABOUT TURN

The ramp for launching the ball is built on a turntable element, and raised up by a 2x2 round brick. This lets you change the angle to give you the best shot.

2x2 round brick

Turntable piece

PICK UP LIGHTSABER STICKS

The lightsaber is the weapon of a Jedi Knight. Not as clumsy as a blaster, it is an elegant weapon for a civilized age. It's also just the thing for... playing pick-up sticks! Play this with one or more friends to find out who has the steadiest nerves – and hands.

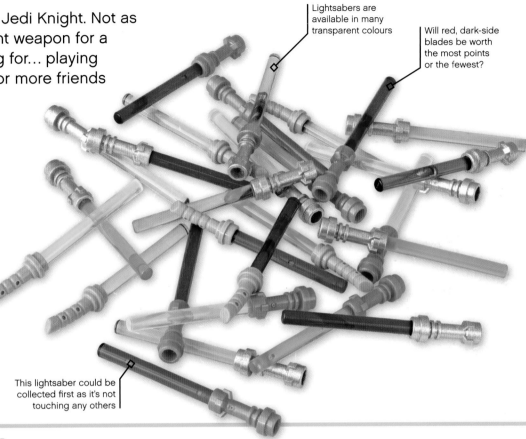

Lightsabers are available in many transparent colours

Will red, dark-side blades be worth the most points or the fewest?

This lightsaber could be collected first as it's not touching any others

HOW TO PLAY

1 Drop lightsabers of different colours onto a flat surface. Agree on a scoring system, allocating points for each colour.

2 Take turns to try and pick up one lightsaber at a time, without touching or moving any others. If you do, your turn is over.

3 Keep playing until all the lightsabers have been picked up. Add up each player's points to find the winner.

Ouch – this game really bowls me over!

Slope pieces set into the floor stop the troopers from falling too easily

Two 1x2 curved slopes make a ramp

Chevrons in the tiles help you to aim the ball

GAME IN ACTION

HOW TO PLAY

1 At the beginning of each turn, put the stormtrooper skittles in position in the bowling alley. Place the ball on the launcher.

2 Position the launcher and roll the ball at the stormtroopers. Remove any fallen troopers. Roll the ball again – each turn consists of two rolls of the ball.

3 The winner is whoever knocks down the most stormtroopers in a single turn.

BUILD FROM MEMORY

Show a friend a build like this Imperial scout trooper and let them study it for one minute. Take it away and give them all the bricks they need and five minutes to try to build it. See how closely they match the original. Ready, set, build!

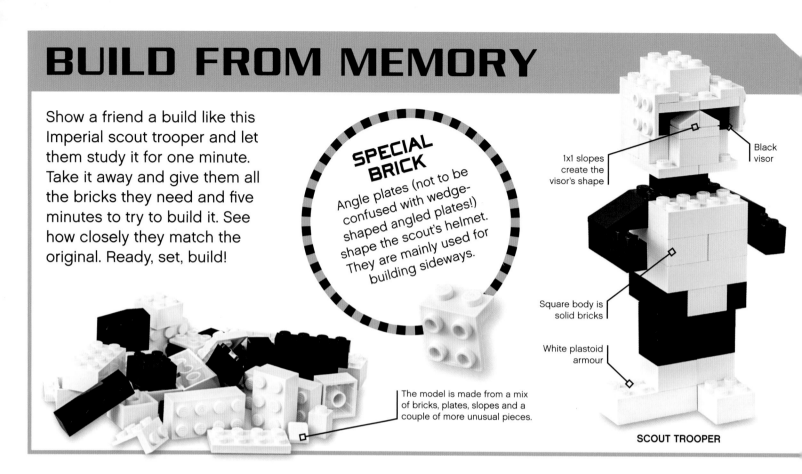

SPECIAL BRICK

Angle plates (not to be confused with wedge-shaped angled plates!) shape the scout's helmet. They are mainly used for building sideways.

1x1 slopes create the visor's shape

Black visor

Square body is solid bricks

White plastoid armour

The model is made from a mix of bricks, plates, slopes and a couple of more unusual pieces.

SCOUT TROOPER

Help Chopper the astromech droid repair the scrambled circuits aboard the *Ghost*. Create the pieces of this LEGO® jigsaw then challenge friends to put it back together.

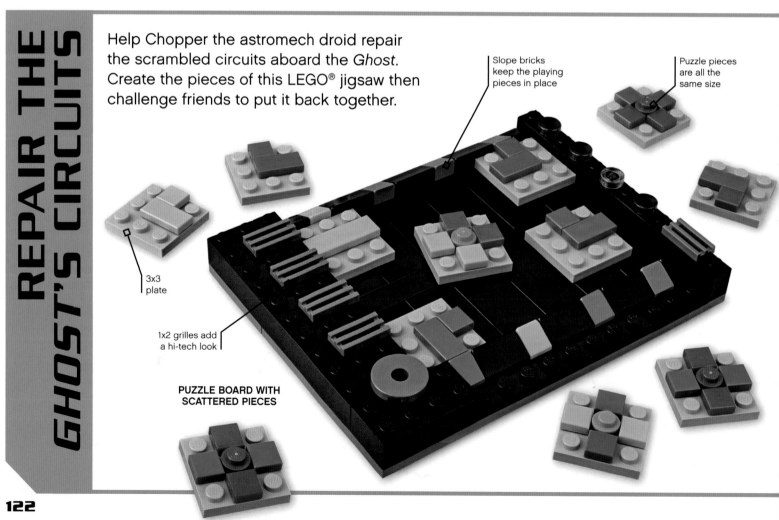

Slope bricks keep the playing pieces in place

Puzzle pieces are all the same size

3x3 plate

1x2 grilles add a hi-tech look

PUZZLE BOARD WITH SCATTERED PIECES

TAKE A BLIND GUESS!

How well do you really know your minifigures? Challenge your friends to feel their way to victory by recognizing characters without seeing them. Telling apart a battle droid from Yoda might be easy, but could you distinguish between Imperial officers?

The box is decorated with an assembly line of droids – including one with C-3PO's head!

HOW TO PLAY

1 One player sits on the walled side of the box and looks away while another places a minifigure in the centre of the box.

2 The first player puts their hands in the sides of the box, feels the figure, and tries to guess who it is.

MADE FOR MYSTERY

Build a simple box, open on three sides to allow plenty of room for hands. This one has been built in the style of a Geonosian droid foundry.

K-2SO droid

Stand for placing a new figure on each round

PICK UP THE PIECES

Create a 9x12 playing space with a raised border around it to hold the 3x3 game tiles in place. You can copy the design of this circuit board, or design your own.

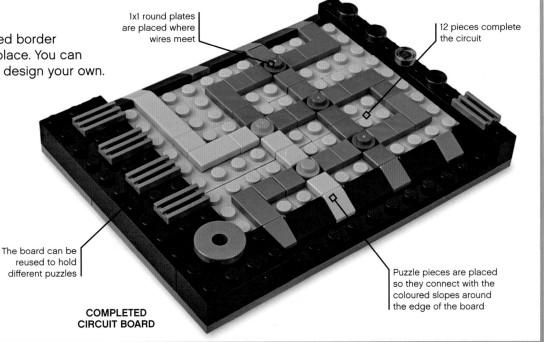

1x1 round plates are placed where wires meet

12 pieces complete the circuit

HOW TO PLAY

1 Take all the circuit pieces off the board and arrange them randomly around the board.

2 Challenge your friends to complete the puzzle. The quickest builder is the winner. If you're doing a solo challenge, try to beat your fastest time.

The board can be reused to hold different puzzles

Puzzle pieces are placed so they connect with the coloured slopes around the edge of the board

COMPLETED CIRCUIT BOARD

READY, SET, PODRACE!

Roll up! Roll up! Welcome to the Boonta Eve Classic! Build your own Mos Espa arena – then race, cheat and sabotage your way around the racecourse. But beware: The Boonta Eve Classic is downright dangerous. It has more fatalities than any other podrace in the Outer Rim!

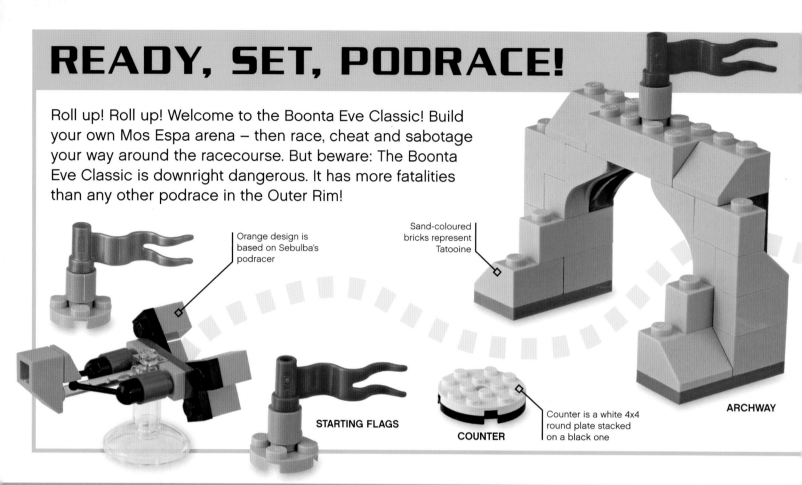

Orange design is based on Sebulba's podracer

Sand-coloured bricks represent Tatooine

STARTING FLAGS

Counter is a white 4x4 round plate stacked on a black one

COUNTER

ARCHWAY

SCAVENGE VALUABLE SCRAP

One person's junk is another's treasure! Help Jakku junk dealer Unkar Plutt find valuable LEGO pieces from scrapped starships, weapons and homes. You decide what's valuable about the pieces you choose to scavenge – it could be their colour, style or usefulness.

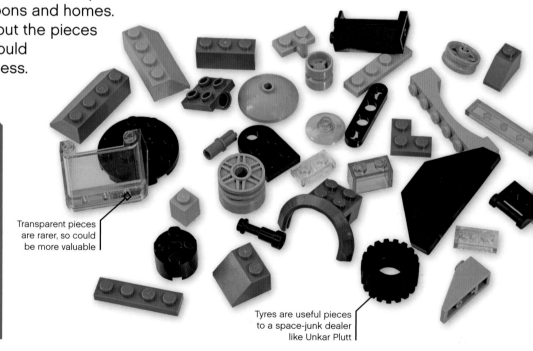

HOW TO PLAY

1 Players find a small container each in which to collect pieces.

2 Decide on the "valuable scrap" in your LEGO collection. All players could be looking for the same pieces or colours, or different ones.

3 Tip out a mixed box of LEGO pieces. Whoever collects the largest amount of valuable scrap in a set amount of time is the winner!

Transparent pieces are rarer, so could be more valuable

Tyres are useful pieces to a space-junk dealer like Unkar Plutt

Flags guide you around the course

TUSKEN RAIDER

FINISH LINE

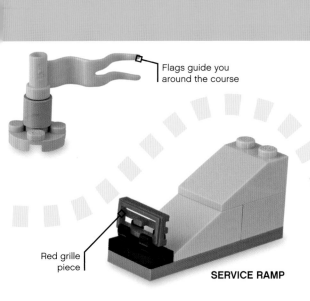

Red grille piece

SERVICE RAMP

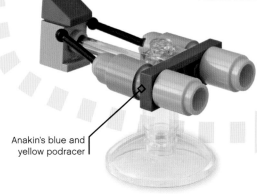

Anakin's blue and yellow podracer

HOW TO PLAY

1 Each object on the course is a "stage." Players take it in turns to flip the counter. White means that you move your podracer two stages and black lets you move three.

2 If you land on a flag, nothing happens. If you land at the archway, you roll again. The Tusken Raider causes you to miss a go. If you are forced onto the service ramp, you have to go back to the start.

3 The winner is the first podracer to complete three laps.

A MOVE IN THE RIGHT DIRECTION

Build a podracer for each player and a simple course that alternates flags with stages, such as an archway, a service ramp and a dangerous Tusken Raider. Build as many stages as you like!

Each player could collect a different colour

This game could also be a fun way to organize your pieces by colour or type!

Bring me your best junk!

SPIN YOUR WAY TO VICTORY

Create a kaleidoscope of colour by building spinning tops, like this one inspired by the Death Star's superlaser. Play against a friend to see whose top can spin the longest. Or you could battle to determine the fate of the galaxy. Can you knock your opponent's top off the table?

Grip the central handle to spin the top

Body can be a hexagonal plate or built from square and corner plates

Inverted radar dish element

Sliding plate in the centre creates minimal friction when spinning

Coloured studs create swirls of colour when top spins

UNDERSIDE

SPINNING TOP

CLOCK UP SOME TARGET PRACTICE

Jedi can hit their target just by using the Force, but everyone else has to put in hours of practice on the firing range. Build a simple game so your minifigures can hone their skills. Collect points for each stud through the holes – the smaller the target, the more points it is worth.

10x10 octagonal plate

Red plates on rings highlight the target areas

Aw shucks! I missed again...

4x4 ring

Minifigure-held stud-shooter

Row of sloped bricks gives stability

Hinge bricks tilt all three targets backward

FIRING RANGE

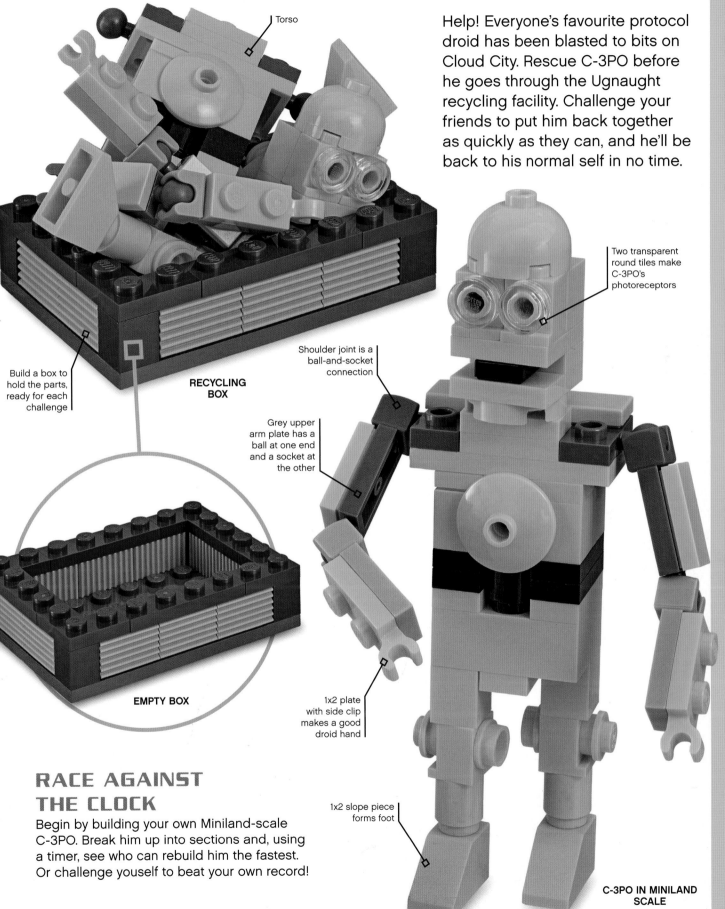

Torso

RECYCLING
BOX

Build a box to
hold the parts,
ready for each
challenge

EMPTY BOX

Help! Everyone's favourite protocol
droid has been blasted to bits on
Cloud City. Rescue C-3PO before
he goes through the Ugnaught
recycling facility. Challenge your
friends to put him back together
as quickly as they can, and he'll be
back to his normal self in no time.

REBUILD C-3PO ON CLOUD CITY

Two transparent
round tiles make
C-3PO's
photoreceptors

Shoulder joint is a
ball-and-socket
connection

Grey upper
arm plate has a
ball at one end
and a socket at
the other

1x2 plate
with side clip
makes a good
droid hand

1x2 slope piece
forms foot

RACE AGAINST
THE CLOCK

Begin by building your own Miniland-scale
C-3PO. Break him up into sections and, using
a timer, see who can rebuild him the fastest.
Or challenge youself to beat your own record!

C-3PO IN MINILAND
SCALE

127

PLAY THE SARLACC PIT GAME

Feed Boba Fett and his villainous buddies to the hungry sarlacc with this fun minifigure-flipping game! It is built by adapting the Desert Skiff Escape set, but you can make a similar game using any LEGO® Star Wars™ elements. All you need is a launcher, some targets and your choice of unfortunate minifigures!

HOW TO PLAY

1 Place your skiff launcher on a flat surface a short distance away from the sarlacc pit target.

2 Keeping the skiff in the same place throughout, try to hit the target by placing a minifigure on the launcher and flipping it with one finger.

3 Score 10 points if your minifigure lands in the sarlacc's mouth, and five points if it lands in one of the dishes surrounding the sarlacc.

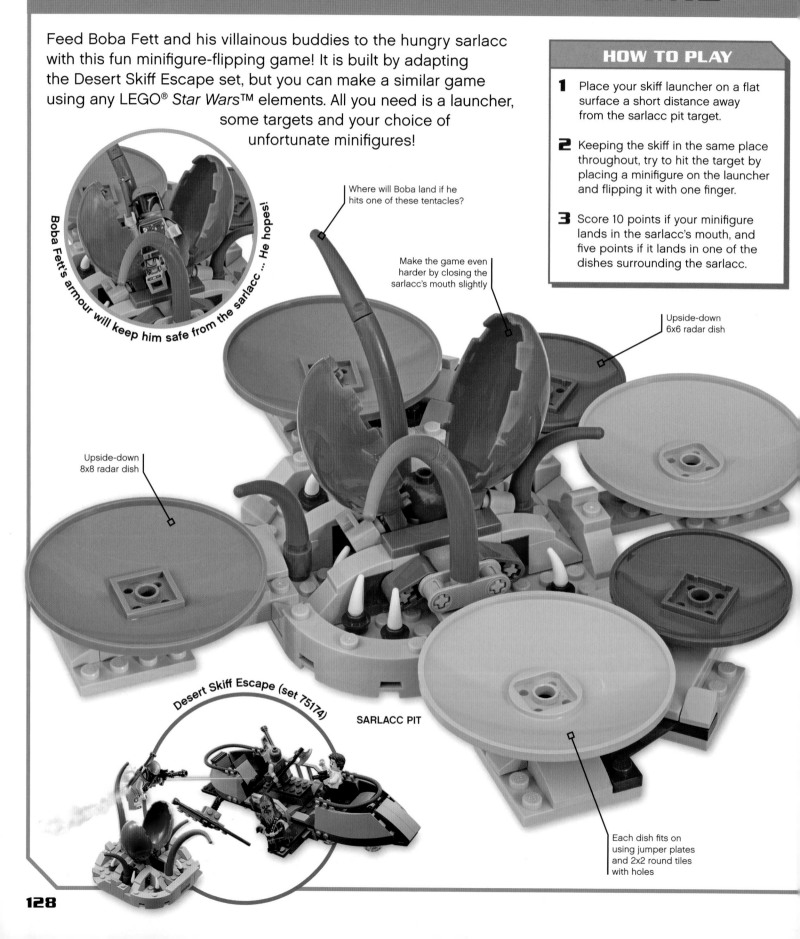

Boba Fett's armour will keep him safe from the sarlacc ... He hopes!

Where will Boba land if he hits one of these tentacles?

Make the game even harder by closing the sarlacc's mouth slightly

Upside-down 6x6 radar dish

Upside-down 8x8 radar dish

Desert Skiff Escape (set 75174)

SARLACC PIT

Each dish fits on using jumper plates and 2x2 round tiles with holes

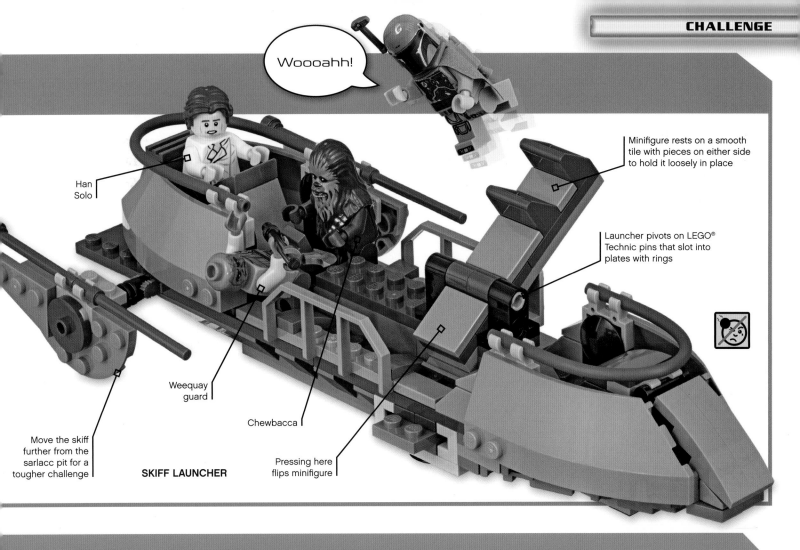

Woooahh!

Han Solo

Minifigure rests on a smooth tile with pieces on either side to hold it loosely in place

Launcher pivots on LEGO® Technic pins that slot into plates with rings

Weequay guard

Chewbacca

Move the skiff further from the sarlacc pit for a tougher challenge

SKIFF LAUNCHER

Pressing here flips minifigure

MAKE A MICRO MONSTER

These little monsters prove that you don't have to be big to be scary! Challenge yourself and your friends to make some classic *Star Wars* monsters with the fewest bricks possible, and then see if you can identify each other's builds.

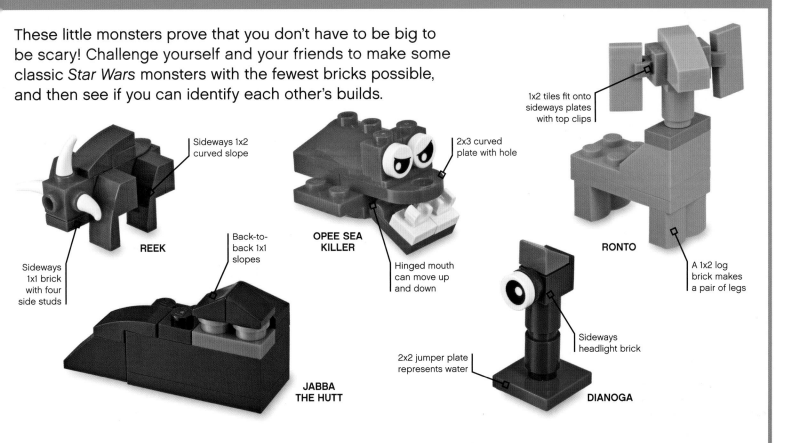

Sideways 1x2 curved slope

REEK

Sideways 1x1 brick with four side studs

Back-to-back 1x1 slopes

JABBA THE HUTT

2x3 curved plate with hole

OPEE SEA KILLER

Hinged mouth can move up and down

2x2 jumper plate represents water

DIANOGA

Sideways headlight brick

1x2 tiles fit onto sideways plates with top clips

RONTO

A 1x2 log brick makes a pair of legs

Who's the most frequent flyer in the *Star Wars* galaxy? See at a glance with this 3-D bar chart. Its minifigures stand on columns built with extra bricks for each planet they have visited. Other achievements you could represent as a chart include battle victories, or languages spoken.

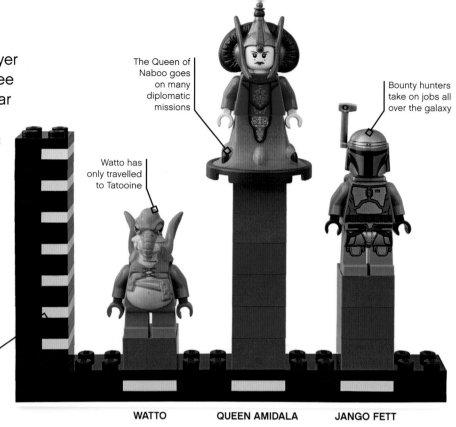

The Queen of Naboo goes on many diplomatic missions

Bounty hunters take on jobs all over the galaxy

Watto has only travelled to Tatooine

Each white bar represents one planet visited

WATTO　　　**QUEEN AMIDALA**　　　**JANGO FETT**

KNOCK DOWN BATTLE DROID SKITTLES

Separatist B1 battle droids make great pins for target practice. How many can you topple with a single shot from your stud shooter? Take it in turns with friends to fire at the "clankers" and send them flying.

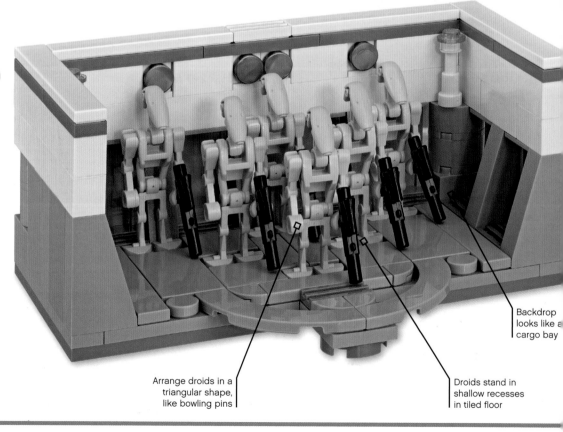

Backdrop looks like a cargo bay

Arrange droids in a triangular shape, like bowling pins

Droids stand in shallow recesses in tiled floor

HOW TO PLAY

1 Lay out the droids in a triangular formation before each go.

2 Players take it in turns to fire a stud at the droids.

3 Whoever knocks down the most droids in a single shot wins.

CREATE A SECRET CODE

A successful rebellion depends on secure communication. Invent your own code and share secret messages with your friends. If your letter is intercepted by anyone, it will be as meaningful to them as Mando is to someone who hasn't visited Mandalore!

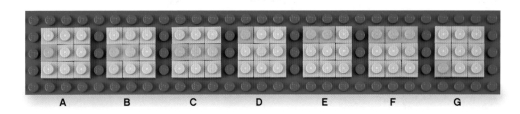

A B C D E F G

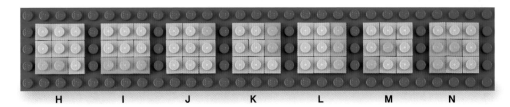

H I J K L M N

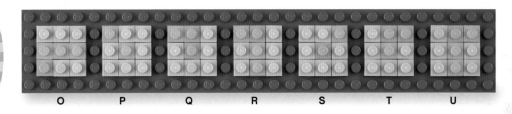

O P Q R S T U

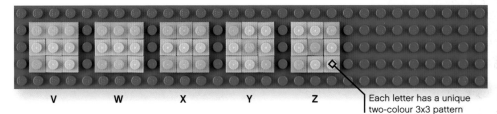

V W X Y Z

Each letter has a unique two-colour 3x3 pattern

CODED SYMBOLS FOR THE LETTERS A TO Z

BUILDER'S TIP

Once you have built a symbol for each letter, you can spell out sentences. If you don't leave spaces between words, messages will be harder for the enemy to decode.

Turn to page 189 to build a coded door sign ▶

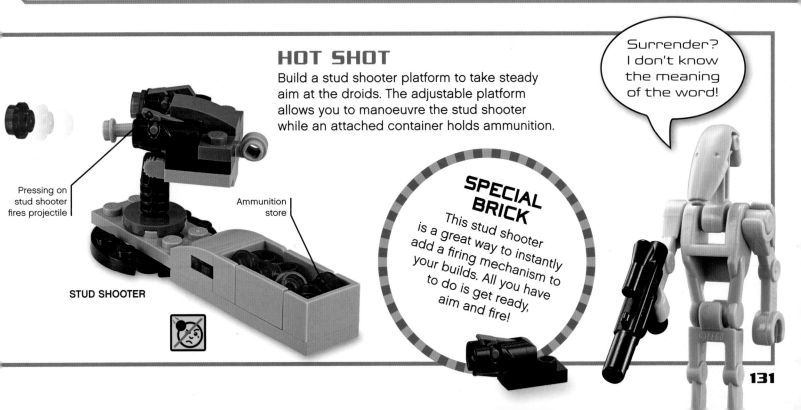

HOT SHOT

Build a stud shooter platform to take steady aim at the droids. The adjustable platform allows you to manoeuvre the stud shooter while an attached container holds ammunition.

Pressing on stud shooter fires projectile

Ammunition store

STUD SHOOTER

Surrender? I don't know the meaning of the word!

SPECIAL BRICK

This stud shooter is a great way to instantly add a firing mechanism to your builds. All you have to do is get ready, aim and fire!

PLAY "WHICH WOOKIEE AM I?"

Wookiees can be hard to tell apart, but each of these hairy heroes has a unique story. Pick your favourite from your minifigure collection, and describe him to your friends. The correct guesser gets to go next!

Turn to page 194 to find who's who... ▶

WOOKIEE A

WOOKIEE B

WOOKIEE C

WOOKIEE D

RACE A RATHTAR!

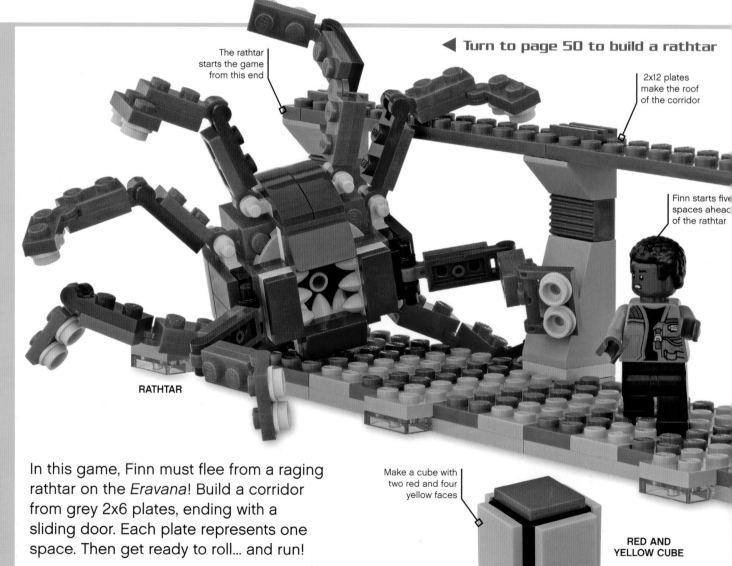

The rathtar starts the game from this end

◀ Turn to page 50 to build a rathtar

2x12 plates make the roof of the corridor

Finn starts five spaces ahead of the rathtar

RATHTAR

In this game, Finn must flee from a raging rathtar on the *Eravana*! Build a corridor from grey 2x6 plates, ending with a sliding door. Each plate represents one space. Then get ready to roll... and run!

Make a cube with two red and four yellow faces

RED AND YELLOW CUBE

TEST YOUR MEMORY

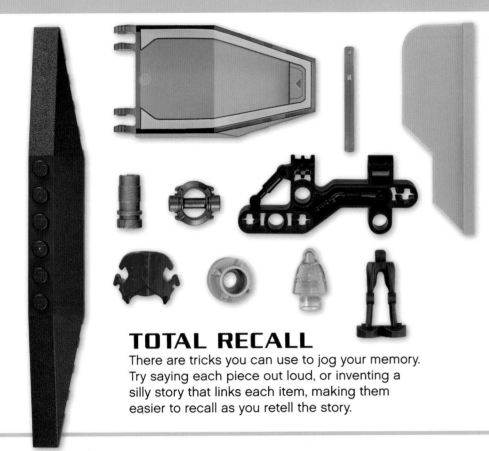

Always forgetting where you've left the keys to the *Millennium Falcon*? Struggle to put names to clone trooper faces? Put your memory to the test with this tricky teaser. If it's too easy, add more pieces or reduce the amount of time you have to study them.

TOTAL RECALL

There are tricks you can use to jog your memory. Try saying each piece out loud, or inventing a silly story that links each item, making them easier to recall as you retell the story.

HOW TO PLAY

1 Ask a friend to lay out a collection of different LEGO elements.

2 Study them for one minute, trying to register as many as you can.

3 Close your eyes while your friend takes a piece away and rearranges the pieces. See if you can work out which one is missing.

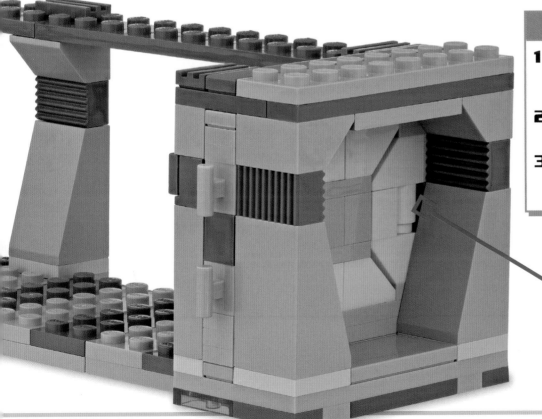

HOW TO PLAY

1 Roll the cube. If it lands on red, the rathtar advances two spaces. If you roll yellow, Finn moves one space.

2 The rathtar will get fewer moves than Finn, but makes bigger jumps.

3 Keep rolling until Finn goes through the door to safety – or the rathtar grabs him!

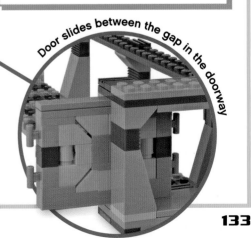

Door slides between the gap in the doorway

PLAY GALACTIC-TAC-TOE

It's *Millennium Falcons* versus lightsabers in this *Star Wars* version of tic-tac-toe. Han Solo's *Falcon* might be the fastest ship in the galaxy, but can it win a game of strategy?

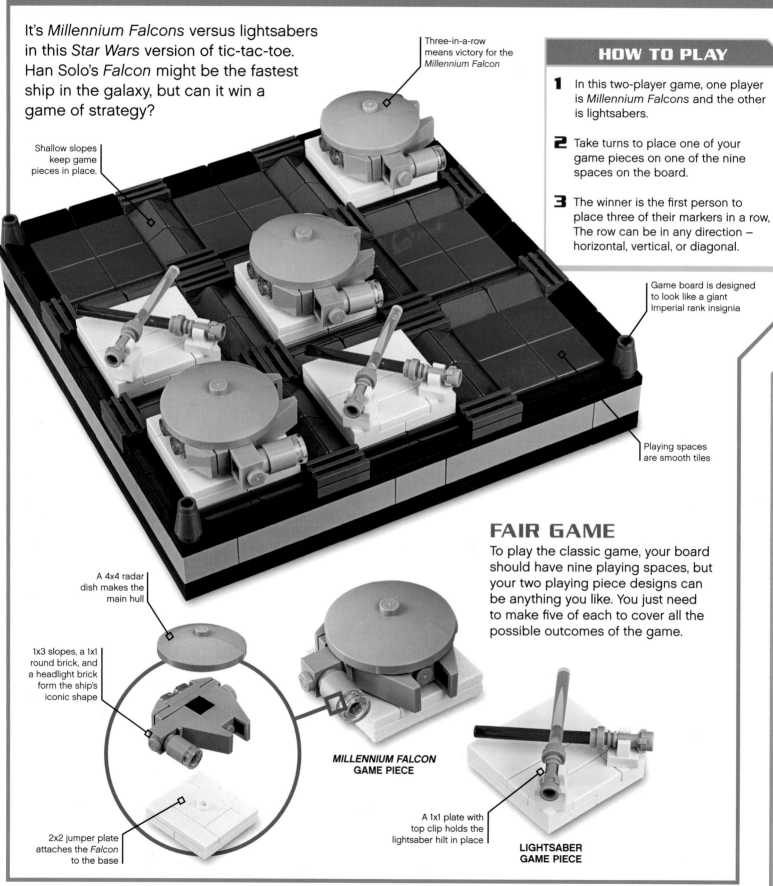

Three-in-a-row means victory for the *Millennium Falcon*

Shallow slopes keep game pieces in place.

A 4x4 radar dish makes the main hull

1x3 slopes, a 1x1 round brick, and a headlight brick form the ship's iconic shape

2x2 jumper plate attaches the *Falcon* to the base

Game board is designed to look like a giant Imperial rank insignia

Playing spaces are smooth tiles

MILLENNIUM FALCON GAME PIECE

A 1x1 plate with top clip holds the lightsaber hilt in place

LIGHTSABER GAME PIECE

HOW TO PLAY

1 In this two-player game, one player is *Millennium Falcons* and the other is lightsabers.

2 Take turns to place one of your game pieces on one of the nine spaces on the board.

3 The winner is the first person to place three of their markers in a row, The row can be in any direction – horizontal, vertical, or diagonal.

FAIR GAME

To play the classic game, your board should have nine playing spaces, but your two playing piece designs can be anything you like. You just need to make five of each to cover all the possible outcomes of the game.

RACE TO THE RESISTANCE

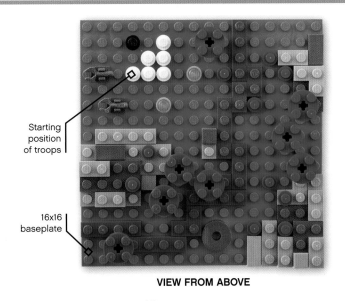

Starting position of troops

16x16 baseplate

VIEW FROM ABOVE

Mix strategic thinking with the roll of the die in this game that can be played on your own or with others. Build a board – like this one set on the forest planet of Takodana – for each player. Use 1x1 round plates to represent troops. Then race to the Resistance base!

The white and orange piece represents a flametrooper

The white piece is a stormtrooper

The blue piece is a First Order officer

HOW TO PLAY

1 Roll the die and then move one piece the corresponding number of steps (each step is one stud on the board).

2 The aim of the game is to move all your troops to the Resistance base in as few rolls of the die as possible. To get onto the base, you must roll the exact number.

3 Pieces can only move into an empty space and they must go around obstacles such as rocks and trees. To cross the river, a piece must be next to it and a 4 rolled on the die.

4 If you roll a 6, you can bring a speeder into play. A speeder attaches to the top of a trooper for the rest of the game. The trooper can then fly over any obstacles instead of going around them.

Speeders can transport troops over obstacles

The river blocks a piece from crossing until a 4 is rolled

Trees block a piece's path

Resistance base

Rocks are impassable except on speeders

MIX UP YOUR MINIFIGURES

What would happen if Darth Vader had to walk in someone else's shoes? Shake things up with this pick and mix of character parts. Can you work out which nine figures these crazy combination characters are built from?

SQUAWK!

1

2

3

I love dress-down Fridays.

4

5

6

I hope the Emperor doesn't see me in this...

7

8

9

Turn to page 194 to see the original minifigures ▶

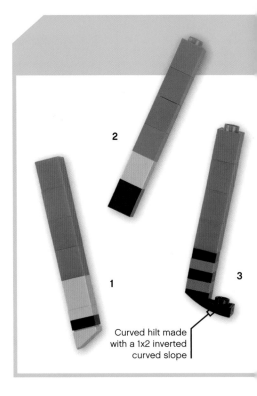

2

1

3

Curved hilt made with a 1x2 inverted curved slope

HOW TO PLAY

1 Place Chewie in the tub, set the catapult so the 2x10 plate is level, and line up the AT-STs.

2 Players take it in turns to fire the catapult and try to knock down the AT-STs.

3 Whoever knocks down the most AT-STs is the winner. If it's too easy, see how many times in a row you can knock them all over.

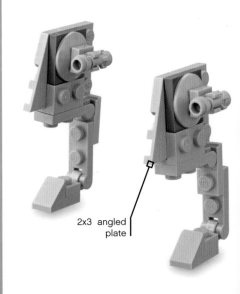

2x3 angled plate

NAME THAT LIGHTSABER

Test your *Star Wars* knowledge as well as your LEGO building skills with this guessing game. Every Jedi and Sith designs their own lightsaber, so each one is unique. Make some simplified lightsabers and see if your friends can guess who owns them.

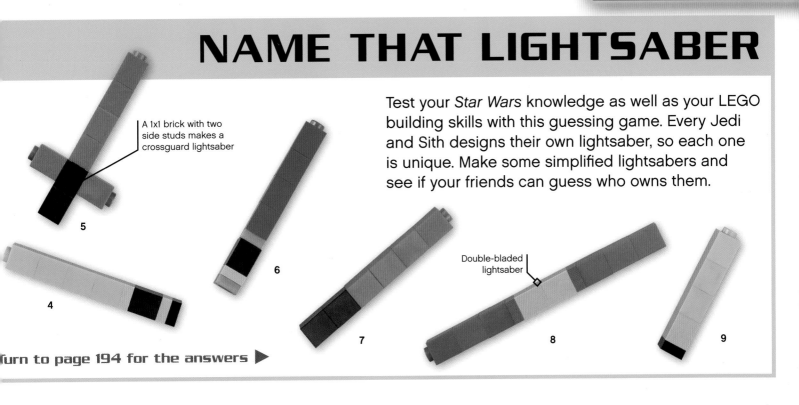

A 1x1 brick with two side studs makes a crossguard lightsaber

5

4

6

Double-bladed lightsaber

7

8

9

Turn to page 194 for the answers ▶

Ferocious, hairy Wookiees are pretty scary at the best of times, but imagine their hefty bulk hurtling at you from above! When it comes to invading Imperial AT-STs, Chewbacca loves to throw his weight around. Help him defeat the Empire in this game of power and skill.

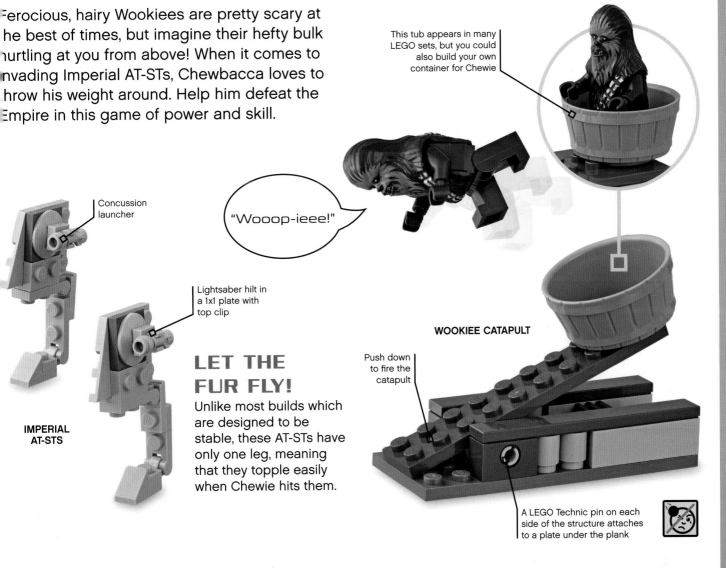

This tub appears in many LEGO sets, but you could also build your own container for Chewie

"Wooop-ieee!"

Concussion launcher

Lightsaber hilt in a 1x1 plate with top clip

LET THE FUR FLY!

Unlike most builds which are designed to be stable, these AT-STs have only one leg, meaning that they topple easily when Chewie hits them.

IMPERIAL AT-STS

WOOKIEE CATAPULT

Push down to fire the catapult

A LEGO Technic pin on each side of the structure attaches to a plate under the plank

SEND CHEWIE FLYING

RADICAL REBUILD

Poe Dameron's X-wing starfighter is an icon of the Resistance, with its unique orange-and-black styling turning heads wherever it lands. But where *does* it land? Here, the set has been reimagined as parts of a Resistance base, where ace pilots may come and go, but there is always important work for the ground crew to do!

DATA FILE

SET NUMBER
75102

LAUNCH DATE
September 2015

PIECE COUNT
717

LEGO STAR WARS

8-14
75102
Poe's X-wing Fighter™

Disney

POWER LIFTER

Resistance ground crew use various small vehicles to keep their prized starfighters ready for action. The power lifter is for loading cargo and extra equipment, such as this sensor array.

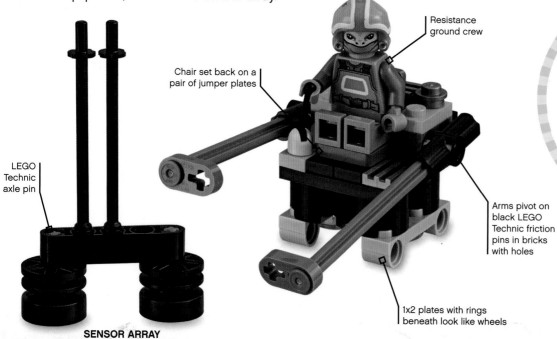

Resistance ground crew

Chair set back on a pair of jumper plates

LEGO Technic axle pin

Arms pivot on black LEGO Technic friction pins in bricks with holes

1x2 plates with rings beneath look like wheels

SENSOR ARRAY

BUILDER'S TIP

LEGO Technic axles are usually hidden as part of the "skeleton" of a complex build, but don't forget that they can be interesting features in their own right, too!

PERIMETER WALKER

A pilot can protect his Resistance pals from the ground in this walker. Its height gives a great view during base patrols, and it stands ready to fire its spring-shooter missiles.

Two sideways wheel arches complete the cockpit top

The shooter section pivots on a pair of 1x2 plates with top clips

Sideways curved slopes give the cockpit its rounded look

LEGO Technic axles run through the legs

Jumper plates hold these pieces in place

LEGO Technic ski pole is an X-wing laser cannon in for repair

Round pieces are power cells and cans of machine lubricant

ENGINEER'S WORKSTATION

The best pilot in the Resistance needs the best engineers. This workstation is where the top technicians repair and enhance starfighter parts to make the ships faster and more ferocious!

Wrench piece fits into a LEGO Technic angle connector

Both LEGO Technic axles are eight-studs long and have end studs

LEGO Technic bushes hold angle connector in place

A 4x6 base plate keeps the crane arm stable

Arm pivots on a click hinge connection

Spring-shooter missiles slot into sideways bricks with side studs

MISSILE LOADER

This mighty mechanical arm does the delicate work of loading highly volatile missiles into Poe's walker and other Resistance vessels. The missiles themselves are kept on a rack with a built-in cooling system.

MISSILE RACK

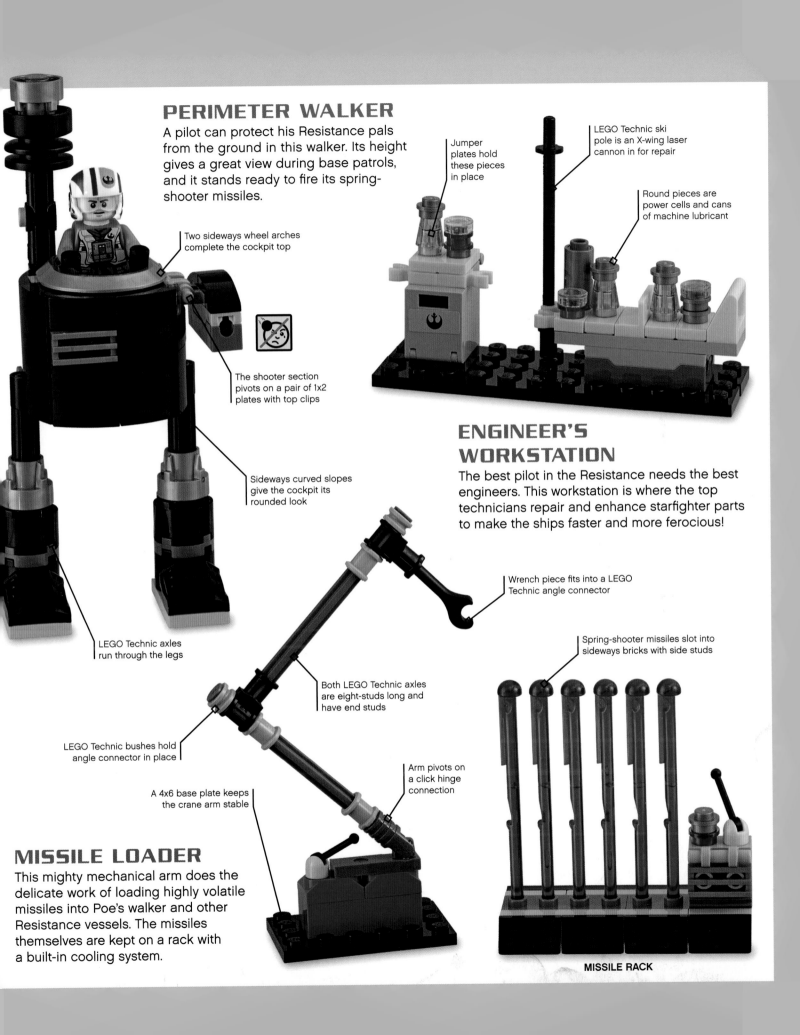

HELP BB-8 DODGE DANGER

Help! BB-8 is stuck on Jakku and needs to get vital information to the Resistance. Determine the droid's fate with this fairground-style game. Will he make it to the safety of the *Millennium Falcon*, be captured by First Order TIE fighters, or disappear into the Sinking Sands?

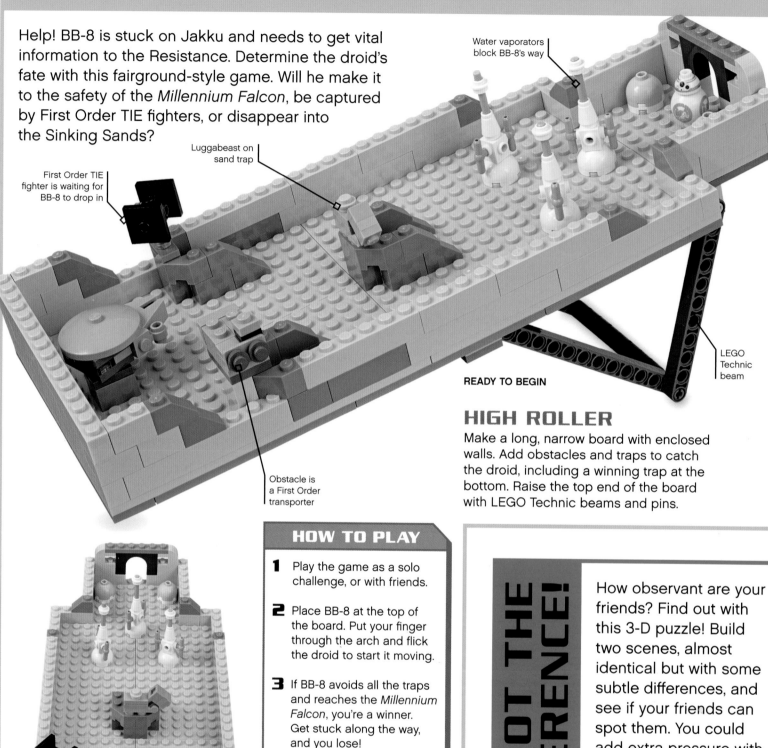

Water vaporators block BB-8's way

Luggabeast on sand trap

First Order TIE fighter is waiting for BB-8 to drop in

LEGO Technic beam

READY TO BEGIN

Obstacle is a First Order transporter

HIGH ROLLER

Make a long, narrow board with enclosed walls. Add obstacles and traps to catch the droid, including a winning trap at the bottom. Raise the top end of the board with LEGO Technic beams and pins.

The *Millennium Falcon* is on standby for escape off-world

BB-8 ABOUT TO REACH SAFETY

HOW TO PLAY

1 Play the game as a solo challenge, or with friends.

2 Place BB-8 at the top of the board. Put your finger through the arch and flick the droid to start it moving.

3 If BB-8 avoids all the traps and reaches the *Millennium Falcon*, you're a winner. Get stuck along the way, and you lose!

SPOT THE DIFFERENCE!

How observant are your friends? Find out with this 3-D puzzle! Build two scenes, almost identical but with some subtle differences, and see if your friends can spot them. You could add extra pressure with a timer, but remember to tell your friends how many changes they're looking for!

TRY YOUR LUCK AT BINGO

Eyes down for a full house! This bingo board matches LEGO® *Star Wars*™ elements instead of numbers. To play, make a grid with nine sections for each player and place a different LEGO piece in each square, making sure that no two grids are exactly the same. Then choose a brick you have plenty of to use as a marker.

HOW TO PLAY

1 Make the grids and nominate someone to be the bingo caller, who will pull a selection of LEGO pieces out of a box.

2 Whenever a piece matches the shape of one on a player's grid (don't worry about the colour), the player can mark it off.

3 The first player to mark off a row of three (in any direction) on their grid shouts "Bingo!" – and is the winner.

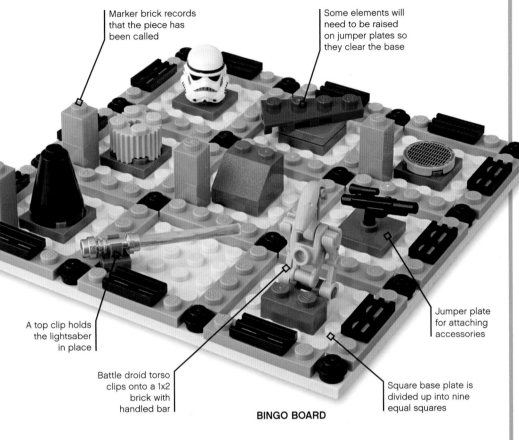

Marker brick records that the piece has been called

Some elements will need to be raised on jumper plates so they clear the base

A top clip holds the lightsaber in place

Battle droid torso clips onto a 1x2 brick with handled bar

Jumper plate for attaching accessories

Square base plate is divided up into nine equal squares

BINGO BOARD

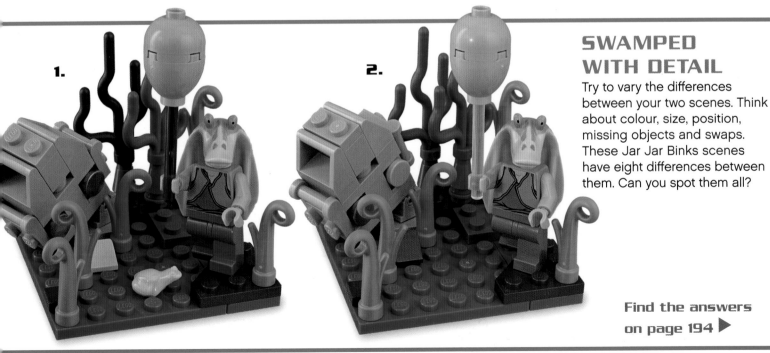

1.

2.

SWAMPED WITH DETAIL

Try to vary the differences between your two scenes. Think about colour, size, position, missing objects and swaps. These Jar Jar Binks scenes have eight differences between them. Can you spot them all?

Find the answers on page 194 ▶

SWING ON A STAR

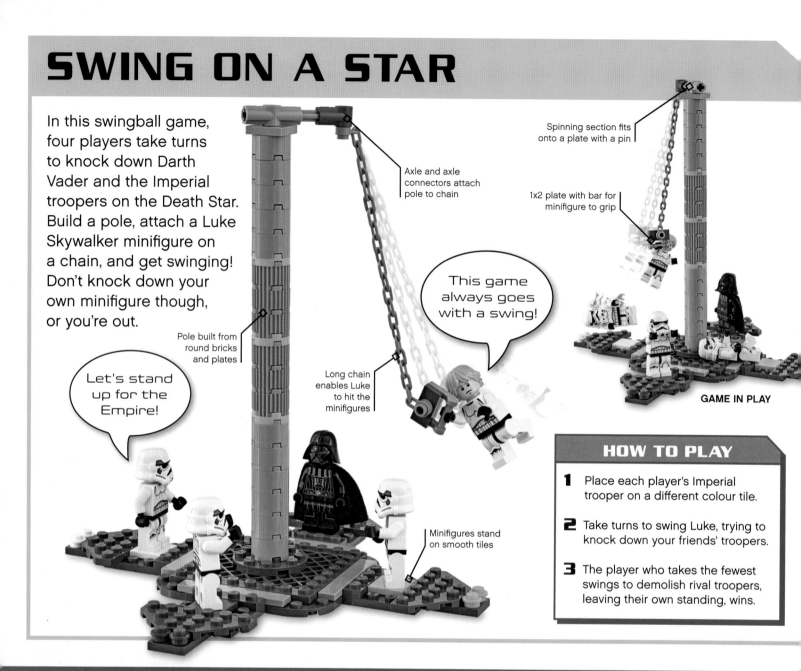

In this swingball game, four players take turns to knock down Darth Vader and the Imperial troopers on the Death Star. Build a pole, attach a Luke Skywalker minifigure on a chain, and get swinging! Don't knock down your own minifigure though, or you're out.

Spinning section fits onto a plate with a pin

Axle and axle connectors attach pole to chain

1x2 plate with bar for minifigure to grip

This game always goes with a swing!

Pole built from round bricks and plates

Let's stand up for the Empire!

Long chain enables Luke to hit the minifigures

Minifigures stand on smooth tiles

GAME IN PLAY

HOW TO PLAY

1 Place each player's Imperial trooper on a different colour tile.

2 Take turns to swing Luke, trying to knock down your friends' troopers.

3 The player who takes the fewest swings to demolish rival troopers, leaving their own standing, wins.

PICK A PLAYER

Who should have the first turn in a two-player game? This spinner will decide for you – as long you and your opponent can agree which droid to be!

LEGO Technic axle connector spins on a plate with a pin

C-3PO minifigure

Oh dear... isn't it rude to point?

4x4 ring

R2-D2

If the pointer lands on this half, C-3PO wins

Challenge your friends to build a *Star Wars* beast or being in just 10 minutes. Set a timer and get building. When the time is up, see if you can identify each other's creations.

BUILDER'S TIP

You don't have much time, so keep it simple! Focus on getting the overall shape and colours right, then add identifying details such as tusks, ears or weapons.

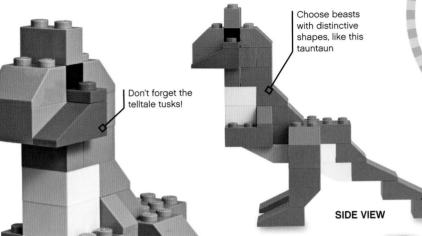

Choose beasts with distinctive shapes, like this tauntaun

Don't forget the telltale tusks!

Stacked slopes make a perfect tauntaun tail

SIDE VIEW

TAUNTAUN

2x3 slopes form big tauntaun feet

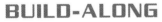
BRICKS FOR TAUNTAUN

PICK YOUR BRICKS

You could pick the bricks you need before setting your timer, or begin gathering bricks only when the countdown has started. It depends how hard you want to make the challenge!

BUILD-ALONG

If you prefer an artistic challenge to a race against the clock, why not get all players to build the same creature, such as an Ewok? At the end, award a prize for the best build.

Can I have my droids back please?

BRICKS FOR EWOK

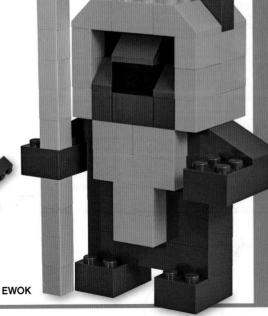
EWOK

Ears made from 1x2 slopes

TAKE THE COOKIE FROM THE WOOKIEE

Build a 3-D board game with a staircase and a simple maze. Then race your friends to the middle, where the Wookiee is waiting to award the winner with a cookie.

HOW TO PLAY

1 Each player's minifigure starts the game on the green square.

2 Take it in turns to roll a die, then move your minifigure the number of spaces shown. If the space you land on is already occupied by another player, go back to the start. If you land on a red square, go back two spaces.

3 The winner is the first to reach the Wookiee and his cookies!

Players move from jumper plate to jumper plate

Starting square

TOP VIEW

Printed cookie tile

Row of bricks stops cheaters taking shortcuts!

If you land on a red square, go back two spaces

Rooooarrrgh ur roo!

The base could be built from solid bricks or from hollow walls with plates across the top

TAKE THE THREE-BRICK JUNKYARD CHALLENGE

One space traveler's trash is another's treasure. Why not try your hand at making something old into gold? Each player chooses three bricks from a pile and upcycles them into something new. Ask a non-player to judge the winner.

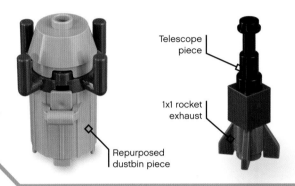

Repurposed dustbin piece

Telescope piece

1x1 rocket exhaust

This roof-tile piece is part of the Sith Nightspeeder (set 7957)

4x4 round brick with holes

SPECIAL BRICK
Round plates with four vertical bars are often used to attach leaves and branches to trees, but they can also add a touch of space tech to builds.

FLIP YOUR MINIFIGURE

I can definitely feel the Force!

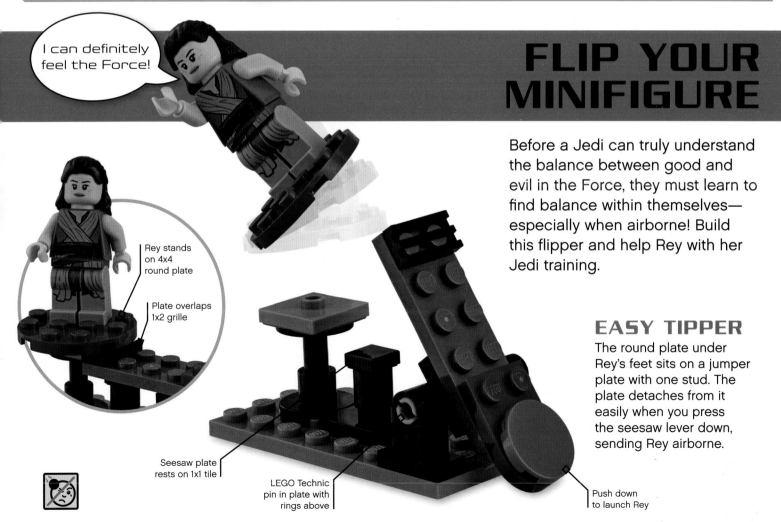

Before a Jedi can truly understand the balance between good and evil in the Force, they must learn to find balance within themselves—especially when airborne! Build this flipper and help Rey with her Jedi training.

Rey stands on 4x4 round plate

Plate overlaps 1x2 grille

EASY TIPPER
The round plate under Rey's feet sits on a jumper plate with one stud. The plate detaches from it easily when you press the seesaw lever down, sending Rey airborne.

Seesaw plate rests on 1x1 tile

LEGO Technic pin in plate with rings above

Push down to launch Rey

PLAY DEATH STAR CRAZY GOLF

Can you hit a tiny target with a small object, as Luke Skywalker did on the Death Star? The space station was covered in details known to modelmakers as greebles. Use this intricate pattern as inspiration to create a crazy golf hole. Then challenge your friends – but no cheating by using the Force!

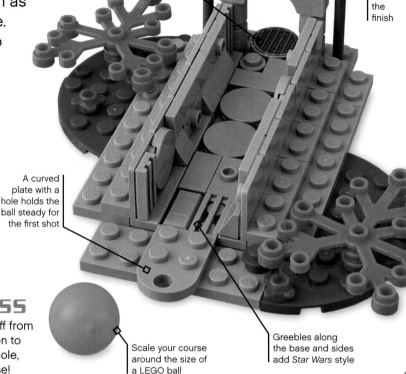

The target is a 2x2 round printed tile

Flags mark the finish

A curved plate with a hole holds the ball steady for the first shot

Scale your course around the size of a LEGO ball

Greebles along the base and sides add *Star Wars* style

HOW TO PLAY

1 Place the ball on the "tee" – the curved plate at the opposite end from the arch. Use your finger to flick the ball forward.

2 The winner is the first player to get a hole in one – by landing the ball on the the printed round tile under the arch.

ON COURSE FOR SUCCESS

Create your crazy golf build with a place to tee off from and a target to aim for – with greebles in between to make it more challenging. Now you've built one hole, you could build an entire 18-hole crazy golf course!

NAME THAT DROID!

Do you know your R4-P44 from your R2-Q5? Can you name each one of these handy helpers? Line up your astromech droid minifigures and challenge your friends to name them all. Gain extra points for naming who they work for, too!

Beep-Beep-Whirr-Beep!

1

2

3

4

5

6

7

8

9

10

Find the answers on page 194 ▶

COVER UP A CRYSTAL

A careful Jedi keeps their precious kyber crystal safe at all times. Hide your crystal under one of three brick-built cups, then challenge a friend to guess which cup it's under. If they guess right, they take the crystal! You'll have to win it back by letting them have a turn at hiding it.

Make sure that the crystal can fit inside the cup

Make all three cups identical

Crystal base attaches to jumper plate

Crystal base is a 2x2 truncated cone

RAISE THE CUPS

Slot your cups onto a made-to-measure stand – a raised border of tiles will keep them aligned. You will need to lift and lower the cups every time somebody has a guess, so attach a strong handle to their tops.

Two back-to-back handle pieces make grips for the cups

SPECIAL BRICK

LEGO crystals come in five-point and four-point variants, and many colours. If you are on the dark side, use a red Sith crystal instead of this silver Jedi one!

I challenge you to find my crystal!

ROLL LOGS LIKE AN EWOK

Ewoks are good at using basic building materials to create impressive traps. They use whatever they can find on the forest moon of Endor – which is usually trees! This brave Ewok has built a device to keep stormtroopers at bay. Why not build one yourself? It's as easy as falling off a log!

Yub nub!

Small leaf elements make the tree

2x2 and 1x1 round bricks form thicker and thinner logs

I'm coming to get you, fuzzball!

Back-to-back 1x6x5 girder panels form the central part of the wall

LOG ROLL – PIN IN PLACE

Forest floor formed by connecting 16x8 and 6x8 baseplates

The axle slots in to hold up the log pile – pulling it out releases them

SLIPPERY SLOPE

The forest hillside is created using two hinges. It's attached at the top, but at the bottom, it just rests on the base plate. You can change the angle of the slope by varying the height of the wall.

LOG ROLL – PIN RELEASED

PLAY TATOOINE CROQUET

Life in the Tatooine desert can get pretty dull. Liven things up with a game of croquet. As well as trying to reach the target, players also try to knock each other's balls out of the way. Watch out for opponents as though there's a TIE fighter on your tail!

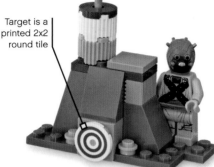

Target is a printed 2x2 round tile

CROQUET TARGET

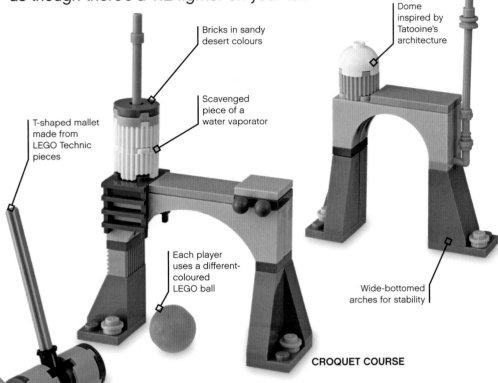

Bricks in sandy desert colours

Scavenged piece of a water vaporator

T-shaped mallet made from LEGO Technic pieces

Each player uses a different-coloured LEGO ball

Dome inspired by Tatooine's architecture

Wide-bottomed arches for stability

CROQUET COURSE

HOW TO PLAY

1 Build a series of hoops and a winning target.

2 Players take turns trying to knock their ball through hoops with a mallet. If you go through a hoop, take an extra shot. If you hit another ball, take two more shots.

3 Once you've completed the course, aim for the target. The first player to hit the target is the winner.

TIMBER!

Removing an axle from the structure causes the L-shaped shelf to fall on its pivot, bringing the whole stack of logs tumbling down on any enemy.

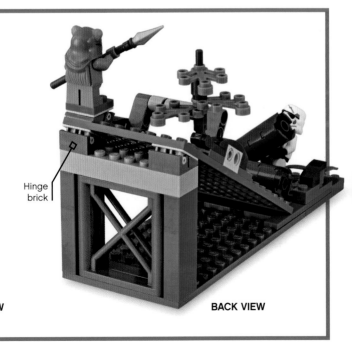

Hinge brick

ACTION VIEW

BACK VIEW

RACE TO WIN A DROID DRIVE

In a droid drive, players take turns to roll a die as they race to make their own brightly coloured droids. Start by building body parts in six colours, and a die with a different one of those colours on each of its six sides.

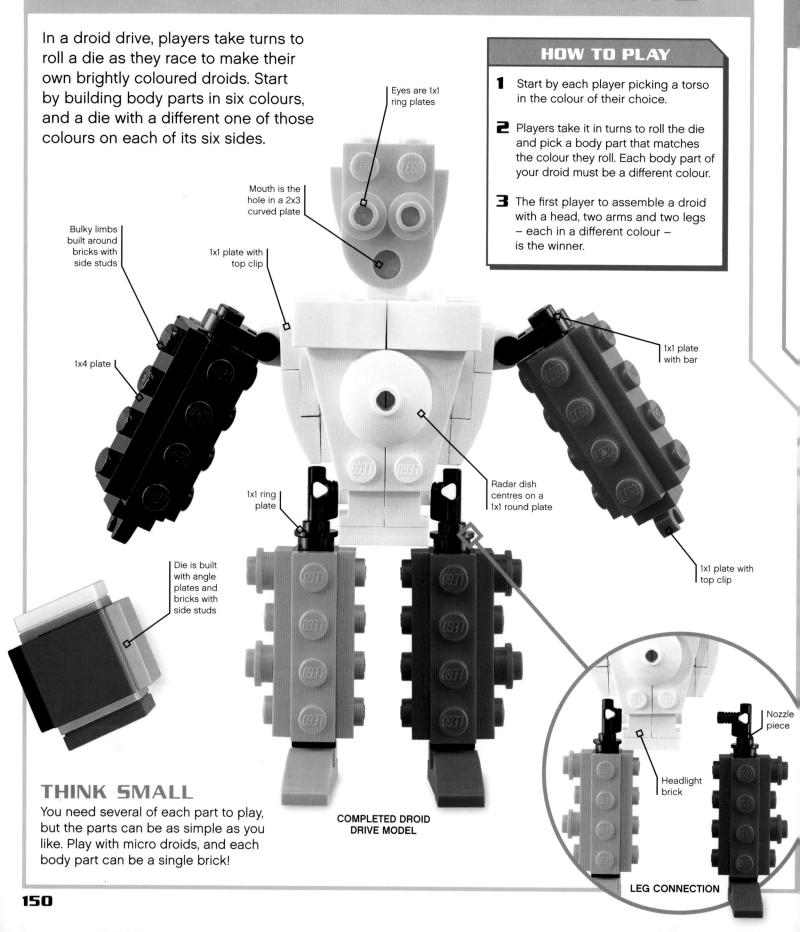

Eyes are 1x1 ring plates

Mouth is the hole in a 2x3 curved plate

Bulky limbs built around bricks with side studs

1x1 plate with top clip

1x4 plate

Die is built with angle plates and bricks with side studs

1x1 ring plate

1x1 plate with bar

Radar dish centres on a 1x1 round plate

1x1 plate with top clip

Headlight brick

Nozzle piece

COMPLETED DROID DRIVE MODEL

LEG CONNECTION

HOW TO PLAY

1 Start by each player picking a torso in the colour of their choice.

2 Players take it in turns to roll the die and pick a body part that matches the colour they roll. Each body part of your droid must be a different colour.

3 The first player to assemble a droid with a head, two arms and two legs – each in a different colour – is the winner.

THINK SMALL

You need several of each part to play, but the parts can be as simple as you like. Play with micro droids, and each body part can be a single brick!

150

DESIGN A SET OF STAR WARS DOMINOS

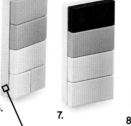

1. 2. 3. 4. 5. 6. 7. 8. 9.

Most of the dominos start with a 2x4 plate

Meesa no sure about any of these!

ICONIC CHARACTER DOMINOS

All these dominos are abstracted versions of classic *Star Wars* characters. Can you identify them all? Which other characters can you build? The trick is to make them as simple as possible, without losing each character's iconic features.

Why not use your designs to make a domino rally?

Turn to page 194 to see the answers ▶

TOPPLED DOMINOS

PLAY THE GEONOSIS PILLAR GAME

On Geonosis, Padmé, Anakin and Obi-Wan are held captive on top of tall stone pillars. But in this game, they build the towers themselves! Play it with friends, or try to beat your personal best.

Anakin is just too good at this!

That's why they call him Skywalker!

Towers are made with 2x2 round bricks and plates

HOW TO PLAY

1 Arrange your round plates and bricks, studs upward, on a flat surface, and set a timer for 30 seconds.

2 Using just one hand, pick up a minifigure and press its feet on to one of the bricks without touching the brick yourself. Start the timer!

3 Keep adding bricks under your minifigure, still using just one hand and without touching the bricks. Build the tallest tower you can before the time runs out.

ROLL LIKE A DROIDEKA

1x2 curved slopes create a rounded shape

Droidekas are deadly battle droids used by the Separatists. They curl up to roll into battle, then unfurl and shoot. Challenge your friends to create fast-rolling droidekas, then race your designs down a purpose-built slope.

A 1x2 plate with radiator adds detail

BUILDER'S TIP

The support is the brick structure under one end of the slope. The higher the support, the steeper the ramp will be, and the faster the droidekas will roll.

Textured bricks add hi-tech detail

SLIPPERY SLOPE

Get the ball rolling with a ramp for the droidekas to race down. Remember to check the size of your droids before you settle on the final dimensions of your slope.

Smooth parallel tracks keep droidekas on course

LAUNCH A COUNTER-ATTACK

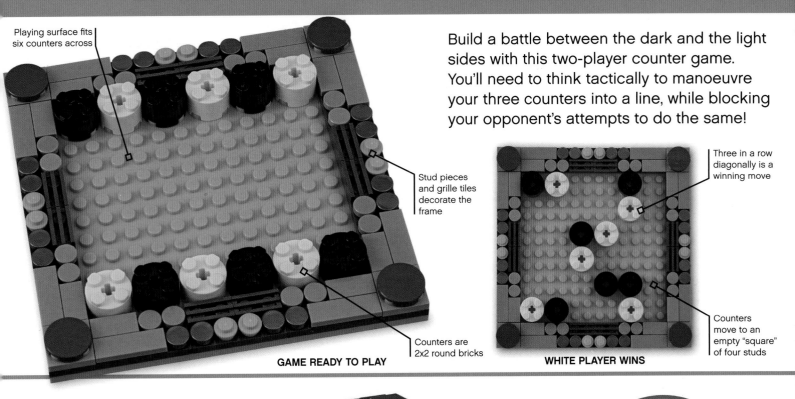

Playing surface fits six counters across

Stud pieces and grille tiles decorate the frame

Counters are 2x2 round bricks

GAME READY TO PLAY

Build a battle between the dark and the light sides with this two-player counter game. You'll need to think tactically to manoeuvre your three counters into a line, while blocking your opponent's attempts to do the same!

Three in a row diagonally is a winning move

Counters move to an empty "square" of four studs

WHITE PLAYER WINS

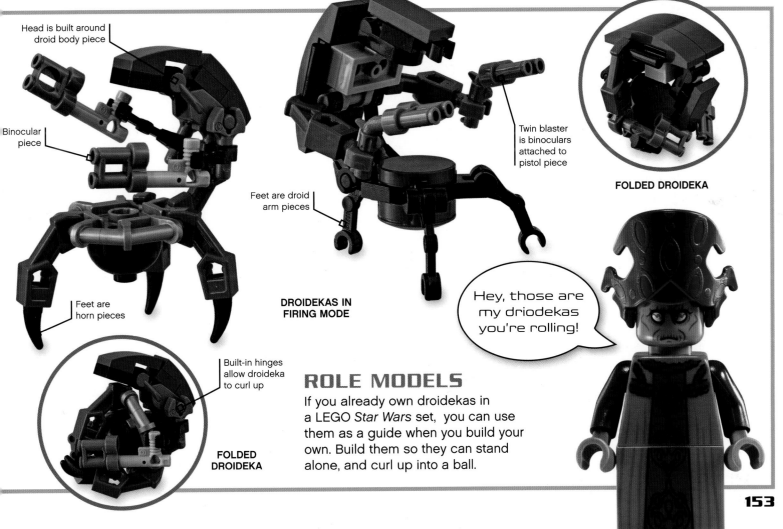

Head is built around droid body piece

Binocular piece

Feet are horn pieces

Built-in hinges allow droideka to curl up

FOLDED DROIDEKA

Feet are droid arm pieces

DROIDEKAS IN FIRING MODE

Twin blaster is binoculars attached to pistol piece

FOLDED DROIDEKA

Hey, those are my driodekas you're rolling!

ROLE MODELS

If you already own droidekas in a LEGO *Star Wars* set, you can use them as a guide when you build your own. Build them so they can stand alone, and curl up into a ball.

PLAY JAR JAR ROULETTE

Never mind Imperial officers, shadow troopers or hairy Wookiees – in this game, it's the Gungan Jar Jar Binks who brings you bad luck! Take turns with your friends spinning the wheel. If Jar Jar lands at the bottom, you're eliminated. Keep going until you have a winner.

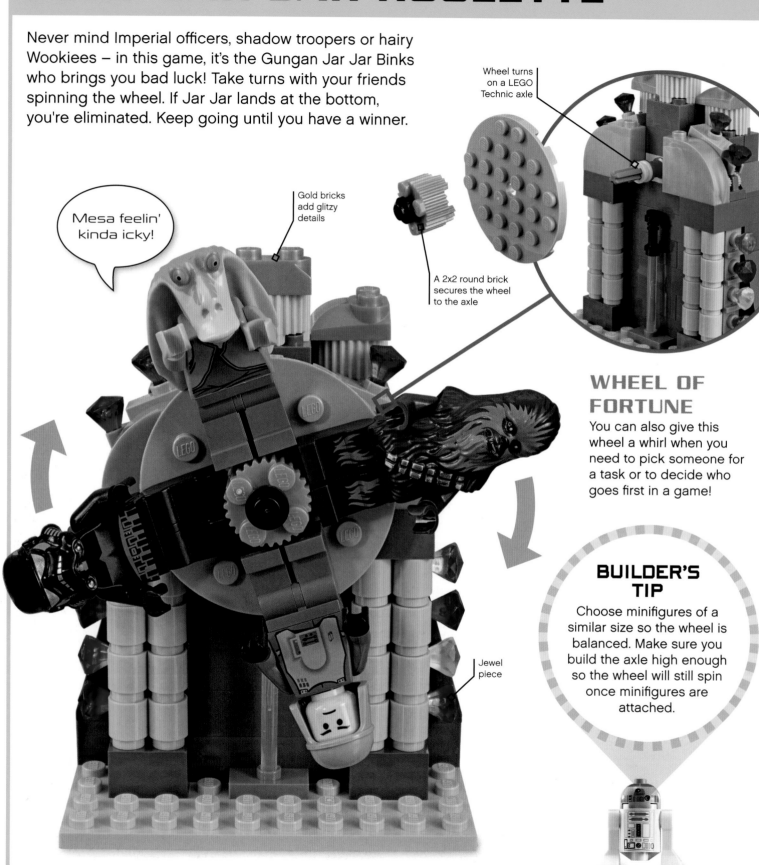

Mesa feelin' kinda icky!

Gold bricks add glitzy details

Wheel turns on a LEGO Technic axle

A 2x2 round brick secures the wheel to the axle

WHEEL OF FORTUNE

You can also give this wheel a whirl when you need to pick someone for a task or to decide who goes first in a game!

Jewel piece

BUILDER'S TIP

Choose minifigures of a similar size so the wheel is balanced. Make sure you build the axle high enough so the wheel will still spin once minifigures are attached.

CAST A LONG SHADOW

In one of the posters for *The Phantom Menace*, young Anakin's shadow takes the shape of Darth Vader. Create unusual, amusing or creepy shadows of your own using your LEGO *Star Wars* minifigures!

Morph two minifigures' shadows together to create a sinister silhouette

Unusual outfits or headgear will cast interesting shapes

JAR JAR BINKS AND WATTO

Tilt and twist the minifigure to create shapes. Can you make the shadow look Vader-like?

YOUNG ANAKIN SKYWALKER

QUEEN AMIDALA

MAKE A MIRROR IMAGE

In this matching game, design one half of a shape – such as Shaak Ti's face – in 2-D, then challenge a friend, or yourself, to build the other half.

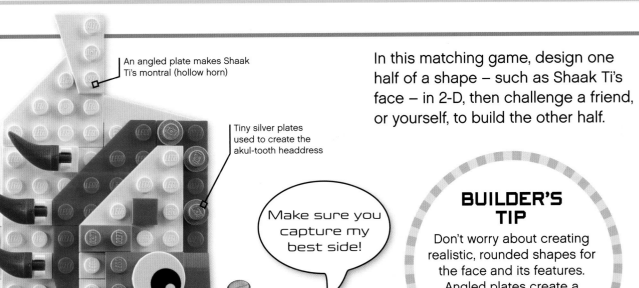

An angled plate makes Shaak Ti's montral (hollow horn)

Tiny silver plates used to create the akul-tooth headdress

Tooth pieces make the stripes on Shaak Ti's lekku (head-tails)

SHAAK TI

Make sure you capture my best side!

BUILDER'S TIP

Don't worry about creating realistic, rounded shapes for the face and its features. Angled plates create a stylized effect while still making the face recognizable.

NAVIGATE THE KAMINO MAZE

Tracking a mysterious villain is never easy, as Obi-Wan finds out. On the trail of the tricky bounty hunter Jango Fett, Obi-Wan discovers the hidden ocean world of Kamino. Why not create a puzzling maze for your friends, complete with twists, turns and frustrating dead ends?

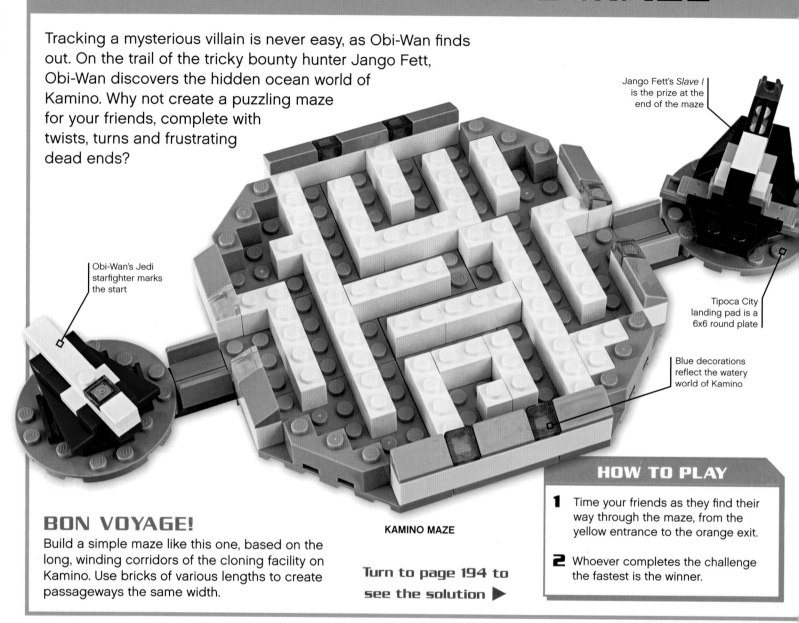

Jango Fett's *Slave I* is the prize at the end of the maze

Tipoca City landing pad is a 6x6 round plate

Obi-Wan's Jedi starfighter marks the start

Blue decorations reflect the watery world of Kamino

KAMINO MAZE

BON VOYAGE!

Build a simple maze like this one, based on the long, winding corridors of the cloning facility on Kamino. Use bricks of various lengths to create passageways the same width.

Turn to page 194 to see the solution ▶

HOW TO PLAY

1 Time your friends as they find their way through the maze, from the yellow entrance to the orange exit.

2 Whoever completes the challenge the fastest is the winner.

COLLECT 3-D TRADING CARDS

Make your minifigures stand out from the crowd with these 3-D frames that show them off and act as collectible, swappable cards. Rate each character's vital statistics so you can compete with friends. Who is braver, Rey or Finn? Whose dark side is strongest, Darth Vader or Kylo Ren? You decide!

Use a 6x8 base plate

IMPERIAL SHOCK TROOPER

There aren't many ducks on Tatooine so why not play hook-a-bantha instead? Banthas are a good choice for this game because of their large, hookable horns. Build micro-scale versions of these cute hairy beasts then try to catch them with a LEGO lasso on a stick. You'll fall for this game hook, line and sinker!

HOW TO PLAY

1 Each player has one minute to hook as many banthas as they can. Lift them out of the herd and into an agreed area. If you drop a bantha, your turn is over.

2 Whoever collects the most banthas wins. Add an element of chance with a coloured plate on the underside of one beast – that one scores double!

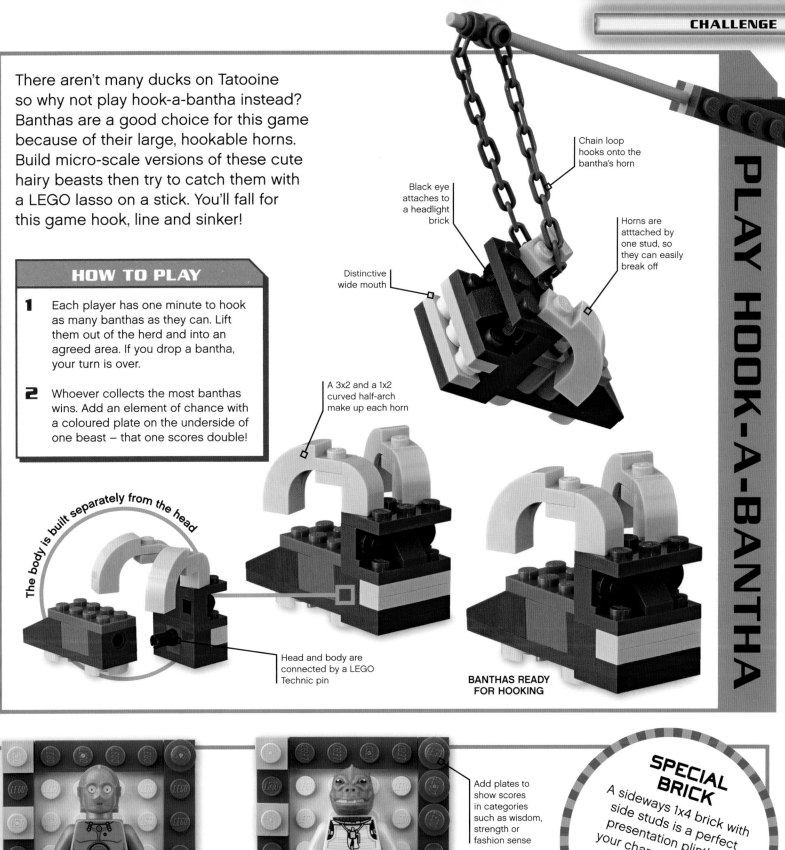

Chain loop hooks onto the bantha's horn

Black eye attaches to a headlight brick

Horns are atttached by one stud, so they can easily break off

Distinctive wide mouth

A 3x2 and a 1x2 curved half-arch make up each horn

The body is built separately from the head

Head and body are connected by a LEGO Technic pin

BANTHAS READY FOR HOOKING

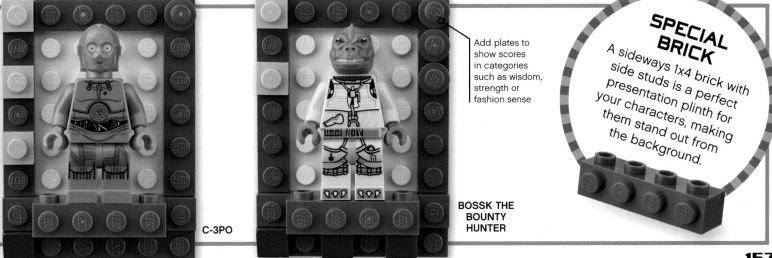

Add plates to show scores in categories such as wisdom, strength or fashion sense

C-3PO

BOSSK THE BOUNTY HUNTER

SPECIAL BRICK

A sideways 1x4 brick with side studs is a perfect presentation plinth for your characters, making them stand out from the background.

TRAIN AS A STORMTROOPER

Could you cut it as a stormtooper? Report for basic training with this two-player game to find out. A board and four stormtroopers is all you need to step into the fray and see if you can take out the enemy while protecting your brother-in-arms.

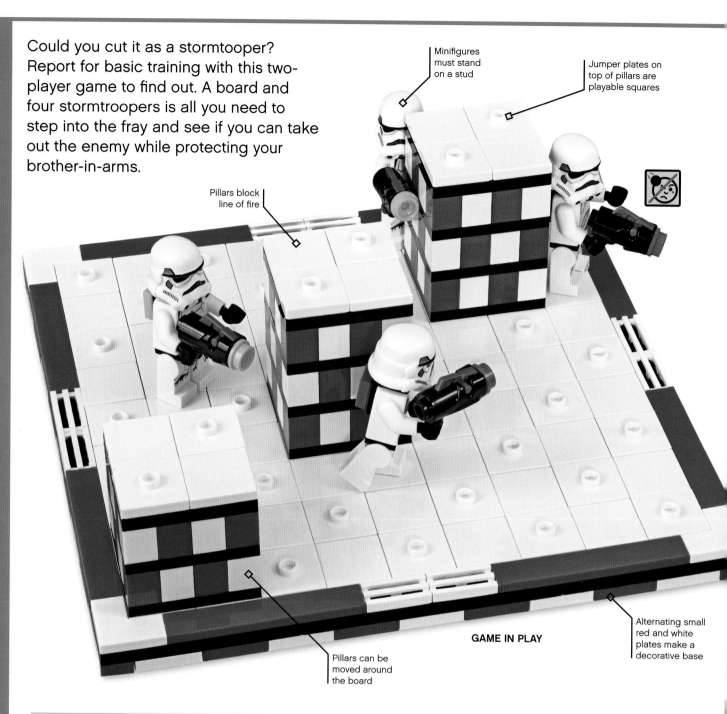

Minifigures must stand on a stud

Jumper plates on top of pillars are playable squares

Pillars block line of fire

Pillars can be moved around the board

GAME IN PLAY

Alternating small red and white plates make a decorative base

HOW TO PLAY

1 One player is "blue team," the other is "yellow team." Each should have two minifigures.

2 At the start of play, place the three pillars in a diagonal line across the board. Place the two teams on either side of the pillars, so that they can't see each other.

3 Players take it in turns to move either one stormtrooper or one pillar one space. You can only move to jumper plates neighbouring your current position.

4 As soon as a player moves a minifigure into a position on the board where the figure has a clear line of sight to an enemy minifigure, they can fire their stud shooter at them. If they hit the stormtrooper, then that figure is taken off the board. A player can move and fire on the same turn.

5 Play continues until there is only one stormtrooper left on the board. The player with the last minifigure standing is the winner!

PLAY *STAR WARS* CHARADES

If you like acting, this charades challenge is for you. First, line up a mix of *Star Wars* characters. Each player picks one in secret, then acts out the character for the others to guess who it is. No talking – you must do it all with mime!

DARTH VADER

JAR JAR BINKS

WICKET W. WARRICK

SALACIOUS B. CRUMB

JABBA THE HUTT

SEND IN THE CLONES

How fast can you generate clones? Take all your clone minifigures apart and time yourself as you reassemble them. Then try to beat your record!

Clone trooper lieutenant

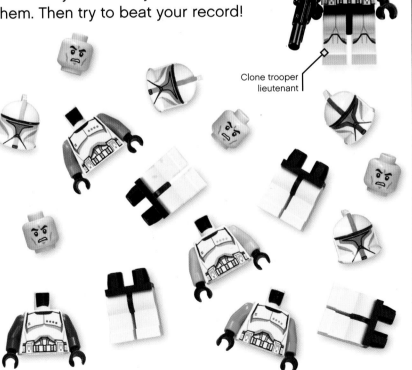

EMPEROR PALPATINE

CHEWBACCA

BB-8

KEEP IT ZIPPED
Growling, squeaking and speaking lines from the movies are not allowed, so rely on gestures and facial expressions to convey your character. Use your hands to indicate clothing or unusual body parts, too.

159

SCAVENGE WITH REY

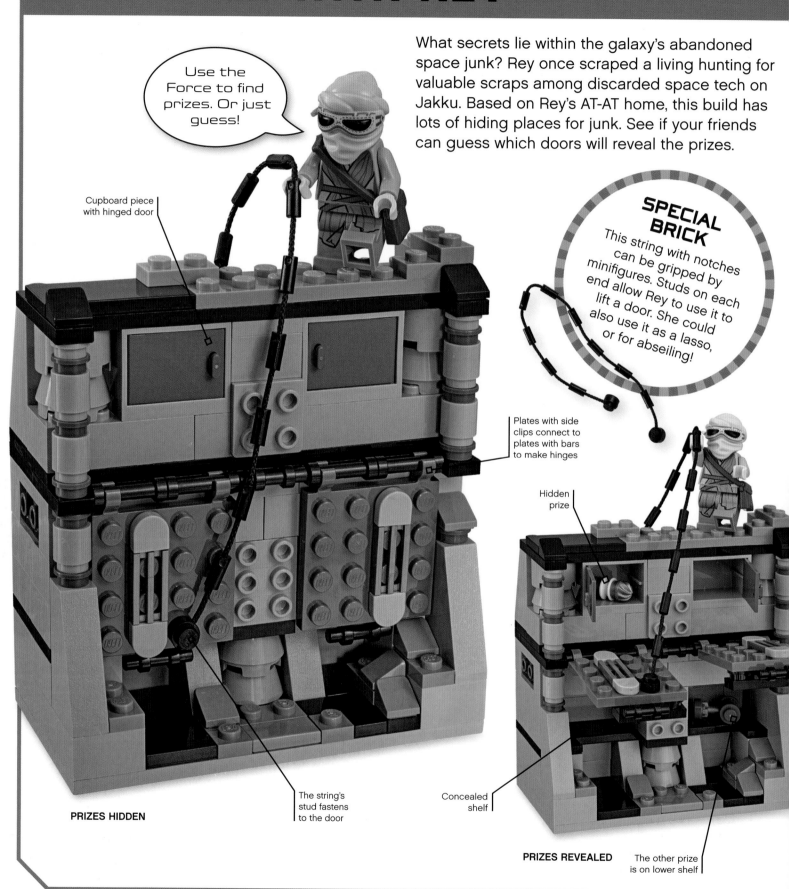

Use the Force to find prizes. Or just guess!

What secrets lie within the galaxy's abandoned space junk? Rey once scraped a living hunting for valuable scraps among discarded space tech on Jakku. Based on Rey's AT-AT home, this build has lots of hiding places for junk. See if your friends can guess which doors will reveal the prizes.

Cupboard piece with hinged door

SPECIAL BRICK
This string with notches can be gripped by minifigures. Studs on each end allow Rey to use it to lift a door. She could also use it as a lasso, or for abseiling!

Plates with side clips connect to plates with bars to make hinges

Hidden prize

The string's stud fastens to the door

PRIZES HIDDEN

Concealed shelf

PRIZES REVEALED

The other prize is on lower shelf

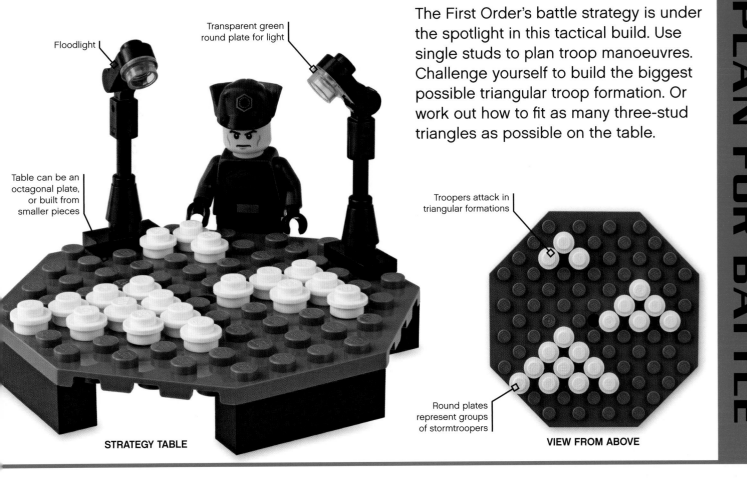

Floodlight

Transparent green round plate for light

Table can be an octagonal plate, or built from smaller pieces

STRATEGY TABLE

The First Order's battle strategy is under the spotlight in this tactical build. Use single studs to plan troop manoeuvres. Challenge yourself to build the biggest possible triangular troop formation. Or work out how to fit as many three-stud triangles as possible on the table.

Troopers attack in triangular formations

Round plates represent groups of stormtroopers

VIEW FROM ABOVE

MAKE A JEDI TABLET

Test your friends' powers of deduction with a tablet based on Mace Windu's Jedi testing screen. A player chooses a piece in one of nine squares, and their friends ask a maximum of 10 "yes" or "no" questions to figure out the shape and colour of the piece in that square.

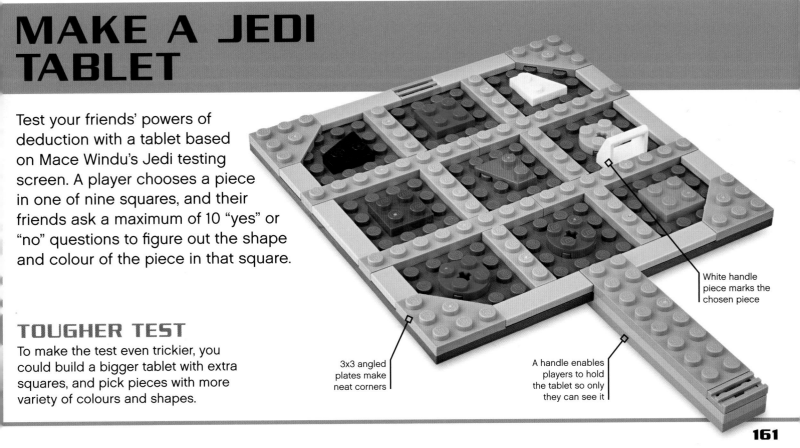

TOUGHER TEST

To make the test even trickier, you could build a bigger tablet with extra squares, and pick pieces with more variety of colours and shapes.

3x3 angled plates make neat corners

A handle enables players to hold the tablet so only they can see it

White handle piece marks the chosen piece

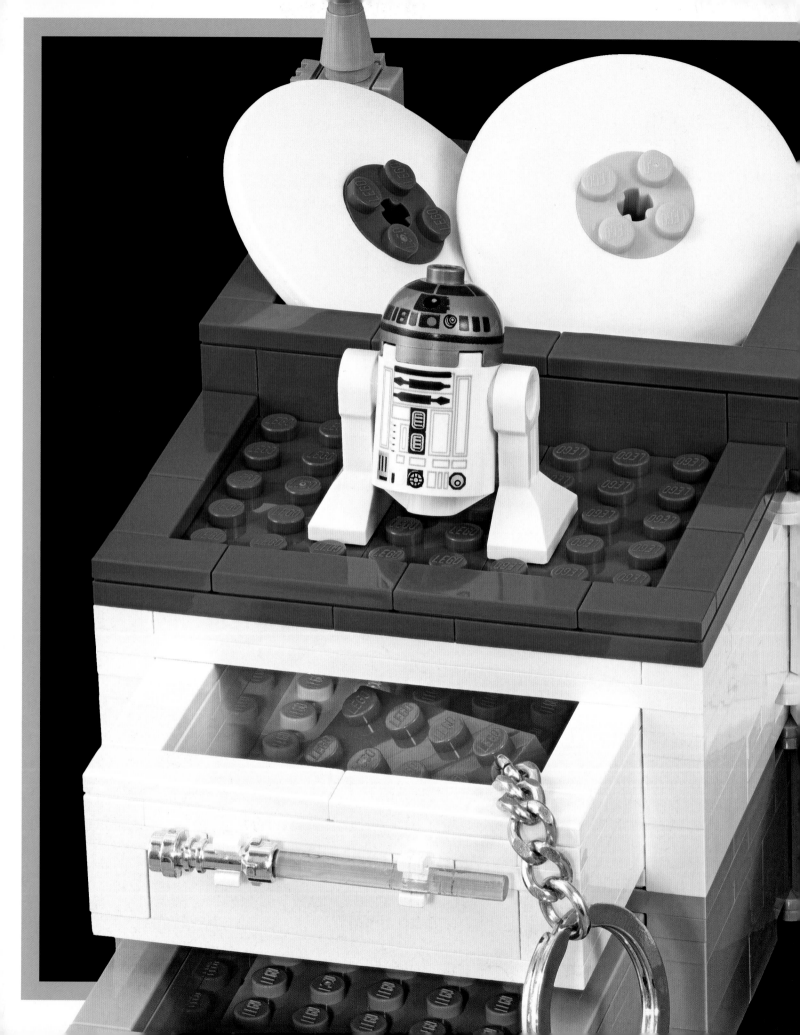

LAUGH ALL THE WAY TO THE PIGGY BANK

You need someone fierce and good at guarding to look after your cash so why not build your own LEGO® Gamorrean piggy bank? You can bet your bottom dollar that this porcine Gamorrean Guard will keep your money safe.

ON THE MONEY

Gamorreans are Jabba the Hutt's preferred guards because of their brute strength and ferocious nature. Not to mention those fearsome horns and tusks!

Jutting eyebrows for a fierc expressic

The money slot is lined with smooth tiles built sideways from bricks with side studs

The lid lifts off easily because it's only connected by four studs

Each of the four legs are made of three 2x2 round plates

Piglike nostrils on upturned nose

Fearsome tusks are horn pieces held in place by clips

GAMORREAN PIGGY BANK

GAMORREAN PIGGY BANK – OPEN

SPECIAL BRICK

First seen in the LEGO® Castle theme, the cow horn is one of several horn-shaped pieces that can add character to your builds as fangs, claws and more.

GIVE YOUR PENS A HEAD START

Isn't it infuriating when your LEGO pens keep disappearing? Try building these colourful containers to keep them safe. Unauthorized borrowers will have to brave Darth Maul and Jango Fett before they can make off with your prized possessions!

Maul's Zabrak horns are cones topped with small horn pieces

Pots can be as tall or short as you like

Glowing eyes are transparent orange round plates

DARTH MAUL PENCIL POT

A double row of round plates form a set of ferocious fangs

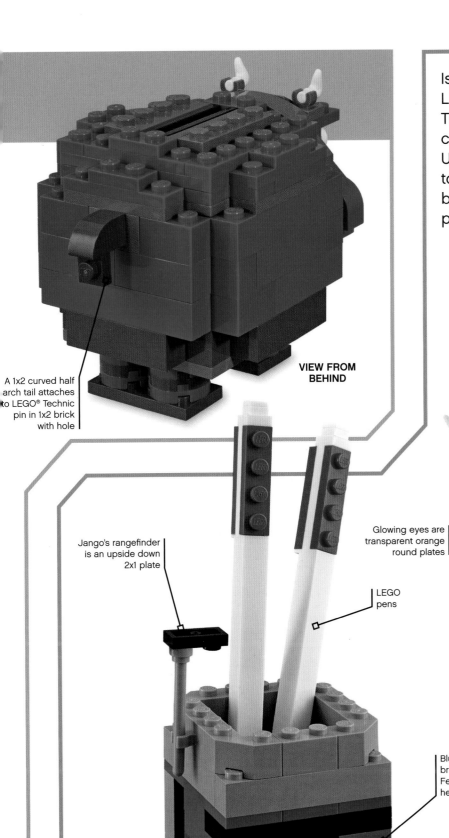

A 1x2 curved half arch tail attaches to LEGO® Technic pin in 1x2 brick with hole

VIEW FROM BEHIND

Jango's rangefinder is an upside down 2x1 plate

LEGO pens

Blue and black bricks recreate Fett's iconic helmet visor

JANGO FETT PENCIL POT

USE YOUR HEAD

These pen pots are based on bounty hunter Jango Fett's helmet, with its "T"-shaped visor, and the tattooed face of sinister Sith apprentice Darth Maul.

MAKE A DEATH STAR DISPLAY UNIT

That's no moon! It's a display cabinet – in the shape of an enormous, planet-destroying battle station. What better place to store your favourite LEGO® *Star Wars*™ minifigures than inside your own version of the iconic Death Star?

Large superlaser

Little droids like BB-8 can fit in these smaller spaces

Transparent yellow bars are fitted into cones, attached to plates with side clips

TIE fighters attached with transparent antenna pieces appear to patrol the exterior

Display shelves are made from a double layer of plates built into the main structure

A 6x16 base plate acts as a sturdy stand for the cabinet

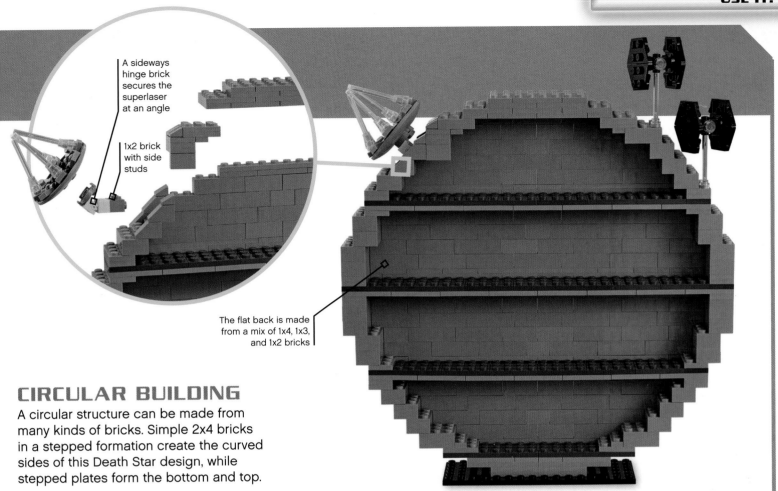

A sideways hinge brick secures the superlaser at an angle

1x2 brick with side studs

The flat back is made from a mix of 1x4, 1x3, and 1x2 bricks

CIRCULAR BUILDING

A circular structure can be made from many kinds of bricks. Simple 2x4 bricks in a stepped formation create the curved sides of this Death Star design, while stepped plates form the bottom and top.

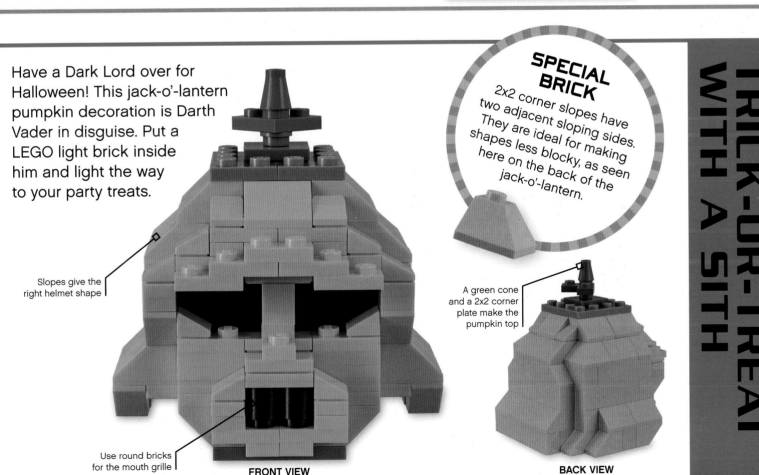

Have a Dark Lord over for Halloween! This jack-o'-lantern pumpkin decoration is Darth Vader in disguise. Put a LEGO light brick inside him and light the way to your party treats.

SPECIAL BRICK
2x2 corner slopes have two adjacent sloping sides. They are ideal for making shapes less blocky, as seen here on the back of the jack-o'-lantern.

Slopes give the right helmet shape

Use round bricks for the mouth grille

FRONT VIEW

A green cone and a 2x2 corner plate make the pumpkin top

BACK VIEW

TRICK-OR-TREAT WITH A SITH

DESIGN THE DESK STAR

While the real Death Star can blow away whole planets, this Desk Star paperweight just stops important papers from blowing away! Make it solid to give it weight, but leave room to attach the superlaser, using a clip and bar to make a hinge.

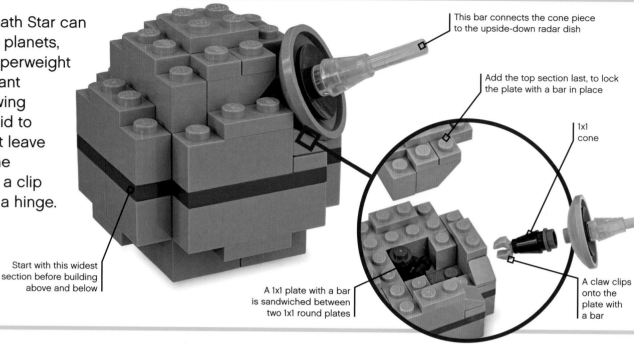

This bar connects the cone piece to the upside-down radar dish

Add the top section last, to lock the plate with a bar in place

1x1 cone

Start with this widest section before building above and below

A 1x1 plate with a bar is sandwiched between two 1x1 round plates

A claw clips onto the plate with a bar

BUILD A MOVIE BACKDROP

A striking LEGO starfield is great for displaying your smaller sets or builds. It also makes a briiliant backdrop for the next LEGO blockbuster you film using a smartphone or other movie-making equipment.

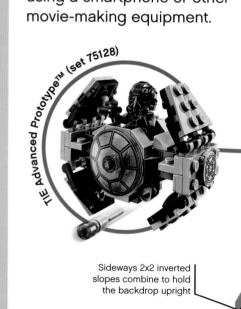

TIE Advanced Prototype™ (set 75128)

Sideways 2x2 inverted slopes combine to hold the backdrop upright

The base lines up with the back section but is not connected to it

BRIGHTEN UP A BOOKSHELF

This cool recreation of the Death Star's trash compactor is just the right size to decorate your bookshelf, desk, or bedside table. What a fun way to add a *Star Wars* scene to your room!

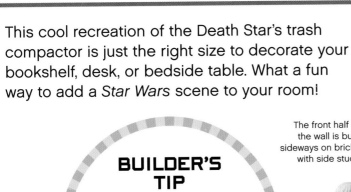

The front half of the wall is built sideways on bricks with side studs

BUILDER'S TIP

The broad base and wall of this build would make a sturdy backdrop for any LEGO *Star Wars* scene. Pick your favourite movie moment to build and display proudly!

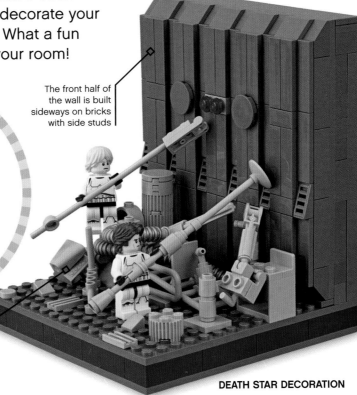

Use the most unusual pieces you can find to make space junk

DEATH STAR DECORATION

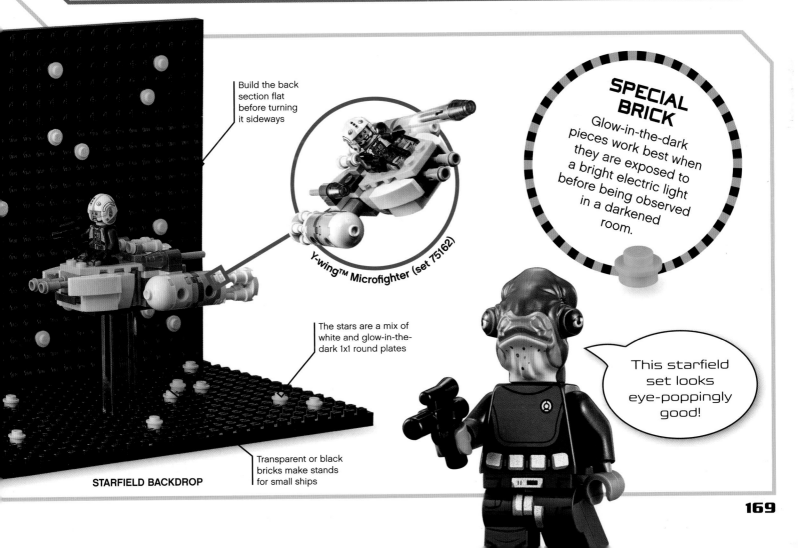

Build the back section flat before turning it sideways

Y-wing™ Microfighter (set 75162)

SPECIAL BRICK

Glow-in-the-dark pieces work best when they are exposed to a bright electric light before being observed in a darkened room.

The stars are a mix of white and glow-in-the-dark 1x1 round plates

This starfield set looks eye-poppingly good!

STARFIELD BACKDROP

Transparent or black bricks make stands for small ships

If your desk space looks like its been blasted by TIE fighters, restore a little order with an out-of-this-world organizer. This one has three drawers, two hidden compartments and an R2-D2 colour scheme. What will your design look like?

BUILDER'S TIP

Start by thinking about what you want to fit inside your organizer. Keep those items nearby so that you can build the compartments to fit them.

Small, round pieces connect to make antennas

Smooth tiles give a finished look

R2-D2 figure keeps watch over your valuables

Antenna base bui around a 1x1 brick with four side stud

Hidden compartments are in this section

Lightsaber drawer handles

R2-D2 DESK TIDY

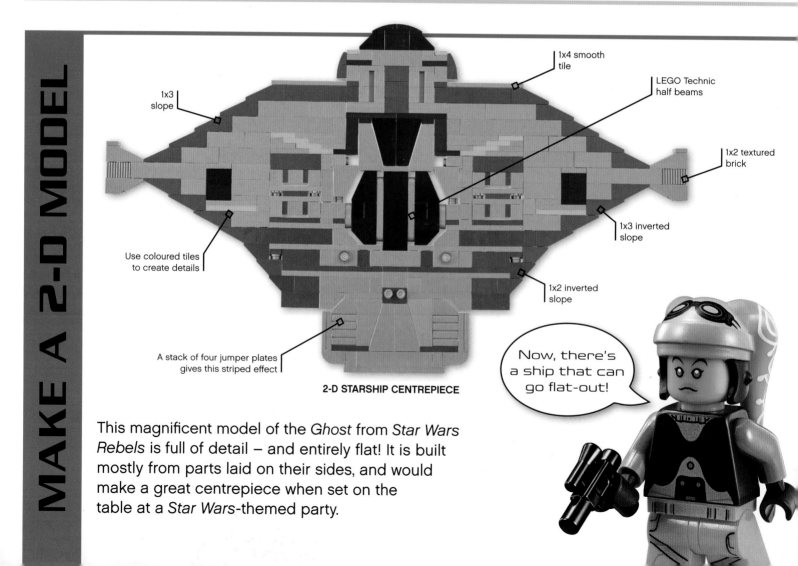

MAKE A 2-D MODEL

1x3 slope

1x4 smooth tile

LEGO Technic half beams

1x2 textured brick

1x3 inverted slope

1x2 inverted slope

Use coloured tiles to create details

A stack of four jumper plates gives this striped effect

2-D STARSHIP CENTREPIECE

Now, there's a ship that can go flat-out!

This magnificent model of the *Ghost* from *Star Wars Rebels* is full of detail – and entirely flat! It is built mostly from parts laid on their sides, and would make a great centrepiece when set on the table at a *Star Wars*-themed party.

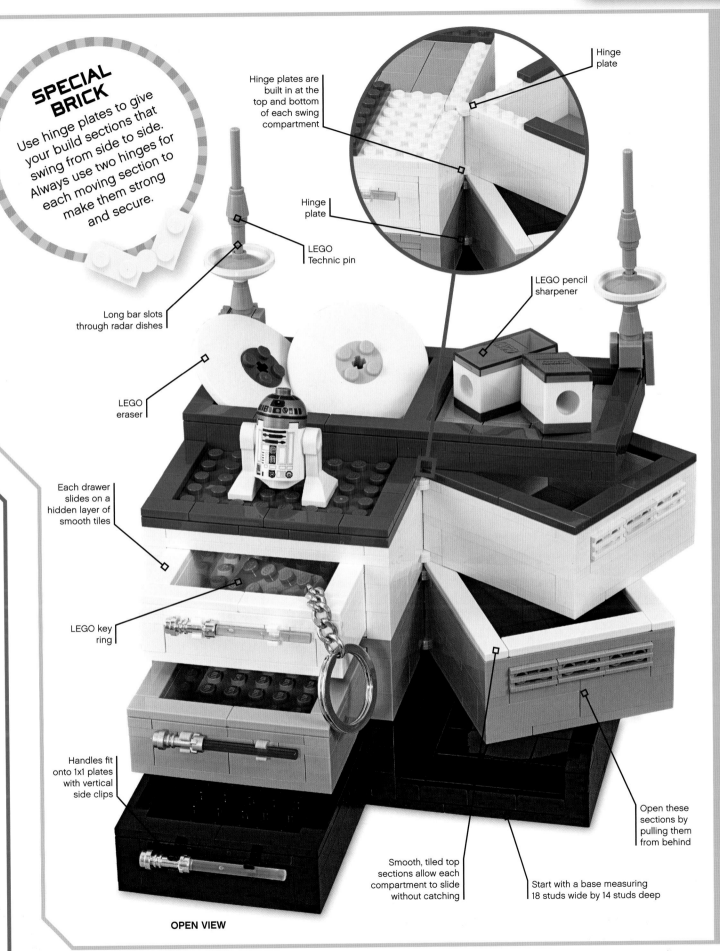

ORGANIZE YOUR GALAXY

SPECIAL BRICK
Use hinge plates to give your build sections that swing from side to side. Always use two hinges for each moving section to make them strong and secure.

Hinge plates are built in at the top and bottom of each swing compartment

Hinge plate

Hinge plate

LEGO Technic pin

LEGO pencil sharpener

Long bar slots through radar dishes

LEGO eraser

Each drawer slides on a hidden layer of smooth tiles

LEGO key ring

Handles fit onto 1x1 plates with vertical side clips

Open these sections by pulling them from behind

Smooth, tiled top sections allow each compartment to slide without catching

Start with a base measuring 18 studs wide by 14 studs deep

OPEN VIEW

171

MAKE A HOTH KEYRING HOLDER

Create your own Echo Base for keys with this Hoth-style keyring holder. With a colour scheme inspired by the icy planet and its inhabitants, plus a miniature marauding AT-AT and a laser-blasting cannon on top, it's a fun place to keep your keys.

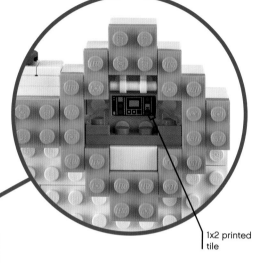

AT-AT's legs are 1x2 plates with end bars

Laser cannon blast is a transparent red lightsaber blade

1x2 printed tile

KEY DESIGN
Orange plates of different sizes form the key shape that signals what this base is used for. Build a control centre within the key's circle to make the base look extra secure.

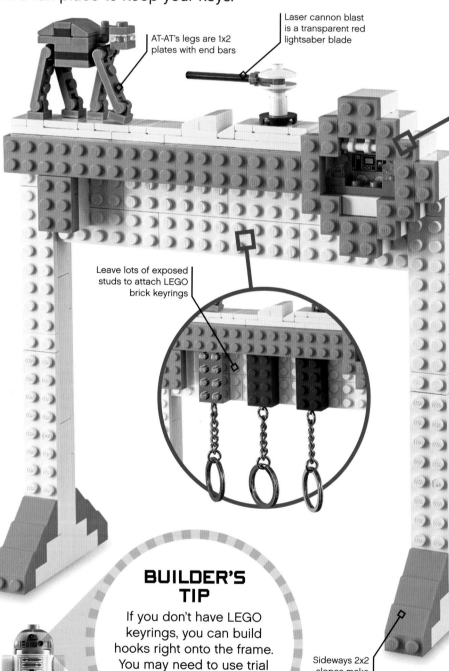

Leave lots of exposed studs to attach LEGO brick keyrings

◀ Turn to page 95 to build fantasy flowers

So now I'm taking orders from... a VASE?

BUILDER'S TIP
If you don't have LEGO keyrings, you can build hooks right onto the frame. You may need to use trial and error to create hooks strong enough to hold your keys.

Sideways 2x2 slopes make stable feet

USE VADER AS A VASE

Many things have gone into Vader's helmet: technology, dark side alchemy, hi-tech materials, medical skill and, of course, Anakin Skywalker's head. But never flowers – until now, that is! What a cool way to display your fantasy blooms.

BUILDER'S TIP

It's a good idea to study Vader's helmet from all sides before you start. Make note of its shape and features, and then make a plan for recreating it with the bricks you have.

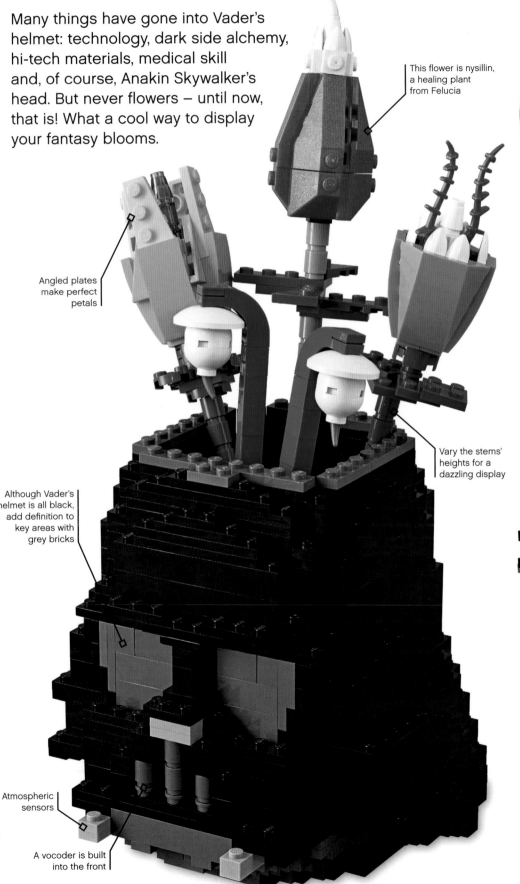

This flower is nysillin, a healing plant from Felucia

Angled plates make perfect petals

Although Vader's helmet is all black, add definition to key areas with grey bricks

Vary the stems' heights for a dazzling display

Atmospheric sensors

A vocoder is built into the front

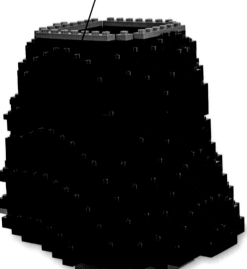

Gradual steps of bricks and plates create a curved effect

SIDE AND REAR VIEW

FLOWER POWER

Nip Vader's plans for galactic domination in the bud with this blooming marvelous vase. Let the life-saving helmet support flowers instead of a Sith Lord. And if galactic gardening isn't your thing, you could use the Vader vase to store pens and pencils.

The Force is strong with the Skywalker family, so why not build them a strong family tree? Put your Kylo Ren minifigure at the bottom, then add branches above for previous generations. Padmé Amidala and Anakin Skywalker should go at the top – they started the whole clan!

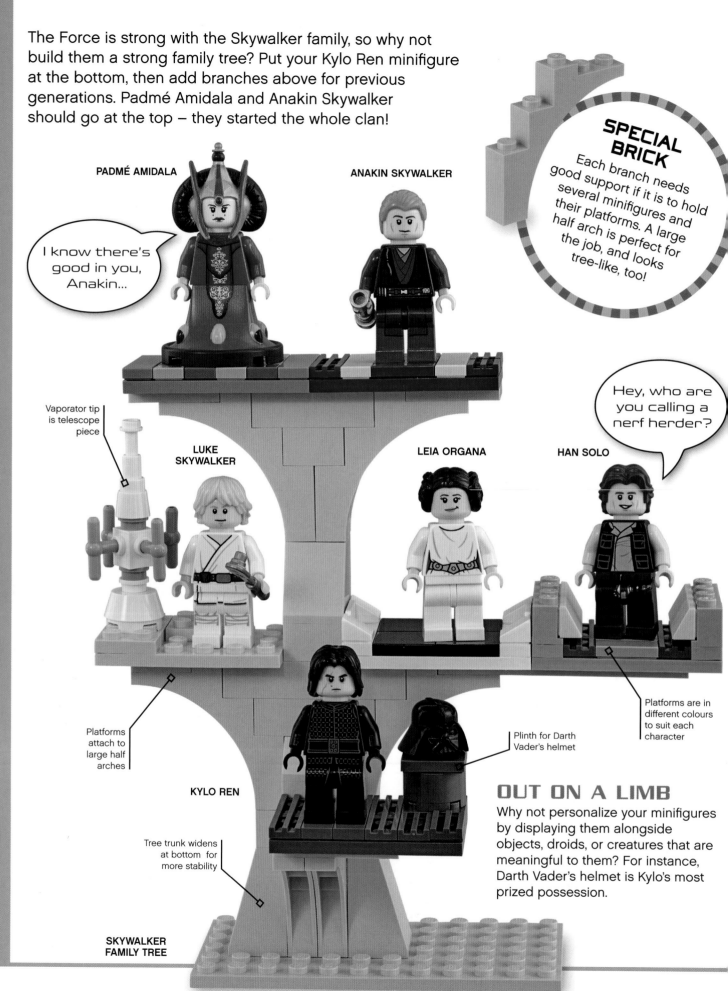

PADMÉ AMIDALA

I know there's good in you, Anakin...

ANAKIN SKYWALKER

SPECIAL BRICK
Each branch needs good support if it is to hold several minifigures and their platforms. A large half arch is perfect for the job, and looks tree-like, too!

Vaporator tip is telescope piece

LUKE SKYWALKER

LEIA ORGANA

HAN SOLO

Hey, who are you calling a nerf herder?

Platforms are in different colours to suit each character

Platforms attach to large half arches

KYLO REN

Plinth for Darth Vader's helmet

Tree trunk widens at bottom for more stability

OUT ON A LIMB
Why not personalize your minifigures by displaying them alongside objects, droids, or creatures that are meaningful to them? For instance, Darth Vader's helmet is Kylo's most prized possession.

SKYWALKER FAMILY TREE

On Jakku, Rey learns that it's wise to store even the smallest scavenged items. You never know when they will come in handy. Why not build this sturdy box to keep all your own little treasures safe? And, for added Rey-appeal, make the box in colours that match her speeder.

STORE YOUR STUFF

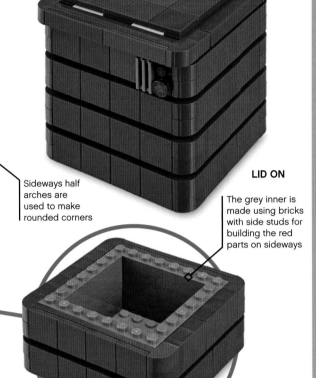

Lid lifts on and off

LID ON

The grey inner is made using bricks with side studs for building the red parts on sideways

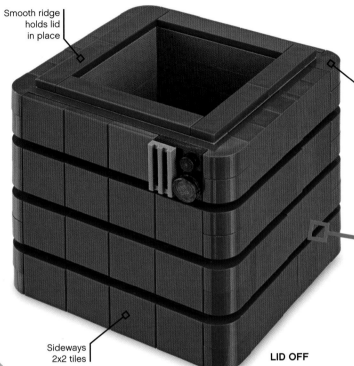

Smooth ridge holds lid in place

Sideways half arches are used to make rounded corners

Sideways 2x2 tiles

LID OFF

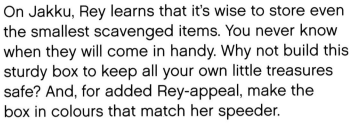

2x2 jumper plate

1x2 plate

2x8 plate supports two platforms

2x2x2 slope brick

Darth Vader's helmet sits on a minifigure head piece

Large, rectangular plate makes a stable base for the tree

BREAKDOWN OF TREE

BUILDER'S TIP

Your tree must be firmly rooted, or it might tip over. Use slope bricks to widen the trunk at the bottom. The taller or wider the tree, the bigger the base should be.

BRANCHING OUT

To build your tree, start with a sturdy base and then add layers, branches and platforms. Your tree can be as tall or wide as you like. Why not invent a family tree for another character?

MAKE A *STAR WARS* MOVIE SET

It's great fun making LEGO *Star Wars* films on a smartphone or tablet – and your mini movies can be even better with a realistic backdrop! This build has tall walls that fold inward to fill your camera's frame. The sections can be swapped easily, so you can make the set look like more than one location!

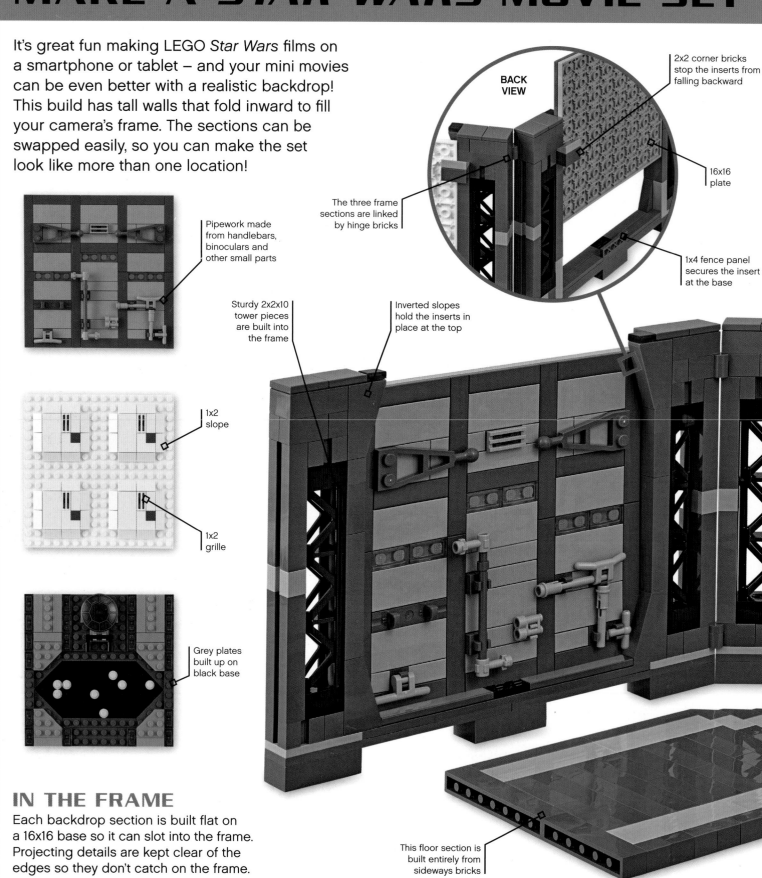

BACK VIEW

2x2 corner bricks stop the inserts from falling backward

16x16 plate

The three frame sections are linked by hinge bricks

1x4 fence panel secures the insert at the base

Pipework made from handlebars, binoculars and other small parts

Sturdy 2x2x10 tower pieces are built into the frame

Inverted slopes hold the inserts in place at the top

1x2 slope

1x2 grille

Grey plates built up on black base

IN THE FRAME

Each backdrop section is built flat on a 16x16 base so it can slot into the frame. Projecting details are kept clear of the edges so they don't catch on the frame.

This floor section is built entirely from sideways bricks

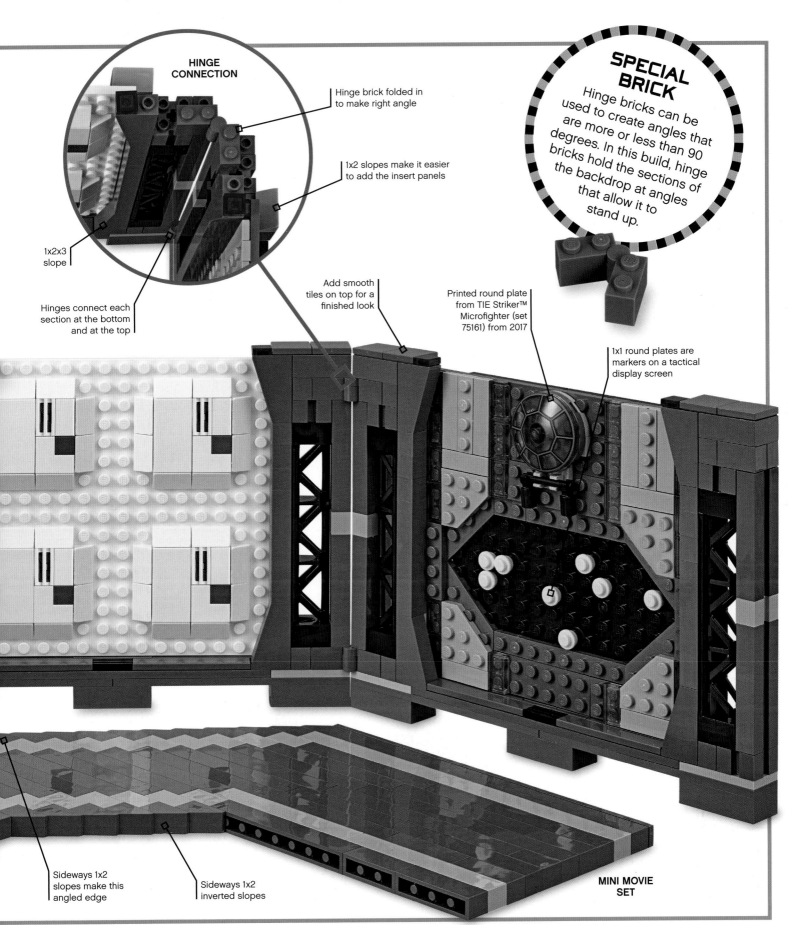

HINGE CONNECTION

Hinge brick folded in to make right angle

1x2 slopes make it easier to add the insert panels

1x2x3 slope

Hinges connect each section at the bottom and at the top

SPECIAL BRICK

Hinge bricks can be used to create angles that are more or less than 90 degrees. In this build, hinge bricks hold the sections of the backdrop at angles that allow it to stand up.

Add smooth tiles on top for a finished look

Printed round plate from TIE Striker™ Microfighter (set 75161) from 2017

1x1 round plates are markers on a tactical display screen

Sideways 1x2 slopes make this angled edge

Sideways 1x2 inverted slopes

MINI MOVIE SET

KEEP YOUR SABER SAFE

Give the gift of good lightsaber storage with this perfectly proportioned presentation box. Or you could keep it yourself and spell out your name in Aurebesh on the lid – you'll find the Aurebesh alphabet on page 55.

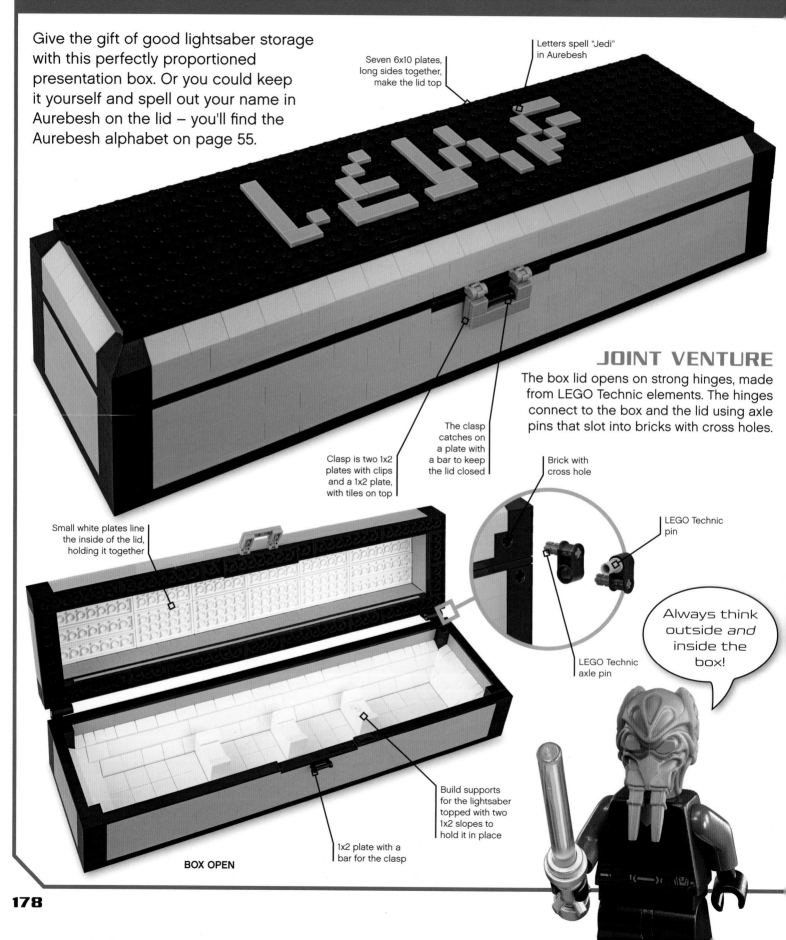

Seven 6x10 plates, long sides together, make the lid top

Letters spell "Jedi" in Aurebesh

JOINT VENTURE
The box lid opens on strong hinges, made from LEGO Technic elements. The hinges connect to the box and the lid using axle pins that slot into bricks with cross holes.

The clasp catches on a plate with a bar to keep the lid closed

Clasp is two 1x2 plates with clips and a 1x2 plate, with tiles on top

Brick with cross hole

LEGO Technic pin

Small white plates line the inside of the lid, holding it together

LEGO Technic axle pin

Always think outside *and* inside the box!

1x2 plate with a bar for the clasp

Build supports for the lightsaber topped with two 1x2 slopes to hold it in place

BOX OPEN

GREEBLE A LETTER

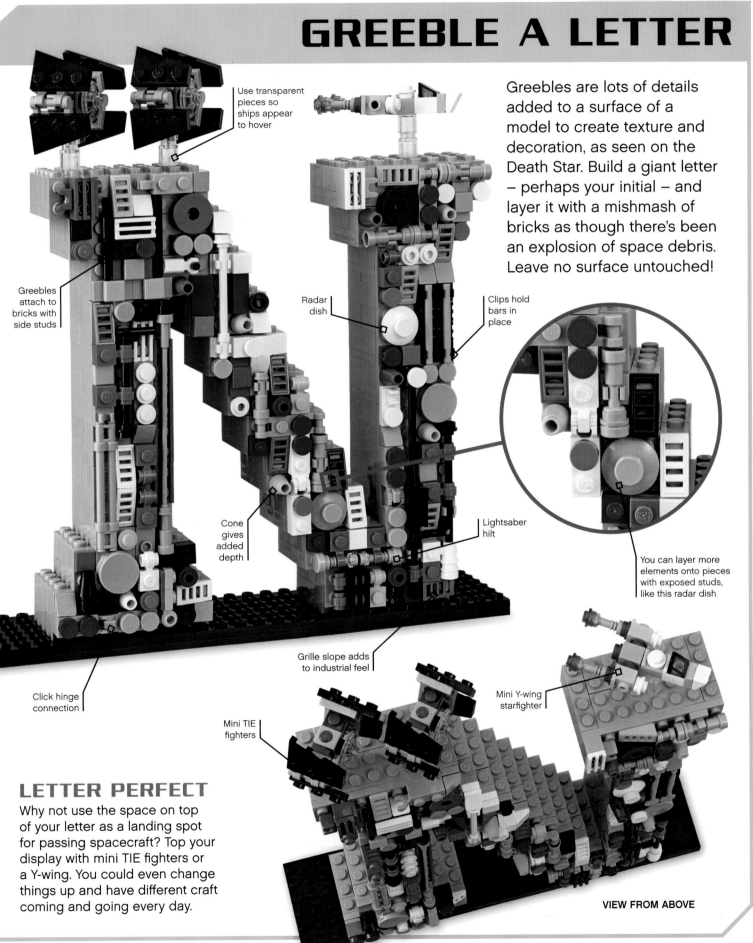

Use transparent pieces so ships appear to hover

Greebles are lots of details added to a surface of a model to create texture and decoration, as seen on the Death Star. Build a giant letter – perhaps your initial – and layer it with a mishmash of bricks as though there's been an explosion of space debris. Leave no surface untouched!

Greebles attach to bricks with side studs

Radar dish

Clips hold bars in place

Cone gives added depth

Lightsaber hilt

You can layer more elements onto pieces with exposed studs, like this radar dish

Grille slope adds to industrial feel

Click hinge connection

Mini Y-wing starfighter

Mini TIE fighters

LETTER PERFECT

Why not use the space on top of your letter as a landing spot for passing spacecraft? Top your display with mini TIE fighters or a Y-wing. You could even change things up and have different craft coming and going every day.

VIEW FROM ABOVE

STAND UP FOR MINIFIGURES

Show off your favourite minifigures on custom-built stands. To pick a theme, just think about their memorable moments. Darth Maul's stand, for example, could be sand coloured, like the Tatooine desert where the Jedi first learned of his existence.

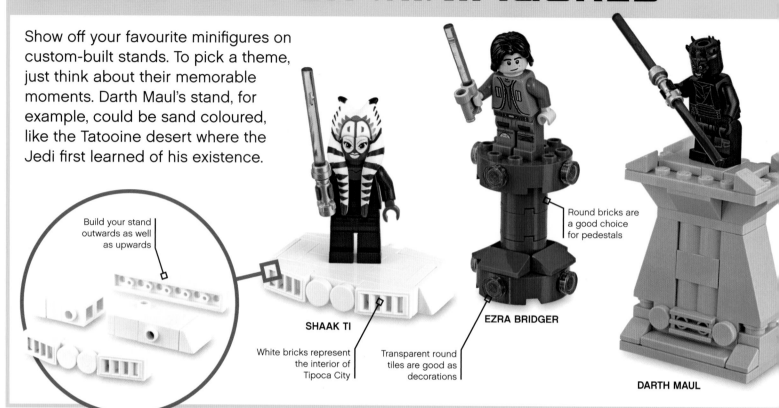

Build your stand outwards as well as upwards

SHAAK TI

White bricks represent the interior of Tipoca City

Transparent round tiles are good as decorations

Round bricks are a good choice for pedestals

EZRA BRIDGER

DARTH MAUL

SHIELD YOUR MAIL

Keep your mail safe in a letter holder that's shaped like the shield generator on Hoth. Envelopes will stay neatly stowed between the shield's two halves. Even a pesky probe droid won't be able to disrupt them!

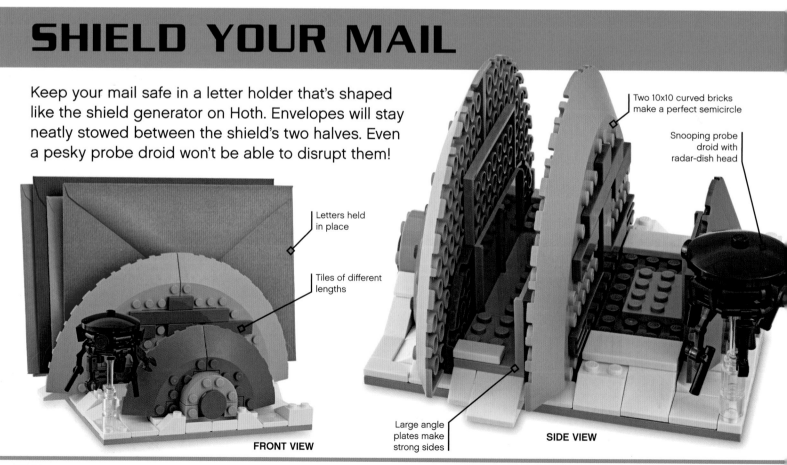

Letters held in place

Tiles of different lengths

Two 10x10 curved bricks make a perfect semicircle

Snooping probe droid with radar-dish head

FRONT VIEW

Large angle plates make strong sides

SIDE VIEW

HANG OUT AT A BIG SPACE BATTLE

This mobile will keep you in suspense! Which way will the battle turn next? Build a hanger from overlapping plates, then hang microfighters from it using strings with studs, so they seem to be floating in space. Why not add a few asteroids, too?

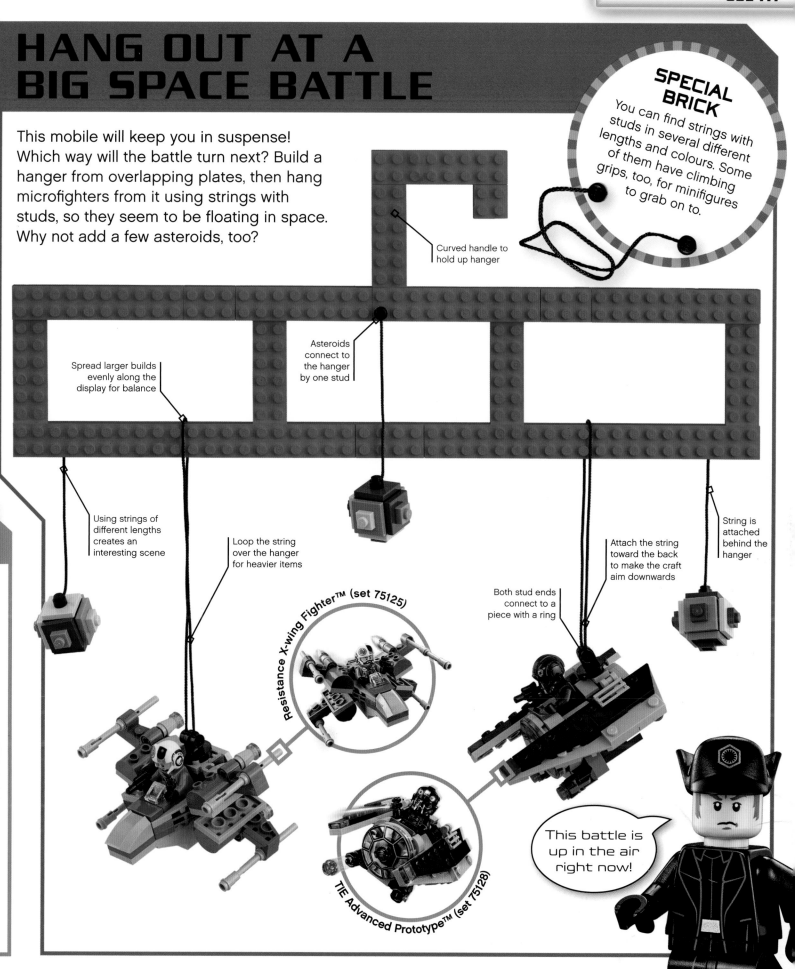

Curved handle to hold up hanger

SPECIAL BRICK
You can find strings with studs in several different lengths and colours. Some of them have climbing grips, too, for minifigures to grab on to.

Asteroids connect to the hanger by one stud

Spread larger builds evenly along the display for balance

Using strings of different lengths creates an interesting scene

Loop the string over the hanger for heavier items

Resistance X-wing Fighter™ (set 75125)

Both stud ends connect to a piece with a ring

Attach the string toward the back to make the craft aim downwards

String is attached behind the hanger

TIE Advanced Prototype™ (set 75128)

This battle is up in the air right now!

LOCK AWAY YOUR VALUABLES

Do you need to secure some top-secret schematics? A plan for a super weapon maybe? Or perhaps you have other precious things to keep safe. Here is the solution: a LEGO box that actually locks with a key!

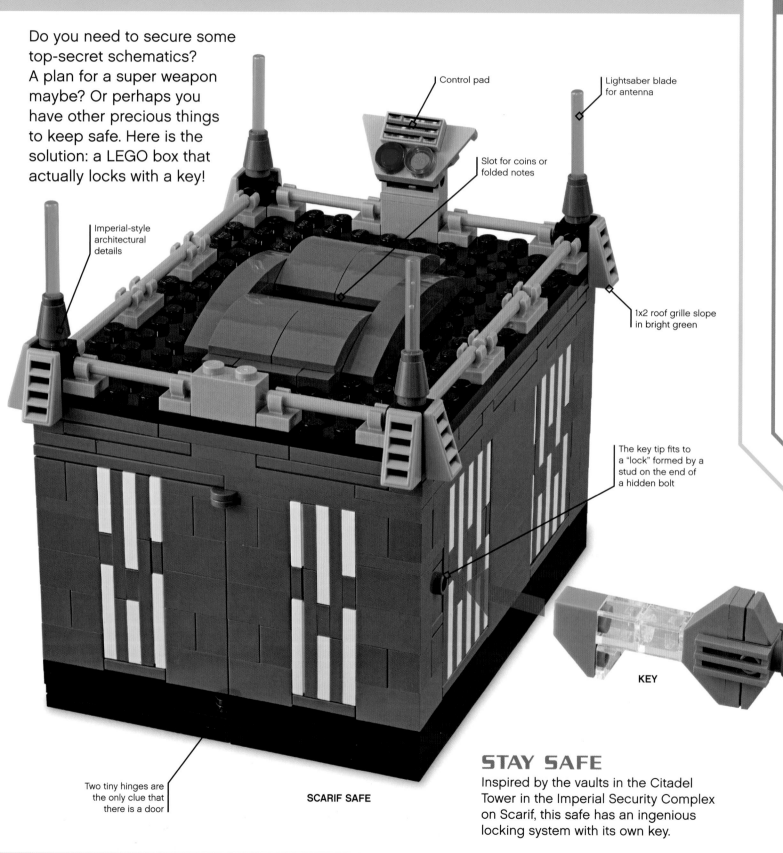

Imperial-style architectural details

Control pad

Lightsaber blade for antenna

Slot for coins or folded notes

1x2 roof grille slope in bright green

The key tip fits to a "lock" formed by a stud on the end of a hidden bolt

Two tiny hinges are the only clue that there is a door

SCARIF SAFE

KEY

STAY SAFE
Inspired by the vaults in the Citadel Tower in the Imperial Security Complex on Scarif, this safe has an ingenious locking system with its own key.

LAY YOUR ALLEGIENCE ON THE TABLE

Are you loyal to the Empire, or rooting for the rebels? Use one of these eye-catching *Star Wars* symbols as a table centrepiece and let everyone know where your allegience lies. If you like, stand a rebel or Imperial minifigure on it for emphasis.

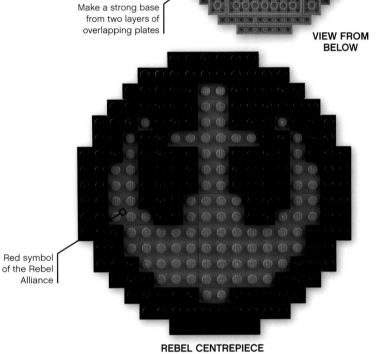

Make a strong base from two layers of overlapping plates

VIEW FROM BELOW

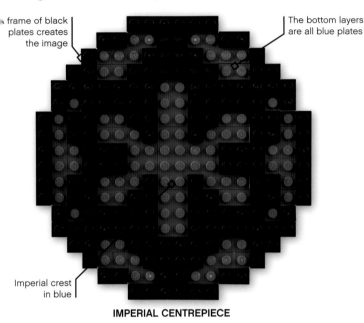

A frame of black plates creates the image

The bottom layers are all blue plates

Imperial crest in blue

IMPERIAL CENTREPIECE

Red symbol of the Rebel Alliance

REBEL CENTREPIECE

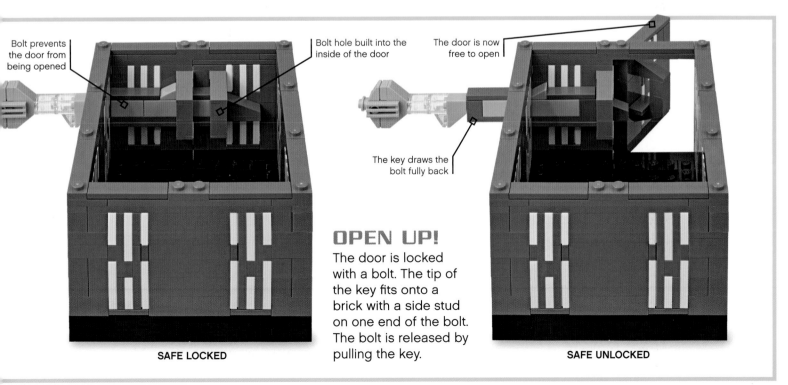

Bolt prevents the door from being opened

Bolt hole built into the inside of the door

The door is now free to open

The key draws the bolt fully back

OPEN UP!

The door is locked with a bolt. The tip of the key fits onto a brick with a side stud on one end of the bolt. The bolt is released by pulling the key.

SAFE LOCKED

SAFE UNLOCKED

MAKE A SCENE ON NABOO

The planet of Naboo is one of the most beautiful in the galaxy, and it has seen some of the most dramatic events in *Star Wars* history. Why not build a frame based on one of its buildings, to display a photo or artwork of your favourite Naboo moment?

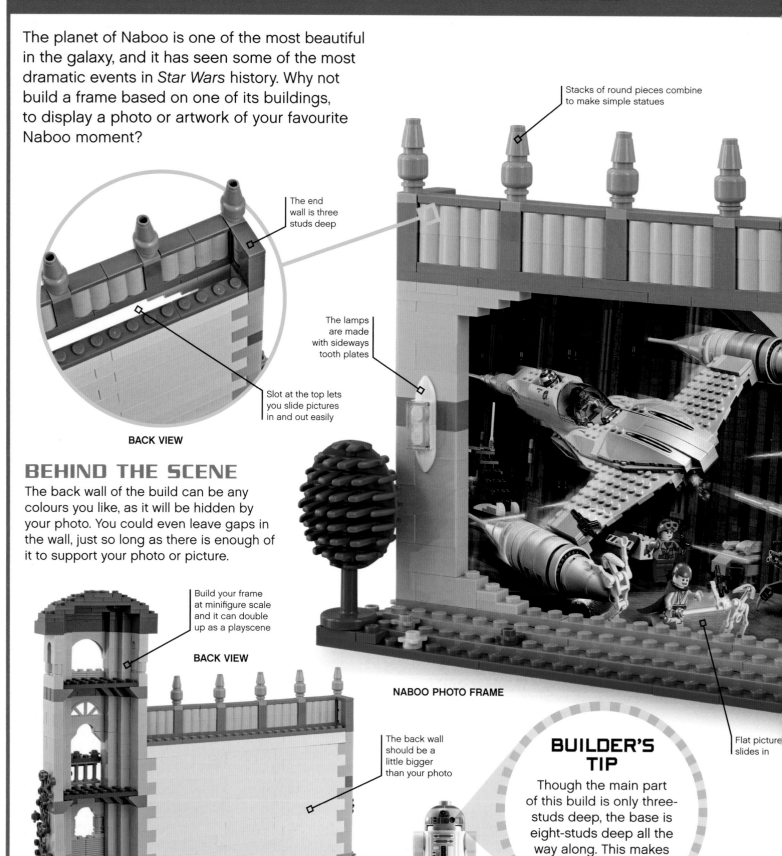

Stacks of round pieces combine to make simple statues

The end wall is three studs deep

The lamps are made with sideways tooth plates

Slot at the top lets you slide pictures in and out easily

BACK VIEW

BEHIND THE SCENE

The back wall of the build can be any colours you like, as it will be hidden by your photo. You could even leave gaps in the wall, just so long as there is enough of it to support your photo or picture.

Build your frame at minifigure scale and it can double up as a playscene

BACK VIEW

The back wall should be a little bigger than your photo

NABOO PHOTO FRAME

Flat picture slides in

BUILDER'S TIP

Though the main part of this build is only three-studs deep, the base is eight-studs deep all the way along. This makes it far less likely to fall and break.

The domed of is built in similar way the planets on page 36

Fanlight piece

Make the framing front wall a little smaller than your photo

Plant pieces connect to make long vines

MAKE A PEN PAL

You can be pen pals with beings from across the galaxy when you build them straight onto your writing tools! Start by finding a pen or pencil and seeing which LEGO parts fit onto the end.

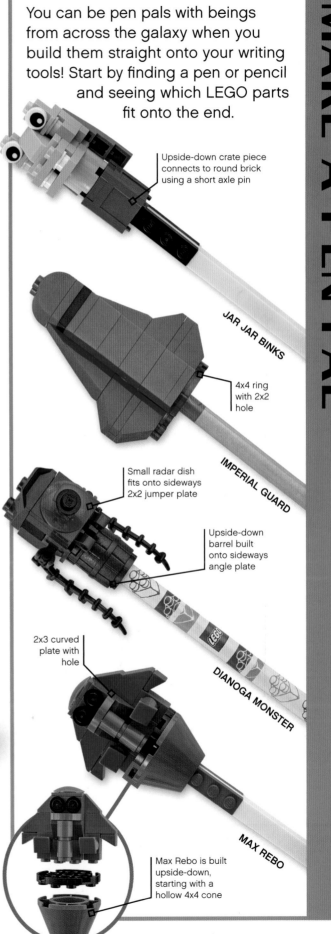

Upside-down crate piece connects to round brick using a short axle pin

JAR JAR BINKS

4x4 ring with 2x2 hole

IMPERIAL GUARD

Small radar dish fits onto sideways 2x2 jumper plate

Upside-down barrel built onto sideways angle plate

DIANOGA MONSTER

2x3 curved plate with hole

MAX REBO

Max Rebo is built upside-down, starting with a hollow 4x4 cone

185

Keep a zen-like level of organization in your house with a container inspired by Darth Vader's meditation chamber. The life-support pod keeps Vader alive when he's not in his suit. This version can keep your stress levels down by making it easy to find your keys!

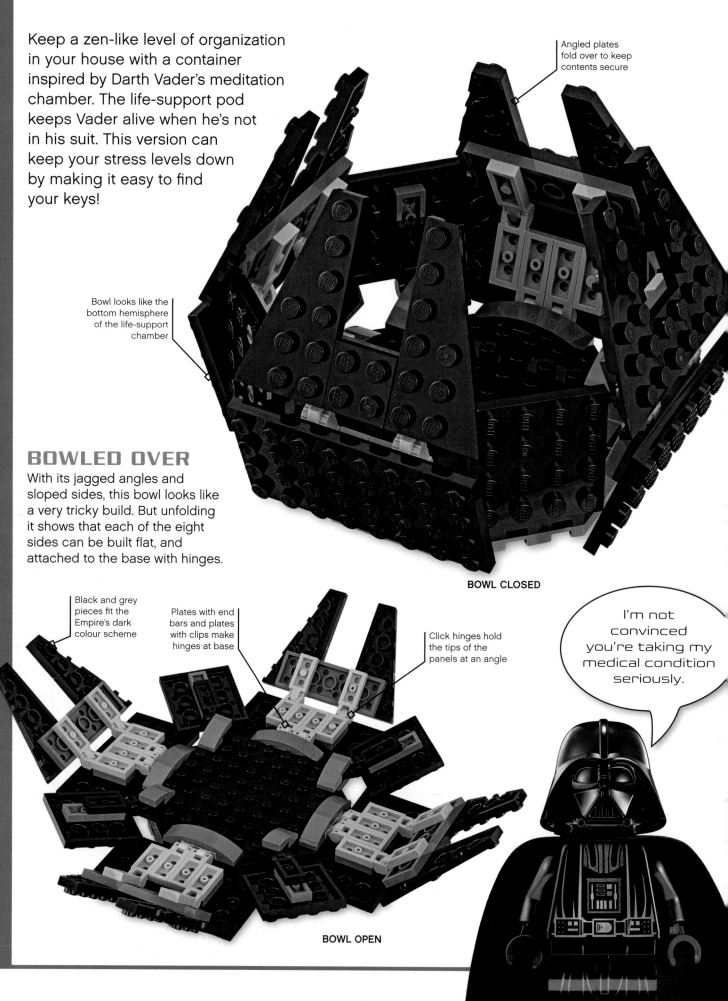

Angled plates fold over to keep contents secure

Bowl looks like the bottom hemisphere of the life-support chamber

BOWLED OVER

With its jagged angles and sloped sides, this bowl looks like a very tricky build. But unfolding it shows that each of the eight sides can be built flat, and attached to the base with hinges.

BOWL CLOSED

Black and grey pieces fit the Empire's dark colour scheme

Plates with end bars and plates with clips make hinges at base

Click hinges hold the tips of the panels at an angle

I'm not convinced you're taking my medical condition seriously.

BOWL OPEN

MAKE AN ECHO BASE PENCIL CASE

Echo the rebels' base on Hoth with a pencil case as cool as a tauntaun in a snowdrift. The sliding lid is based on the doors to Echo Base's hangar. Your stationery will be safe inside – as long as the Empire doesn't track it down!

LID UNDERSIDE

Each half of the lid is made using a mix of different plate shapes

Plates with a side rail all the way along the edge

Both halves of the lid slide outward

Box could store minifigures instead of stationery

LID OPEN

Sliding bricks have a groove along one side so that a plate with a rail can slide along inside them

INSIDE VIEW

Build your pencil case at least three bricks high

LID CLOSED

A pattern of tiles and grille pieces gives the doors an industrial look

The join is hidden when the lid is closed

SPECIAL BRICK

Plates with side rails fit into slider bricks to make a smooth sliding mechanism.

CELEBRATE THE HOLIDAYS WITH *STAR WARS*

Why not celebrate the holiday season with your favourite characters from the *Star Wars* galaxy? Create festive scenes with a *Star Wars* twist. You could draw inspiration from the LEGO *Star Wars* advent calendar sets, or come up with your own.

Sand-stained helmet from a Tatooine stormtrooper

Snowtrooper helmet

Brown carrot-top piece

Transparent dark-blue tiles for a frozen pond

SNOWMEN ON HOTH

Slope bricks of different angles form a tree shape

1x1 round plates are tree decorations

Santa hat appears in 13 LEGO sets, including two LEGO *Star Wars* advent calendars

I can feel the presents of the Force.

ABOMINABLE SNOWMEN

No, this isn't a battle scene on Hoth, they're snowmen built for the holidays. With abandoned Imperial helmets available, who needs carrots and coal?

Minifigures stand on jumper plates

The season for giving it is.

SECRET SANTA

Brighten up the grey of the Death Star with a festive tree and colourful gifts. After all, it is the season of goodwill to all beings – even Sith!

TABLE CENTREPIECE

2x2 corner tile

HANG A CODED SIGN ON YOUR DOOR

Hang a message from your door handle with this customizable sign. Use LEGO plates to write your own message. It could be your name or a secret, coded message like this one, that only those in the know will understand!

◀ Turn to page 130 to find out how to make a coded message

Add decorative details like this Sith lightsaber

Overlap the plates to make a sturdy sign

Sign is two plates deep

The coded message reads "Jedi enter"

KEEP YOUR PENCILS SAFE

Your friends will think twice about stealing pencils from this pot! Built in the style of a laser gun turret on the Death Star, it has two moveable guns at the top. Grab your grey bricks to build a pencil pot with a heavily armoured look.

LEGO Technic elements can make great cannons

1x1 brick with bar

Attach plates sideways and leave their studs exposed to add texture

Pot is built up from a square 8x8 base plate

PENCIL POT BASE

Cannons pivot on sideways round bricks with holes

DETACHABLE TOP

Use the handle to aim guns up or down

MAKE A KYBER CRYSTAL CHEST

If you have treasures you need to keep from prying eyes, this chest is the perfect place for them. The design is based on the armoured crates used by the Empire to hold kyber crystals in transit. Your riches will be well protected!

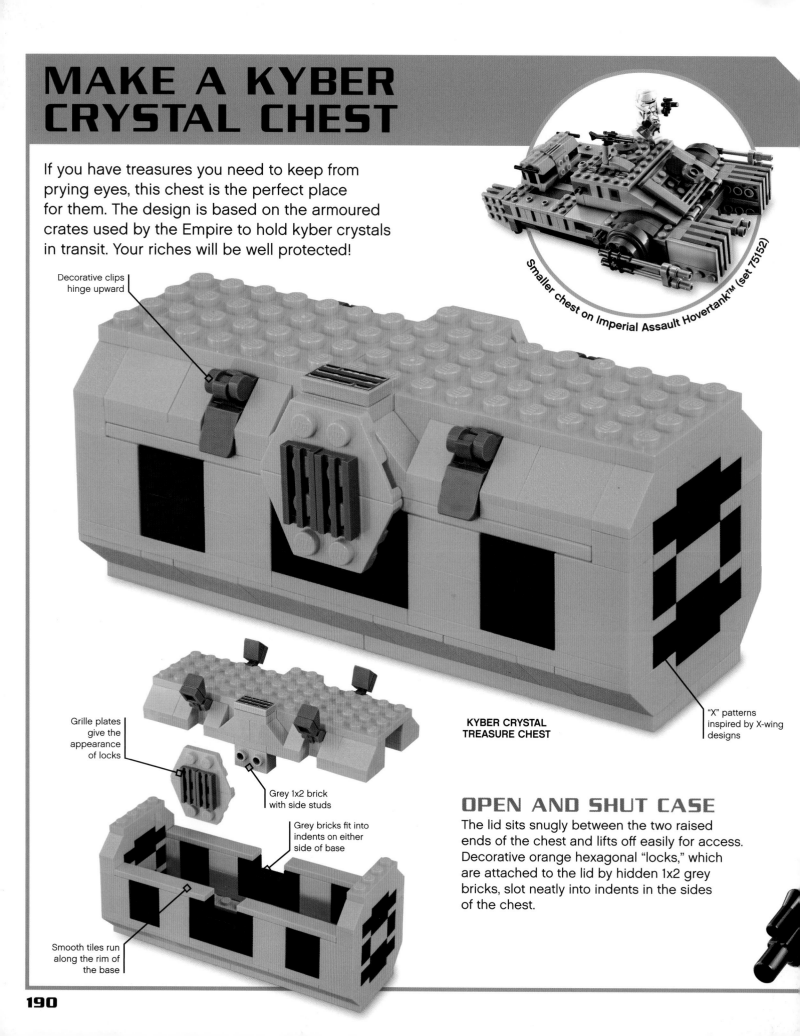

Smaller chest on Imperial Assault Hovertank™ (set 75152)

Decorative clips hinge upward

Grille plates give the appearance of locks

Grey 1x2 brick with side studs

Grey bricks fit into indents on either side of base

KYBER CRYSTAL TREASURE CHEST

"X" patterns inspired by X-wing designs

Smooth tiles run along the rim of the base

OPEN AND SHUT CASE

The lid sits snugly between the two raised ends of the chest and lifts off easily for access. Decorative orange hexagonal "locks," which are attached to the lid by hidden 1x2 grey bricks, slot neatly into indents in the sides of the chest.

SHOW LOVE FOR *STAR WARS*

Do you love *Star Wars*? Show your fondness for the galaxy far, far away, as well as for a loved one, with this 3-D framed heart picture. It's the perfect Valentine's gift! This example shows Princess Leia and Han Solo, but you could choose any minifigures you like.

Heads are turned to look lovingly at each other

Small, detailed elements add a touch of *Star Wars* technology

SPECIAL BRICK

One curved plate with a hole has many uses, but two together make an unexpected heart shape! The holes could be used to thread it onto a necklace.

This chest is worth its weight in kyber crystals!

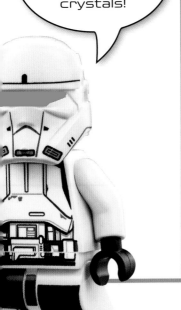

Minifigure stands on a 2x2 bracket plate

FRAMED HEART PICTURE

BUILDER'S TIP

This build makes a great display piece. Build the frame flat first before displaying it on its side. Make sure the items inside do not protrude past the frame.

Tile printed with Rebel Alliance symbol

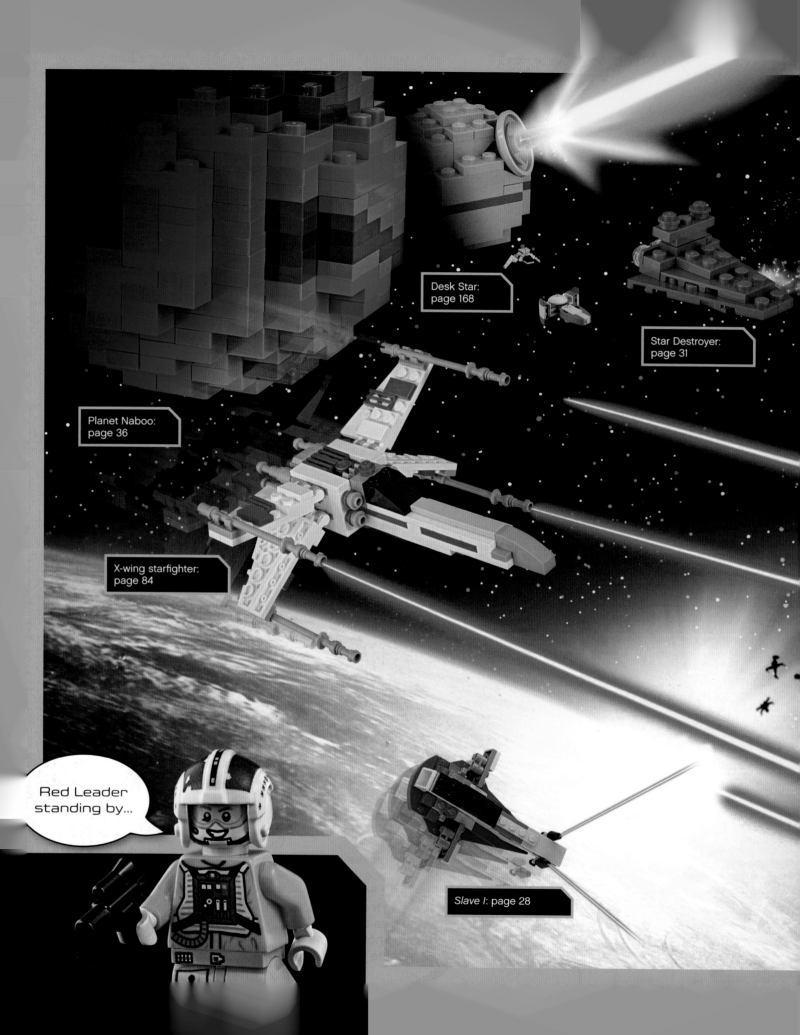

Desk Star:
page 168

Star Destroyer:
page 31

Planet Naboo:
page 36

X-wing starfighter:
page 84

Red Leader
standing by...

Slave I: page 28

Planet Mustafar:
page 36

Vader's TIE:
page 84

SOLUTIONS

PAGE 132: PLAY "WHICH WOOKIEE AM I?"

WOOKIEE WARRIOR

WULLFFWARRO

CHIEF TARFFUL

CHEWBACCA

PAGE 136: MIX UP YOUR MINIFIGURES

ROSE

PORG

POE

PHASMA

VADER

REY

LEIA

HUX

LUKE

PAGE 137: NAME THAT LIGHTSABER

1. DARTH SIDIOUS

2. LUKE SKYWALKER

3. COUNT DOOKU

4. LUKE SKYWALKER

5. KYLO REN

6. MACE WINDU

7. DARTH VADER

8. DARTH MAUL

9. YODA

These puzzles have blown my logic circuits!

PAGE 140: SPOT THE DIFFERENCE

1. Swamp plant is a different colour
2. Frog missing from the floor
3. Mud tile is a different colour
4. Trousers are a different colour
5. Balloon string is a different colour
6. Plant is lighter green
7. One ear is attached sideways
8. One eye is lighter grey

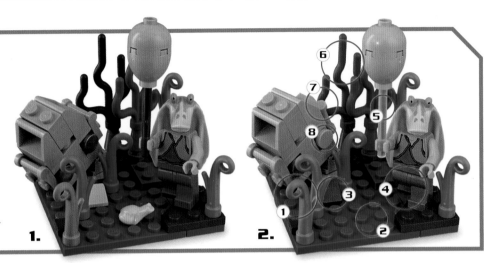

1.

2.

PAGE 146: NAME THAT DROID!

1. R2-Q5

2. R8-B7

3. R5-D4

4. R2-Q2

5. R4-P44

6. R2-A3

7. R3-D5

8. C1-10P (CHOPPER)

9. R4-P17

10. R5-J2

PAGE 150: DESIGN A SET OF *STAR WARS* DOMINOS

1. Chewbacca
2. Darth Vader
3. Boba Fett
4. Stormtrooper
5. Han Solo
6. Luke Skywalker
7. Princess Leia
8. C-3PO
9. R2-D2

PAGE 156: NAVIGATE THE KAMINO MAZE

The models in this book were conceived and built by a talented team of builders, all of whom are huge fans of *Star Wars* and, of course, crazy about LEGO® bricks. We asked them to share some of their secrets with us...

RHYS KNIGHT

WHY DID YOU CHOOSE THIS MINIFIGURE?

The Cassian Andor minifigure looks a little like me!

WHAT'S YOUR "DAY JOB"?

I'm a full-time LEGO modelmaker.

THE FIRST STAR WARS MOVIE YOU EVER SAW

A New Hope. I was four years old.

FAVOURITE STAR WARS MOMENT

A New Hope, when Han shoots Greedo. (Han shot first!)

FAVOURITE PIECE

The 1x1 brick with four side studs, because it's so versatile.

DID YOU KNOW?

My wedding cake was in the shape of a 2x4 LEGO brick!

◀ Turn to page 57 to see this build by Rhys!

ALICE FINCH

WHY DID YOU CHOOSE THIS MINIFIGURE?

Rey is spirited, works hard, and fights for just causes.

WHAT'S YOUR "DAY JOB"?

Freelance LEGO artist, mother, educator and social justice advocate.

THE FIRST STAR WARS MOVIE YOU SAW

The Empire Strikes Back, when I was six. I was terrified by the AT-ATs!

FAVOURITE STAR WARS MOMENT

Rey flying the *Millennium Falcon* on Jakku. It's a great planetary skirmish with awesome piloting skills.

FAVOURITE PIECE

1x1 round plate with hole, because it can be used in so many ways.

DID YOU KNOW?

The first gift my boyfriend (now husband) gave me was a LEGO set – I still have it!

◀ Turn to page 45 to see this build by Alice!

TIM GODDARD

WHY DID YOU CHOOSE THIS MINIFIGURE?

Like Chewie, I don't say much, I like to help others and I have good mechanical skills – at least with LEGO elements!

WHAT'S YOUR "DAY JOB"?

I manage an analytical chemistry laboratory.

THE FIRST STAR WARS MOVIE YOU SAW

Return of the Jedi. I was seven years old.

FAVOURITE STAR WARS MOMENT

The Battle of Hoth in *The Empire Strikes Back*. The AT-ATs look so menacing, marching across the snow!

FAVOURITE PIECE

1x1 plate with clip, great for connecting anything with a bar to anything with a stud.

DID YOU KNOW?

I won the first UK LEGO Robot Wars contest with my robot, the Brick Separator!

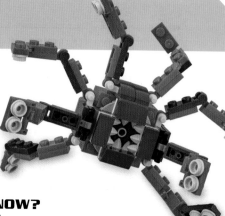

◀ Turn to page 50 to see this build by Tim!

ROD GILLIES

WHY DID YOU CHOOSE THIS MINIFIGURE?

Han Solo is a bit of a rascal and doesn't take things too seriously. Here, he's dressed for going out in the snow – which I also love to do.

FAVOURITE *STAR WARS* MOMENT

"Lock S-foils into attack position!" (from *A New Hope*). The first time I saw the rebel fighters form up for their attack on the Death Star, it was so exciting.

WHAT'S YOUR "DAY JOB"?

I work for a drinks company, in innovation and marketing.

THE FIRST *STAR WARS* MOVIE YOU SAW

The original *Star Wars* (*A New Hope*), back in 1977. I was seven years old.

FAVOURITE PIECE

The headlight brick. It's so useful, especially if you build a lot of microscale models.

DID YOU KNOW?

I've recently started building a microscale model of Edinburgh, Scotland, which is my home town.

◀ Turn to page 99 to see this build by Rod!

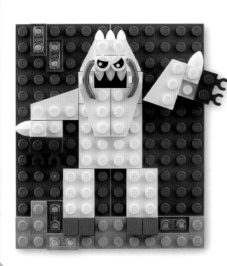

BARNEY MAIN

WHY DID YOU CHOOSE THIS MINIFIGURE?

As a child, I had my face painted to look like Darth Maul and have wanted to be him ever since. Plus – he has a double lightsaber!

WHAT'S YOUR "DAY JOB"?

I'm a design engineer.

THE FIRST *STAR WARS* MOVIE YOU SAW

The Phantom Menace, when I was six years old.

FAVOURITE *STAR WARS* MOMENT

It has to be Anakin's Boonta Eve Classic podrace in *The Phantom Menace* – very fast, very dangerous and very exciting!

FAVOURITE PIECE

1x2/2x2 angle plate. It's really useful for building sideways and detailing – and it's strong, too.

DID YOU KNOW?

At our wedding last year, my family decorated our wedding car to look like a giant yellow LEGO brick!

◀ Turn to page 118 to see this build by Barney!

KEVIN HALL

WHY DID YOU CHOOSE THIS MINIFIGURE?

As a child, I thought the Ewoks were funny, mischievous and brave.

WHAT'S YOUR "DAY JOB"?

I run my own LEGO modeling company and I am a LEGO artist.

THE FIRST *STAR WARS* MOVIE YOU SAW

The Empire Strikes Back, when I was seven years old.

FAVOURITE *STAR WARS* MOMENT

The final lightsaber duel in *Return of the Jedi,* where Luke defeats his father, Darth Vader.

FAVOURITE PIECE

The basic 2x4 brick, as you can create anything your imagination desires with it.

DID YOU KNOW?

When I was six years old I decided I wanted to work with LEGO bricks when I grew up – and that is exactly what I have been able to achieve!

◀ Turn to page 179 to see this build by Kevin!

INDEX

ACKNOWLEDGMENTS

Penguin
Random
House

Senior Editors
Emma Grange, Laura Palosuo, Rona Skene

Editors
Pamela Afram, Julia March, Rosie Peet

Senior Designers
Lisa Robb, Joe Scott

Designers
Jenny Edwards, James McKeag, Toby Truphet

US Editor
Megan Douglass

Senior Pre-Production Producer
Jennifer Murray

Print Producer
Louise Daly

Managing Editor
Paula Regan

Managing Art Editor
Jo Connor

Publisher
Julie Ferris

Art Director
Lisa Lanzarini

Publishing Director
Simon Beecroft

Inspirational models built by
Alice Finch, Rod Gillies, Tim Goddard,
Kevin Hall, Rhys Knight, Barney Main

Photography by
Gary Ombler

Dorling Kindersley would like to thank Randi K. Sørensen,
Heidi K. Jensen, Martin Leighton Lindhardt, Paul Hansford,
Henrik Andersen, and Charlotte Neidhart at the LEGO
Group as well as Jennifer Heddle, Mike Siglain,
Leland Chee, Derek Stothard, Julia Vargas, Stephanie
Everett, and Chelsea Alon at Lucasfilm. Many thanks also
to Thorin Finch and Hadrian Finch for their help with
building the models and to Hannah Gulliver-Jones
at DK for editorial assistance.

First published in Great Britain in 2018 by
Dorling Kindersley Limited
80 Strand, London WC2R 0RL
A Penguin Random House Company

10 9 8 7 6 5 4 3 2 1
001–307688–Sep/2018

Page design copyright © 2018 Dorling Kindersley Limited

LEGO, the LEGO logo, the Brick and Knob configurations,
and the Minifigure are trademarks of the LEGO Group.
©2018 The LEGO Group.

Manufactured by Dorling Kindersley under licence
from the LEGO Group.

© & TM 2018 LUCASFILM LTD

A CIP catalogue record for this book
is available from the British Library.
ISBN 978-0-24131-425-8

Printed and bound in China

A WORLD OF IDEAS:
SEE ALL THERE IS TO KNOW

www.dk.com
www.starwars.com